Microsoft® SQL Server™ 2000 For Dummies®

W9-BGL-477

Microsoft SQL Server 2000 Datatypes

Datatype	Explanation
BigInt	New for SQL Server 2000, this datatype stores whole number integers in the range of −9,223,372,036,854,775,808 to +9,223,372,036,854,775,807. The BigInt datatype requires 8 bytes to store data.
Binary	Holds up to 8,000 bytes of binary data. Binary data is any data that is stored in a stream of 1s and 0s. The data stored in a Binary column must be fixed in length.
Bit	Used to hold either a 1 or a 0, commonly used as a True/False or Yes/No indicator, or a flag that indicates that something is "switched on or off." A bit datatype takes 1 byte in storage.
Char	Holds up to 8,000 bytes (characters) of data. The data stored in a Char column must be fixed in length.
Cursor	Special datatype that holds a reference to a cursor. These variables are typically used in stored procedures.
Datetime	Stores a date and time value. A Datetime column takes two 4-byte integers of storage. The date range available in the 4-byte configurations are between 1/1/1753 and 12/31/9999. The time range spans the full range of the clock, accurate to within 3/100 of a second.
Decimal	Stores numeric data. The storage space required for the Decimal datatype range is from 2 to 17 bytes, depending on the precision and scale of the data. Precision indicates the number of digits required by the number. Scale indicates the number of decimal places required by the number.
Float	Stores numeric data with floating-point numbers. The range of data that can be stored is from −1.79E +308 to 1.79E +308. The amount of space required to store a Float datatype is up to 8 bytes.
Image	Stores binary data represented by an image. The Image datatype can store more information than a Binary datatype but requires more space. An Image datatype holds variable-length binary data. The amount of space required varies, based on the amount of data. It can store more than 2GB (gigabytes) of binary data.
Int	Stores whole number integers in the range of −2,147,483,648 to +2,147,483,647. The Int datatype requires 4 bytes to store data.
Money	Stores monetary values in the range of −922,337,203,685,477.5808 to +922,337,203,685,477.5807. The Money datatype requires 8 bytes to store data.
nChar	Holds up to 4,000 bytes (characters) of Unicode data. The data stored in an nChar column must be fixed in length. Unicode data is used for international characters.
nText	Stores variable-length Unicode character data. The nText datatype can store up to 1,073,741,823 bytes (or characters).
Numeric	Same as the decimal datatype, but the Numeric datatype is preferred.
nVarchar	Holds up to 4,000 bytes (characters) of Unicode data. The data stored in an nVarchar column is variable-length. Unicode data is used for international characters.

Microsoft® SQL Server™ 2000 For Dummies®

Cheat Sheet

Microsoft SQL Server 2000 Datatypes *(continued)*

Datatype	Explanation
Real	Stores numeric data with floating-point numbers. The range of data that can be stored is from 1.18E–38 to 3.40E 38 for positive numbers. The range of data that can be stored is from –1.18E–38 to –3.4E 38. The amount of space required to store a Real datatype is 4 bytes, which is half the size (and range) of the Float datatype.
Rowversion	New for SQL Server 2000, this datatype formerly known as a Timestamp, stores binary data representing the current date and time. The data in a Timestamp column is automatically inserted or updated every time the data in a row is changed.
Smalldatetime	Stores a date and time value. A Datetime column takes 4 bytes of storage. The date range available is between 1/1/1900 and 6/6/2079. The time range spans the full range of the clock, accurate to within one minute.
Smallint	Stores whole number integers in the range of –32,768 to 32,767. The Smallint datatype requires 2 bytes to store data.
Smallmoney	Stores monetary values in the range of –214,748.3648 to 214,748.3647. The Smallmoney datatype requires 4 bytes to store data. Decimal places are rounded to two places.
SQL_Variant	New for SQL Server 2000, this datatype allows you to not specifically define a datatype when storing values. This is because any valid value of any datatype except text, ntext, and rowversion can be used.
Sysname	Used to store the name of system tables. The Sysname datatype is automatically defined as being varchar(30) and therefore takes no more than 30 bytes to store.
Table	New for SQL Server 2000, this special datatype allows you to temporarily store result sets for later processing.
Text	Stores variable-length character data. The Text datatype can store up to 2,147,483,647 bytes (or characters).
Tinyint	Stores whole numbers in the range from 0 to 255 and requires only 1 byte to store.
Uniqueidentifier	Stores a globally unique identifier. The Uniqueidentifier datatype requires 16 bytes of storage.
Varbinary	Holds up to 8,000 bytes of binary data. Binary data is any data that is stored in a stream of 1s and 0s. The data stored in a varbinary column is variable-length.
Varchar	Holds up to 8,000 bytes (characters) of data. The data stored in a Varchar column is variable-length.

For Dummies: Bestselling Book Series for Beginners

Microsoft® SQL Server® 2000 FOR DUMMIES®

by Anthony T. Mann, MCT, MCDBA, MCSD

Wiley Publishing, Inc.

Microsoft® SQL Server® For Dummies®

Published by
Wiley Publishing, Inc.
909 Third Avenue
New York, NY 10022

www.wiley.com

Copyright © 2001 by Wiley Publishing, Inc., Indianapolis, Indiana

Published by Wiley Publishing, Inc., Indianapolis, Indiana

Published simultaneously in Canada

For general information on our other products and services or to obtain technical support, please contact our Customer Care Department within the U.S. at 800-762-2974, outside the U.S. at 317-572-3993, or fax 317-572-4002.

Wiley also publishes its books in a variety of electronic formats. Some content that appears in print may not be available in electronic books.

Library of Congress Control Number: 00-109065

ISBN: 0-7645-0775-3

Manufactured in the United States of America

10 9 8 7 6

About the Author

Anthony T. Mann has been designing, developing, and instructing in the field of web-based systems and Client/Server architecture and technology for many years. He holds the Microsoft Certified Database Administrator (MCDBA), Microsoft Certified Solution Developer (MCSD), and Microsoft Certified Trainer (MCT) certifications.

Anthony is a principal architect for Internosis, a premier Microsoft consulting organization. He specializes in designing and developing e-commerce and Microsoft .NET applications, using Windows DNA-based architectures and frameworks. For more information about Internosis, see Appendix A.

Anthony is a veteran author (or co-author) of many other technical books, including *Microsoft SQL Server 7 for Dummies*, *Real-World Programming with Visual Basic*, *Visual Basic 4 Developer's Guide*, *Real-World Programming with Visual Basic 4*, *Visual Basic 5 Developer's Guide,* and *Visual Basic 5 Development Unleashed.*

If you have any questions for him about this book or to find out what Internosis can do for your organization, he can be e-mailed at tmann@ vbasic.com.

He lives in beautiful southeastern New Hampshire with his wife and three shelties (Shetland Sheepdogs).

Dedication

Once again, I could not write this (or any) book without the love and support of my beautiful wife of 6 years, Alison. She gives me the inspiration that I need to accomplish anything I set my mind to. To the love of my life and best friend, I dedicate this book.

Acknowledgments

There are so many people I want to thank and acknowledge for efforts in putting this book together. Putting one of these things together requires so much effort by me (of course), everyone at IDG Books Worldwide, Inc., and all the people who put up with me during the process.

I wish to extend an extra special thanks to Judy Brief (Senior Acquisitions Editor), Susan Christophersen (Project Editor), Stephen Giles (Technical Editor), and the rest.... (from Gilligan's Island). The very close interaction with all these people is critical to the success of the book. Susan did an outstanding job making sure that all my T's were crossed and my I's were dotted. Stephen also did an outstanding job in helping me make sure that this book is technically accurate. He came up with some great suggestions and even pointed out where I was wwwwwrrrooong (as "The Fonz" used to say).

Publisher's Acknowledgments

We're proud of this book; please send us your comments through our online registration form located at www.dummies.com/register/.

Some of the people who helped bring this book to market include the following:

Acquisitions, Editorial, and Media Development

Project Editor: Susan Christophersen

Acquisitions Editor: Judy Brief

Technical Editor: Stephen Giles

Editorial Manager: Constance Carlisle

Media Development Manager:
Laura Carpenter

Media Development Supervisor:
Richard Graves

Production

Project Coordinator: Nancee Reeves

Layout and Graphics: Amy Adrian, Brian Massey, Jacque Schneider, Kendra Span, Brian Torwelle, Julie Trippetti, Jeremey Unger, Erin Zeltner

Proofreaders: Laura Albert, Susan Moritz, Nancy Price, York Production Services, Inc.

Indexer: York Production Services, Inc.

General and Administrative

Wiley Technology Publishing Group: Richard Swadley, Vice President and Executive Group Publisher; Bob Ipsen, Vice President and Group Publisher; Joseph Wikert, Vice President and Publisher; Barry Pruett, Vice President and Publisher; Mary Bednarek, Editorial Director; Mary C. Corder, Editorial Director; Andy Cummings, Editorial Director

Wiley Manufacturing: Carol Tobin, Director of Manufacturing

Wiley Marketing: John Helmus, Assistant Vice President, Director of Marketing

Wiley Composition Services for Branded Press: Debbie Stailey, Composition Services Director

Contents at a Glance

Introduction *1*

Part 1: An Introduction to Microsoft SQL Server 2000 ..... *7*
Chapter 1: What's New with You? New Features in SQL Server 2000 9
Chapter 2: A Quick Tour of Microsoft SQL Server 2000 Tools 19

Part 11: Database Design *41*
Chapter 3: Understanding the Relational Data Model 43
Chapter 4: Creating Base-Level SQL Server Objects 75
Chapter 5: Creating Advanced SQL Server Objects 99
Chapter 6: Programming SQL Server 2000 125
Chapter 7: Fun with Stored Procedures 143

Part 111: Interface Design *157*
Chapter 8: Making Microsoft SQL Server 2000 Work by Using SQL 159
Chapter 9: Now That I Have a Structure, How Do I Use It? 201
Chapter 10: Maintaining Flexibility by Importing and Exporting Data 223

Part 1V: Enterprise Issues *239*
Chapter 11: Preventing the Inevitable Disaster (Losing Data) 241
Chapter 12: So You Want to Be Published? 257
Chapter 13: Distributed Queries 277

Part V: Administrative Issues *291*
Chapter 14: Using Jobs and Alerts to Make SQL Server Work for You 293
Chapter 15: Maintenance Plans 311

Part V1: The Part of Tens *331*
Chapter 16: Ten Microsoft SQL Server Resources 333
Chapter 17: Ten Popular Ways to Give SQL Server More Pizzazz 337

Part VII: Appendixes 343
Appendix A: Wizard Flowcharts 345
Appendix B: About the CD 365

Index 369

End-User License Agreement 383

Installation Instructions...386

Cartoons at a Glance

By Rich Tennant

"For further thoughts on that subject, I'm going to download Leviticus and go through the menu to Job, chapter 2, verse 6, file J. It reads..."

page 157

"One of the first things you want to do before installing NT Server, is for the users to keep them calm during the procedure."

page 7

"We sort of have our own way of mentally preparing our people to take the MCSE NT workstation exam."

page 41

Okay young man, it's time to wash your hands, brush your teeth, and defrag your hard disk.

page 343

"YOU KNOW KIDS – YOU CAN'T BUY THEM JUST ANY WEB AUTHORING SOFTWARE."

page 239

"OK, make sure this is right. 'Looking for caring companion who likes old movies, nature walks and quiet evenings at home. Knowledge of configuring a 32-bit Microsoft Client for NetWare Networks in Windows 98, a plus'."

page 331

"Look, I've already launched a search for 'reanimated babe cadavers' three times and nothing came up!"

page 291

Cartoon Information:
Fax: 978-546-7747
E-Mail: richtennant@the5thwave.com
World Wide Web: www.the5thwave.com

Table of Contents

Introduction *1*

About This Book 1
Help Me, Help Me! 2
Expanding the Tree 3
Conventions Used in This Book 3
Who Should Read This Book? 4
Organization Is the Key to Life 4
    Part I: An Introduction to Microsoft SQL Server 2000 4
    Part II: Database Design 4
    Part III: Interface Design 5
    Part IV: Enterprise Issues 5
    Part V: Administrative Issues 5
    Part VI: The Part of Tens 5
    Part VII: Appendixes 5
What about All Those Icons? 6

Part 1: An Introduction to Microsoft SQL Server 2000 7

Chapter 1: What's New with You? New Features in SQL Server 2000 9

Introducing Analysis Services Enhancements 9
Announcing New Architectural Features 10
Finding Out about Data Transformation Services
    (DTS) Enhancements 12
Discovering New Documentation Features 12
Enhancing English Query 13
Enabling New Enterprise Features 13
Finding Out about Language Enhancements 14
Mining New Metadata Services 15
Discovering Miscellaneous Enhancements 16
Trying New Tools 16
Wondering about New Wizards 17

Chapter 2: A Quick Tour of Microsoft SQL Server 2000 Tools 19

SQL Server Service Manager 19
SQL Server Enterprise Manager 21
Tracing Problems with SQL Server Profiler 22
    Opening and running an existing trace 23
    Creating a new trace 24

SQL Server Query Analyzer 31
Microsoft English Query 32
SQL Server Performance Monitor 32
Server Network Utility 33
    Entering general information 34
    Viewing network libraries 35
Client Network Utility 36
    Selecting protocol information 36
    Defining aliases 37
    Selecting options 38
    Viewing network libraries 39
Wonderful Wizards 39
Help Me, Help Me! 40

Part II: Database Design 41

Chapter 3: Understanding the Relational Data Model 43

Schema Objects 43
    Keys 44
    Rules 47
    Defaults 47
    Triggers 48
    Indexes 48
What Is a Relational Model? 49
Designing the Model 51
Datatypes 57
    Standard datatypes 57
    User-defined datatypes 60
The "Tier" Buzzword 63
Naming Conventions 64
Relationships 66
    One-to-one relationships 66
    One-to-many relationships 67
    Many-to-many relationships 67
Locking 68
Transactions 71
    Transaction principles 71
    Distributed transactions 72
    Isolation 72

Chapter 4: Creating Base-Level SQL Server Objects 75

Filegroups 75
Building Databases 76
    Using the Create Database Wizard 76
    Relying on the SQL Server Enterprise Manager 81
    Enlisting SQL Server Query Analyzer 86

Designing Tables 87
    Using the SQL Server Enterprise Manager 88
    Turning to the SQL Server Query Analyzer 91
Falling Back on Default Values 93
    DEFAULTing with the SQL Server Enterprise Manager 94
    Maintaining control over defaults with SQL 95
Deleting Database Objects 96
Security on Database Objects 97

Chapter 5: Creating Advanced SQL Server Objects 99

Laying Down the Law: Setting Up Rules in SQL Server 2000 99
    Creating rules with SQL Server Enterprise Manager 100
    Creating rules with SQL 103
An Alternative to Creating Rules: Check Constraints 104
    Creating check constraints with SQL
      Server Enterprise Manager 104
    Creating check constraints with SQL 106
Defining Foreign Key Relationships 107
Creating Indexes 108
    Discovering the Create Index Wizard 109
    Using SQL Server Query Analyzer 112
The Safe Way to Pull the Trigger 113
    Creating triggers with the SQL Server Enterprise Manager 114
    Creating triggers with SQL 116
Full-Text Catalogs 119
    Creating a full-text catalog with the SQL
      Server Enterprise Manager 120

Chapter 6: Programming SQL Server 2000 125

Declaring Variables 125
    Declaring local variables 126
    Declaring cursors 126
    Declaring table definition variables 127
Going with the Flow 127
    IF...ELSE 128
    BEGIN...END 129
    RETURN 130
    CASE...WHEN...ELSE...END 130
    WHILE 131
    GOTO 131
    BREAK 132
    WAITFOR 133
    CONTINUE 134
Additional Transact-SQL Programming Statements 134
    Comments 135
    Displaying information 135
    Executing Transact-SQL code 136
    What about errors? 137

Conjunction-Junction, What's Your Function? 138
System functions 138
User-defined functions 139

Chapter 7: Fun with Stored Procedures **143**

System Procedures 144
Discovering available system procedures 144
Viewing the SQL for a system procedure 145
Executing a system procedure 146
Extended Procedures 146
Unveiling available extended procedures 147
Viewing the properties for an extended procedure 148
Executing an extended procedure 149
Creating extended procedures 150
Creating User-Defined Stored Procedures 152
Stored Procedure Security 155

Part III: Interface Design *157*

**Chapter 8: Making Microsoft SQL Server 2000 Work
by Using SQL** **159**

The Categories of SQL 160
Using Data Definition Language (DDL) Statements 160
Creating a database: The mother of all containers 161
Where do I put all my data? 163
How do I speed up my queries? 166
Seeing things differently 169
Ruling the world 170
Whose default is it, anyway? 171
Horsing around with triggers 173
Using Data Manipulation Language (DML) Statements 175
Getting data in 177
It's your prerogative to change your data 179
Wiping data out 182
Querying data 184
Using transactions with your queries 191
Using Data Control Language (DCL) Statements 192
Statement permissions 193
Object permissions 194
Full-Text Queries 195

Chapter 9: Now That I Have a Structure, How Do I Use It? **201**

Using SQL Server Query Analyzer 201
Executing queries 202
Browsing objects 206
Using templates 206

Technologies to Connect to SQL Server 2000 208
Navigating with Cursors 210
    Declaring the cursor 212
    Opening the cursor 213
    Using the cursor 213
    Closing the cursor 216
    Removing the cursor 216
    Putting it all together 217
Examining SQL Server from an ASP Web Page 218

Chapter 10: Maintaining Flexibility by Importing and Exporting Data 223
What is DTS, Anyway? 224
Importing Data to a SQL Server Database 225
Exporting Data from a SQL Server 2000 Database 232

Part 1V: Enterprise Issues 239

Chapter 11: Preventing the Inevitable Disaster (Losing Data) 241
Why Back Up? 241
Failover Clustering 242
Setting Up a Backup Device 242
Performing the Backup 245
    Specifying general data about the backup 246
    Specifying optional data about the backup 248
Restoring Your Data 250
    Specifying general data about the restore 251
    Specifying optional data about the restore 254
You No Longer Have to Ship Your Logs by UPS! 255

Chapter 12: So You Want to Be Published? .257
Publishing Web Data 257
    Harnessing the power of the Microsoft SQL Server 2000
    Web Assistant 257
    Accessing your published data 266
Publishing to Another Computer 268
    Configuring publishers, distributors, and subscribers 269
    Configuring publications 270
    Subscribing to articles 273

Chapter 13: Distributed Queries 277
How Do Distributed Queries Work? 277
    Distributed nontransactional queries 277
    Distributed transactional queries 278

Linking Your Servers Together 279
Entering general data for the linked server 281
Securing your data 281
Choosing options 282
Accessing Remote Data 284
Distributed nontransactional queries 285
Distributed transactional queries 287

Part V: Administrative Issues 291

Chapter 14: Using Jobs and Alerts to Make SQL Server Work for You 293
Creating a Job 294
Entering general data 294
Creating the sequence of steps 295
Scheduling the frequency of the job 299
What do I do when the job completes? 301
Hello . . . Operator? 303
Entering general data . . . one more time 304
Viewing an operator's notifications 305
Using Alerts 305
Defining alert conditions 307
Defining alert responses 308

Chapter 15: Maintenance Plans 311
What in the World . . .? 311
Creating a Maintenance Plan 312
Launching the Maintenance Plan Wizard 312
Using the wizard 313
Editing a Maintenance Plan 325
Deleting a Maintenance Plan 326
Viewing Maintenance Plan History 327

Part VI: The Part of Tens 331

Chapter 16: Ten Microsoft SQL Server Resources 333
Consulting 333
Web Page Research 334
The mother of all SQL sites: Microsoft SQL Server 334
Microsoft's .NET strategy and products
(including SQL Server) 334
Microsoft files for downloading 334

Microsoft's TechNet site 335
Microsoft Developer Network (MSDN) Online 335
The Development Exchange 335
Discussion Groups 335
microsoft.public.sqlserver.programming 336
microsoft.public.sqlserver.misc 336
comp.databases.ms-sqlserver 336

**Chapter 17: Ten Popular Ways to Give SQL Server
More Pizzazz** **337**
Microsoft — Visio 337
Seagate Software — Crystal Reports 338
Sylvain Faust — SQL Programmer 338
Quest Software — SQL Navigator for SQL Server 339
BEI Corporation — Ultrabac 339
Embarcadero Technologies — DBArtisan 339
Embarcadero Technologies — ER/Studio 340
Great Plains Software — Dynamics 340
Legato Systems — Networker 341
TNT Software — Event Log Monitor 341

Part VII: Appendixes *343*

Appendix A: Wizard Flowcharts **345**
Configure Publishing and Distribution 346
Copy Database 347
Create Alert 348
Create Database 349
Create Database Backup 350
Create Index 351
Create Job 352
Create Login 353
Create Publication 354
Create Stored Procedure 355
Create View 356
Database Maintenance Plan 357
Disable Publishing and Distribution 358
DTS Import/Export 359
Full-Text Indexing 360
Pull Subscription 361
Push Subscription 362
Web Assistant 363

Appendix B: About the CD 365
 System Requirements 365
 Using the CD with Microsoft Windows 366
 What You'll Find 366
  Microsoft SQL Server 2000 120-Day Evaluation 366
 If You've Got Problems (Of the CD Kind) 367

Index *369*

End-User License Agreement *383*

Installation Instructions *386*

Introduction

*W*elcome to the wonderful world of Microsoft SQL Server 2000. This latest version of the very popular relational database management system (RDBMS) is extremely exciting. Microsoft has spent much time and effort (not to mention money) in improving the prior version, 7.0.

If you are new to Microsoft SQL Server, you will find that creating and administering databases is extremely easy. If you are an old hand with Microsoft SQL Server or any other RDBMS, you'll find the improvements to be second to none. Microsoft has established itself (once again) as the industry leader.

SQL Server 2000 comes in seven different editions:

- ✔ Enterprise Edition: Used in the enterprise for Web and data warehouse applications, as well as other very large-scale database applications.

- ✔ Standard Edition: Can be used in a smaller environment, and lacks some of the features of the Enterprise Edition.

- ✔ Personal Edition: Used for developers that need access only to one server or use the server in a mobile environment.

- ✔ Developer Edition: Supports exactly the same functionality as the Enterprise Edition, but can be used only by a single person in a development environment.

- ✔ Desktop Engine: The database engine that can be redistributed if you have applications that require just the engine with no tools.

- ✔ Windows CE Edition: The version of SQL Server 2000 that can actually run on Windows CE devices. This is really cool!

- ✔ Enterprise Evaluation Edition: Allows organizations to download and try out SQL Server for 120 days to see how they like it. However, I've provided this edition on the CD-ROM in the back of the book. This saves you lots of download time!

About This Book

I've spent much time writing this book so that you can benefit from my years of experience. I present the material in an easy-to-read format that will have you up and running in no time. If you have read my prior book, *Microsoft SQL Server 7 For Dummies,* you'll find that I added many new chapters to this book. Some things are, of course, the same, but I spent MUCH time reviewing and updating the book, so I know you'll find it useful. I've also incorporated many of the suggestions from the e-mails that I receive so that I can bring you a better product. I hope you enjoy it. Please send me an e-mail and let me know what you think. My e-mail address is tmann@vbasic.com.

One issue that I always face when I write is to know when to quit! Most of the time, it is the publisher that has to tell me not to cover a topic because it would just make the book too big. This one is no different. If I didn't cover a topic that you wanted me to, I'm sorry, but if I were to cover every possible issue in depth, the book would be from 1,500 to 2,000 pages long. The casualty of all the "slicing and dicing" that had to occur to fit this book into its compact size is that two chapters that were originally included were cut. They are chapters on installation and security. However, all is not lost. These chapters are available on the Web at www.dummies.com/goto/fd-0764507753.htm.

I have multiple computers that I used in the creation of the text and screen shots in this book. You may see any of the following machine names, which are my machine names. Yours will be different. I used any of the following: AMANN, HAWKEYE, POTTER, HOTLIPS, RADAR, TRAPPER, or FERRETFACE. If you are a M*A*S*H fan, you'll notice a trend . . . .

I wrote this book to be equally useful to beginners and intermediate users alike. I don't cover many advanced topics, such as complex database design issues and considerations — I just don't have the space in this book. With this book, however, I do show you how to:

- ✔ Use many of the built-in wizards
- ✔ Find out about data modeling
- ✔ Create database objects
- ✔ Discover stored procedures
- ✔ Much, much more!

With this in mind, I hope you enjoy reading the book as much as I enjoyed writing it.

Help Me, Help Me!

What if you need additional help beyond what I show you in the book? Well, fortunately, Microsoft thought of that. A very easy-to-use help system is available, called Books Online. If you are new to Books Online, you'll find that you can't live without it.

To start Books Online, choose Start⇨Programs⇨Microsoft SQL Server⇨Books Online.

Expanding the Tree

In almost every chapter throughout this book, I mention, "expand the tree." How do you do this? To expand the tree, click the highest-level plus sign (+). The plus sign is located just to the left of the text describing the level in the tree. This plus sign indicates that there are items listed within its hierarchy. *Hierarchy* is a way of categorizing and grouping related items under a specific topic. Those topics may have subtopics that, in turn, have other subtopics. This very much follows an outline format.

Clicking the plus sign expands the tree to show the current level and all of the immediate *child* items. These child items may show other child items, and if they do, the child item will have a plus sign shown to the left of the text describing the level in the tree. If an item doesn't have a plus sign, the currently selected item has no child entries. This is sometimes referred to as a leaf entry, or simply, a leaf. A *leaf* entry is one that cannot be expanded any further.

To use Books Online, you can navigate the left side of the screen by expanding the tree to get to the topic you want. Also, you can search on any keyword by clicking either the Index or Search tabs, typing in the word(s) to search on, and then pressing Enter.

Conventions Used in This Book

I use some terms throughout the book that you should know about:

Select: You highlight an item by clicking it. This usually affects an item in a list box or grid.

Click: This describes an action where you use the left-mouse button to press and release while the mouse is positioned over an area of the screen. For example, if I say, "Click the OK button," I mean that you must press and release the left-mouse button, positioned anywhere over the OK button.

Double-click: You must click the left-mouse button twice in rapid succession. This action either selects an item and closes a dialog box, or expands an item in a hierarchical tree (see earlier in this Introduction for information about expanding trees).

Right-click: This means the same as a "click action," except that you use the right mouse button to click instead of the left mouse button.

Who Should Read This Book?

The answer is simple — everyone interested in SQL Server 2000. You don't need to be a Database Administrator (DBA) or even a programmer to use Microsoft SQL Server 2000. Microsoft has incorporated many wizards to help you do numerous everyday tasks in a very fast and efficient manner. At one time, you needed to be a database genius to perform even the simplest tasks. With the new wizards, virtually anyone can use SQL Server. If I've piqued your interest, you've picked up the right book.

Organization Is the Key to Life

If you are thumbing through this book in the bookstore, you'll want to know how the book is organized before you take the financial plunge. If you already bought it, you can use this section as a quick reference.

Part I: An Introduction to Microsoft SQL Server 2000

Here I give you an overview of Microsoft SQL Server 2000. I give you an introduction to the tools available to you, such as Enterprise Manager, Query Analyzer, and others. Because I know many of you aren't new to Microsoft SQL Server, I also show you what's new in the latest and greatest version of Microsoft's flagship database product.

Part II: Database Design

This is what it's all about! The difference between a good database and a poor database is its design. A well-designed database is fast and efficient. If you design your databases well, you'll also get the approval of your peers (something everybody needs).

In this part, I show you what the relational data model is all about and how it works. I tell you all about primary and foreign keys and how to use database objects. In addition, I show you how to create all sorts of database objects such as tables, indexes, rules, defaults, and triggers.

If all of that doesn't get you going, I discuss stored procedures, extended procedures, and the new user-defined function.

Part III: Interface Design

Interface design is the term I use to describe what you do with Microsoft SQL Server after you've created all the objects and designed your database. After all, what's a database if you can't use it?

In this part, I show you how to use Structured Query Language (or SQL). SQL is an inevitable part of using any relational database. In case that isn't enough, I show you how to use the Query Analyzer in detail, as well as cursors.

Part IV: Enterprise Issues

Well, well, well. This is a particularly interesting section (if I do say so myself). I discuss views and users. I also include how to back up in case the worst happens (losing your data), as well as restoring from backups. However, due to space limitations, I was forced to remove the chapter on security, as it can be considered an advanced topic. If you want to learn about security, refer to the Web address www.dummies.com/goto/fd-0764507753.htm for this deleted chapter. On the Web site, I discuss security and authentication models.

Also, for use in an enterprise situation, you'll need to know how to get data out of multiple databases, so I show you that, too.

Part V: Administrative Issues

Every product has some administrative overhead that needs to be dealt with. In this part, I show you how to deal with the issues such as creating maintenance plans, jobs, alerts, and English Query models.

Part VI: The Part of Tens

As with all . . .For Dummies books, this book contains Part of Tens chapters. This section contains valuable information about the best top-ten resources for use with Microsoft SQL Server 2000. In addition, you can find here ten ways to give SQL Server 7 more pizzazz with add-ons and other programs.

Part VII: Appendixes

Here I show you flowcharts of how many of the wizards work and what's on the CD.

What about All Those Icons?

To help you identify key pieces of text, I put these icons in the margins throughout the book:

This icon indicates a tip that I give you, based on my experience. Paying attention to this icon can save you lots of time.

You don't want to miss any of these. This icon indicates that you need to look out for something. Generally, a warning icon points out something that is critical to the process.

This icon flags a piece of text that is technical in nature but is not critical to reading the book. You could actually skip over this text if you are short of time. However, if you are a curious sort, you won't want to miss this.

Here's where I introduce a new term to you. Most of the terms associated with a lingo icon are also noted in the Glossary.

I use this icon to point out information that you may want to take note of, but this information is not always critical to perform a task. This information is also not technical in nature. On the icon scale, the Note icon is between Warning and Technical Stuff.

I use this icon to point out specific security-related concerns that you may want to know about. Security is such a hot topic, I want these items to stand out.

Here's where I show you new features, functions, statements, or any other bit of information that I can give you to illustrate what is new for this version of SQL Server.

Part I

An Introduction to Microsoft SQL Server 2000

"One of the first things you want to do before installing NT Server, is fog the users to keep them calm during the procedure."

In this part . . .

I talk about the features of Microsoft SQL Server 2000 and give you an overview of how to use the tools that come with this software. I also show you what features are new to this version of SQL Server.

Chapter 1

What's New with You? New Features in SQL Server 2000

In This Chapter

▶ Introducing analysis services enhancements

▶ Announcing new architectural features

▶ Finding out about Data Transformation Services (DTS) enhancements

▶ Enhancing English Query

SQL Server 2000 is the best release of SQL Server yet. Not to sound like a marketing guy, but it is the fastest, most robust relational database management system (RDBMS) on the market today. SQL Server 2000 includes many cool new features that go beyond its predecessor, SQL Server 7. In this chapter, I discuss all the great new enhancements of SQL Server 2000.

I categorize each of the enhancements under headings that I think are appropriate. Some of these enhancements can be considered to span multiple categories, but I had to place them somewhere :-).

In addition to briefly discussing the enhancements herein, I also tell you whether the specific feature (or at least the topic) is covered elsewhere in the book. So, grab a cup of coffee and let's get to it.

Introducing Analysis Services Enhancements

Many new changes have been made to analysis services. Analysis services were previously called OLAP. Analysis services are also sometimes referred to as business analytics. Unfortunately, because of space limitations, I do not cover analysis services in this book. Table 1-1 shows the analysis services enhancements available in SQL Server 2000.

Table 1-1	Analysis Services Enhancements in SQL Server 2000
Feature	*Description*
Data mining	New for SQL Server 2000, data mining allows for very fast processing of Business Analytics (OLAP) cubes.
Dimensions	Many new dimensions can be added to cubes, allowing for better "slicing and dicing" of data.
Security	New security features allow for implementing better security on cubes, cells, and dimensions.
Pivot tables	The Pivot Table service includes enhancements that allow a greater degree of flexibility when using pivot tables and analysis services.
HTTP support	HTTP is now supported to allow communication between Web browsers and the analysis server.
Miscellaneous features	Many new miscellaneous features have been added to analysis services, such as the ability to link cubes on other servers, hide cube elements. Additionally, you now have the ability to alias tables.

Announcing New Architectural Features

The vast majority of the changes made in SQL Server 2000 fall under the category of architectural enhancements. Table 1-2 shows the architectural enhancements available in SQL Server 2000.

Table 1-2	Architectural Enhancements in SQL Server 2000
Feature	*Description*
Federation	Allows groups of servers to process requests for data using distributed partitioned views. Federation is not covered in this book.
User-defined functions	I've been waiting for this feature to be implemented in SQL Server for some time. User-defined functions allow you to create a function that can be called from within your Transact-SQL code. User-defined functions are covered in Chapter 6.
Indexed views	Views can now be indexed.

Feature	*Description*
Indexed computed columns	Computed columns can also be indexed.
New datatypes	Three new datatypes have been added: `bigint`, `table`, and `sql_variant`. These new datatypes are covered in Chapter 3.
New triggers	Two new types of triggers were added in SQL Server 2000. They are `INSTEAD OF` and `AFTER` triggers. Both are discussed in Chapter 5.
Multiple instances	Prior to SQL Server 2000, you could run only a single instance of SQL Server on a single computer. Now, multiple instances can be run. Each instance has a specific name, allowing you to connect to that instance just as if were another server. Multiple instances are not covered in this book.
Text in row data	In prior versions of SQL Server, if you used the `text`, `ntext`, or `image` datatypes, each stored data in separate data pages from the rest of the data in the table. In SQL Server 2000, the data for these three datatypes can be stored along with the rest of the table. This type of storage can help performance if the amount of data is small. For more information on text in row data, see Chapter 4.
64 GB Memory	SQL Server 2000 (only the Enterprise Edition) can use up to 64 gigabytes of physical memory in a server. Extended memory is not covered in this book.
Collation	Collation is the process that SQL Server 2000 uses to determine sort orders for characters, based on the chosen language. Collation is covered in Chapter 4.
New OLE DB providers	OLE DB providers are now supported for Exchange and Microsoft Directory Services. These OLE DB providers allow distributed queries to access Microsoft Exchange or Active Directory data stores. The new OLE DB providers are not covered in this book.
Full-text searching	Change tracking and image filtering are now supported in SQL Server 2000. Full-text searching is briefly covered in Chapter 8.
Net-Library	The SQL Server 2000 Net-Library has been modified to allow Secure Sockets Layer (SSL) connections and eliminates the need to configure the client computer at all. Net-library is mentioned briefly in Chapter 9.

Finding Out about Data Transformation Services (DTS) Enhancements

Data Transformation Services (DTS) were introduced in SQL Server 7. Simply put, DTS allows you to move data from point A to point B, altering that data in some way along the line. This alteration can be as simple or complex as desired. There have been some improvements made to DTS, as shown in Table 1-3.

Table 1-3	DTS Enhancements in SQL Server 2000
Feature	*Description*
Custom tasks	If you are going to use the programming model available within DTS, you can create custom tasks. These custom tasks allow you to perform virtually any action, or task, on your data.
DTS saving	DTS packages can now be saved to a Visual Basic (VB) script file. This allows the "source code" of the transformation to be stored in a repository or some other source code control mechanism. In addition, these VB script files can be used in Web pages, within the Microsoft BizTalk product, or any other places that VB script files are allowed.
Keys and constraints	Prior to version 2000 of SQL Server, the Import and Export wizards (which use DTS) would create only database objects, like tables and views, but not primary keys, foreign keys, or constraints. Now these keys and constraints can be included in your choices for using the import and export wizards.

Discovering New Documentation Features

A few enhancements have been made to the documentation available in SQL Server 2000. Table 1-4 shows the enhancements to the documentation in SQL Server 2000.

Table 1-4   Documentation Enhancements in SQL Server 2000

Feature	Description
Books Online subsets	Subsets are a new feature of Books Online that allow you to limit searches to only desired specific parts of Books Online.
Glossary links	Within Books Online, glossary items are shown in colored text, much as an Internet link is. When this text is clicked, a pop-up window shows you the definition of the term shown in colored text.

Enhancing English Query

English Query is a product that allows you to create queries by using the English language rather than Structured Query Language (SQL). Table 1-5 shows the enhancements made to the English Query tool in SQL Server 2000. English Query is not covered in this book.

Table 1-5   English Query Enhancements in SQL Server 2000

Feature	Description
Integration	English Query now can be integrated with Visual Studio, analysis services, and full-text searches. This integration is not covered in this book.
Graphical User Interface	A graphical user interface can now be used to author English Queries.
XML Support	English Query models are now stored as XML.
Oracle Support	English Query now supports the Oracle database (if you must!).

Enabling New Enterprise Features

Many important features have been added to the Enterprise category of enhancements. This category generally affects large businesses that have to concern themselves with security, performance, and fault tolerance. Table 1-6 shows the enterprise enhancements available in SQL Server 2000.

Table 1-6	Enterprise Enhancements in SQL Server 2000
Feature	*Description*
Failover clustering	Many advances have been made in the area of failover clustering, such as administration and performance. Failover clustering is not covered in this book.
Distributed queries	Distributed queries existed in SQL Server 7, but they have been expanded to take advantage of new OLE DB data sources as well as new datatypes and other features. Distributed queries are discussed in Chapter 13.
Security delegation	Security delegation is the concept of using the Windows 2000 Kerberos security scheme to allow one server to pass the client's authentication credentials on to multiple servers.
Backup and restore	Many improvements have been made in the areas of backup and restore. If you can't wait, you can jump ahead to Chapter 11.
Utility scalability	Some utility operations, such as database consistency checking (DBCC), backup, and restore can take advantage of scalability features such as multiple processors.
Passwords for backup	Backup files can now be password protected. Backing up is discussed in Chapter 11.
Log shipping	Log shipping is a great new feature that allows you to back up transaction logs on a constant basis to another server. Log shipping is covered in Chapter 11.

Finding Out about Language Enhancements

Microsoft did not add too many things in the way of language enhancements into SQL Server 2000. Table 1-7 shows the language enhancements available in SQL Server 2000.

Table 1-7	Language Enhancements in SQL Server 2000
Feature	*Description*
XML support	One of the most exciting features of SQL Server 2000 is its support for Extensible Markup Language (or XML). XML is a relatively new language that allows data to be easily transmitted over the Web. XML is covered in Chapter 8.
Cascading constraints	You are now allowed to control what happens to referential integrity when a related table (declared with foreign keys) has data updated or deleted.

Mining New Metadata Services

Some enhancements have been made in the area of metadata services, which were previously known as the repository. The repository is a database used by SQL Server to manage or administer SQL Server itself. Table 1-8 shows the enhancements made to metadata services in SQL Server 2000. Metadata services are not covered in this book.

Table 1-8	Metadata Services Enhancements in SQL Server 2000
Feature	*Description*
Metadata browser	A new browser has been included in SQL Server 2000 that allows you to browse for metadata objects.
XML encoding	XML encoding allows for metadata to be encoded as XML.
Programming	Programming enhancements have been made to metadata services, such as the ability to control performance by specifying hints, integration with the Distributed Transaction Coordinator (DTC), and the automatic generation of views.
Modeling	Modeling refers to the ability to store information models. These modeling enhancements are well beyond the scope of this book.

Discovering Miscellaneous Enhancements

There have been a couple of enhancements that I can't seem to categorize anywhere else. Table 1-9 shows the miscellaneous enhancements in SQL Server 2000.

Table 1-9	Miscellaneous Enhancements in SQL Server 2000
Feature	*Description*
Windows CE Edition	This new (and quite incredible) edition of the SQL Server 2000 product is designed to run on Windows CE devices. Microsoft has worked very hard to take up only about 800KB of space. Obviously, it doesn't contain every bit of functionality as the full-fledged product does, but it does fully support the ANSI SQL standard. It also has full support for replication to synchronize with the full products. The Windows CE Edition is not covered in this book.
Replication enhancements	There are too many new replication enhancements to mention in this brief chapter. Numerous enhancements have been made in the areas of snapshot, merge, and transactional replication. There have been some new cool features added as well, such as the ability to queue SQL statements on published data. Additionally, Data transformation services (DTS) can be applied to published data. Replication is covered in Chapter 12. Not all of these enhancements are touched upon.

Trying New Tools

There have been a couple of enhancements to the tools that come with SQL Server 2000 over SQL Server 7. Table 1-10 shows the enhancements to the tools in SQL Server 2000.

Table 1-10	SQL Server Tools Enhancements in SQL Server 2000
Feature	*Description*
Query Analyzer	Many new features have been added to the SQL Server Query Analyzer. The Query Analyzer is an indispensable tool to query the database. Version 2000 includes an integrated debugger for troubleshooting stored procedures. Also, the Query Analyzer supports scripting and templates for fast creation of different types of SQL Server objects. The Query Analyzer is described in Chapter 2 and used extensively throughout this book.

Feature	Description
SQL Profiler	The SQL Profiler has been completely redesigned to support the government-defined security level of C2. As such, auditing events have been added to the SQL Profiler. The SQL Profiler is briefly described in Chapter 2.

Wondering about New Wizards

Microsoft added many new wizards to help you with the administration and configuration of SQL Server 2000. Table 1-11 shows the new wizards available in SQL Server 2000 that did not exist in SQL Server 7. I have created flow-charts of each of the wizard options and placed them in Appendix A. These flowcharts help you understand the ramifications of choosing the different options on the wizard screens. Note that Table 1-11 shows only new wizards, not a listing of all possible wizards in SQL Server 2000.

Most of the new wizards relate to analysis services (the service formerly know as OLAP). This is because the concepts surrounding analysis services can be quite complex. These wizards help to simplify the process.

Table 1-11	New Wizards Available in SQL Server 2000
Feature	**Description**
Action	Allows you to define actions on a business analytics (OLAP) cube based on requests from client applications.
Copy Database	Allows you to copy from a source database to a target database. Databases are covered in Chapter 4.
Create Database Backup	Makes it very easy to create backups for databases. Backups are covered in Chapter 11.
Create Login	Assists you in creating logins for SQL Server and specific databases at the same time.
Cube	Allows you to define business analytics (OLAP) cubes.
Data Transformation Services	Prompts you on importing and exporting data using SQL Server 2000's data transformation services. DTS is covered in Chapter 10.
Database Maintenance Plan	Aids you in maintaining your database on a consistent basis by automatically performing many database administrator (DBA) functions. Maintenance plans are covered in Chapter 15.

(continued)

Table 1-11 *(continued)*

Feature	Description
Define Transformation of Published Data	For data replication, after data has been configured for publication, you can transform the data using this wizard. Data replication is covered in Chapter 12.
Dimension	Allows you to define business analytics dimensions for your cubes.
Disable Publishing and Distribution	Allows you to easily and rapidly disable an existing publication and/or distribution on a server. Data replication is covered in Chapter 12.
Full-Text Indexing	Helps you to configure a table for full-text searching. Full-text search is discussed in Chapter 8.
Incremental Update	Allows you to update a cube with new data. This is part of analysis services.
Index Tuning	Recommends and tunes indexes on tables to help increase performance. Indexes are discussed in Chapters 3 and 5.
Migrate Repository	Allows you to migrate the default Microsoft Access database used as the analysis services repository to a SQL Server 2000 repository.
Mining Model	Allows you to easily create a data-mining model.
OLAP Project	Creates entities and relationships for selected analysis services cubes in the English Query.
Partition	Separates a single logical analysis services cube into multiple physical partitions, perhaps on separate disks.
Project	Separates a single logical analysis services cube into multiple physical partitions, perhaps on separate disks.
SQL Project	Creates entities and relationships for selected tables in the English Query.
Storage Design	Used in analysis services, allows you to specify performance and storage considerations for cubes.
Usage Analysis	Generates an on-screen report of the usage of analysis services cubes.
Usage-Based Optimization	Tunes performance of analysis services cubes, based on how they are used.
Virtual Cube	Creates a superset of selected analysis services cubes. This is known as a virtual cube.

Chapter 2

A Quick Tour of Microsoft SQL Server 2000 Tools

In This Chapter

▶ Introducing the Enterprise Manager (the mother of all SQL Server tools)

▶ Tracing with the SQL Server Profiler

▶ Using other great SQL Server 2000 tools

▶ Getting help with Books Online

*W*ell, they keep getting bigger and better! SQL Server 2000 is the best release of SQL Server yet. Not only does it extend the tradition of being a very high-performance relational database management system (RDBMS) at an extremely reasonable price, but it just keeps getting better. In this chapter, I show you how to use the tools that come with SQL Server 2000. What good is a great database without great tools?

SQL Server Service Manager

SQL Server 2000 runs in the background either on Windows 2000, Windows NT, or Windows 98. Because SQL Server 2000 runs in the background, it's called a service, and you need some type of program to administer the starting and stopping of the service. If you're familiar with Windows 2000 or Windows NT, you know that it handles services differently than Windows 98, but the tools used to control the service is the same. In Windows 98, SQL Server 2000 runs as an application and not a service.

For more information about services, refer to *Windows NT 4 For Dummies* by Andy Rathbone and Susan Crawford (from IDG Books Worldwide, Inc.).

SQL Server 2000 uses the following services:

- ✔ **SQL Server:** Service that is the relational database itself. Without this service, you will not be able to issue queries to the server. This service is shown in the Services control panel applet as `MSSQLSERVER`.

- ✔ **SQL Server Agent:** Service that controls scheduling features of SQL Server 2000. This service is shown in the Services control panel applet as `SQLSERVERAGENT`.

- ✔ **Distributed Transaction Coordinator:** Service that controls distributed (across servers) transactions and queries. This service is shown in the Services control panel applet as `Distributed Transaction Coordinator`.

- ✔ **Microsoft Search:** Service that controls the searching and index generation with full-text queries. This service is shown in the Services control panel applet as `Microsoft Search`.

- ✔ **Analysis Services:** Service that controls analysis services, formerly known as OLAP. This service is shown in the Services control panel as `MSSQLServerOLAPService`.

The services in the preceding list can be started and stopped by using the services control panel within the operating system itself. Alternatively, it is much easier to use the SQL Server Service Manager. Before you can continue with any example in this book, SQL Server must be running. To start the SQL Server Service, follow these steps:

1. **Choose Start⇨Programs⇨Microsoft SQL Server⇨Service Manager to start the SQL Server Service Manager (see Figure 2-1).**

Figure 2-1:
The SQL
Server 2000
Service
Manager.

2. **Choose the correct server or server instance in the Server drop-down list box.**

3. **Choose the SQL Server service in the Services drop-down list box.**

4. **Click the Start/Continue button.**

   After you click the Start/Continue button, the service shown in the Services drop-down list starts, which could take a few seconds, depending on the speed of your computer and the amount of memory you have.

   If you want to use the scheduling services for SQL Server 2000, you need to ensure that the SQL Server Agent service is running. Perform the preceding Steps 2-4, but substitute SQL Server Agent for SQL Server service.

   Likewise, start the other services listed previously in the same manner.

SQL Server Enterprise Manager

The SQL Server Enterprise Manager is an application that comes with SQL Server 2000 that enables you to control all aspects of your schema. To start the SQL Server Enterprise Manager, choose Start⇨Programs⇨Microsoft SQL Server⇨Enterprise Manager (see Figure 2-2).

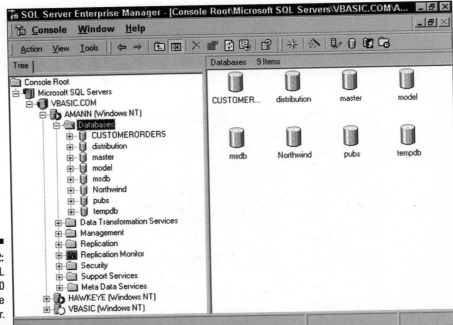

Figure 2-2:
The SQL Server 2000 Enterprise Manager.

The SQL Server Enterprise Manager enables you to control and manipulate databases, tables, indexes, users, and much more. As a matter of fact, you will quickly find that the SQL Server Enterprise Manager is the tool you use most often.

Many chapters in this book show specifically how to use the different aspects of the SQL Server Enterprise Manager, so I'll leave you with this brief introduction (this way you're forced to read the rest of my book). :)

Tracing Problems with SQL Server Profiler

The SQL Server Profiler is an excellent tool to use to help you trace problems with SQL Server, such as login problems, record locking issues, or performance problems. Profiler is also a great tool to help you monitor the activity that's taking place on the server in real-time. SQL Server Profiler works by running in the background while users connect to SQL Server and go about their everyday lives. SQL Server Profiler listens for specific events, such as logons and database transactions, that you specify. An *event* is an action that occurs within SQL Server 2000. SQL Server 2000 responds to these events by trapping them. When it traps the event, SQL Server 2000 reacts in a way that you define. When SQL Server Profiler responds to these defined events, it displays them to the Profiler screen, and optionally writes the results to a file and/or a table. To start the SQL Server Profiler, choose Start⇨Programs⇨ Microsoft SQL Server⇨Profiler (see Figure 2-3). You can also launch the Profiler from within the Enterprise Manager by choosing the Tools⇨SQL Server Query Analyzer menu option.

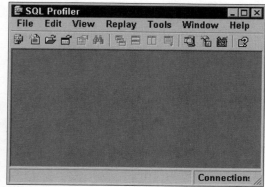

Figure 2-3: The SQL Server 2000 Profiler.

The SQL Server Profiler enables you to store different configurations relating to what you want to trace. For example, one such configuration may be to trace the logins into SQL Server. Another configuration may be to trace all the locks on a given table. These different configuration choices are known as *traces*. You can store and reuse multiple traces within the SQL Server Profiler. In fact, multiple traces can run simultaneously.

SQL Server Profiler is also the tool that will allow you to capture events on a production server and replay them on a development server so you can look for problems. A captured trace is also the prerequisite for the Index Tuning Wizard.

Opening and running an existing trace

You can store trace configurations so that you can recall them later. To open an existing trace, follow these steps:

1. **Choose Start⇨Programs⇨Microsoft SQL Server⇨Profiler to start the SQL Server Profiler (refer to Figure 2-3).**

2. **Choose File⇨Open⇨Trace File to bring up the Open dialog box (see Figure 2-4).**

   Alternatively, you can open a trace that is stored in a table by choosing File⇨Open⇨Trace Table.

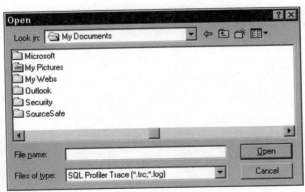

Figure 2-4:
The SQL
Server 2000
Open Dialog
Box.

3. **Choose the desired trace to run.**

   Click the trace that you want to open. You can open multiple traces within the Profiler, but you have to open them one at one time and click OK. The trace is opened into the Profiler.

4. **Click Replay⇨Start to run the traces.**

   You are prompted to log on to the server that the trace will run on.

5. **Select Replay Options (see Figure 2-5).**

   You can specify the following replay options:

   ✔ **Replay SQL Server:** Select the name of the server to log into. By default, the server name selected in the previous step is shown. If you want to change the name of the server, click the button to the right of the text box and select the desired server.

   ✔ **Output File Name:** If you want to write the results of the trace to a file, click the button to the right of the text box and choose a folder and filename.

   ✔ **Replay Events in the Order They Were Traced:** This option is the default and allows you to debug your traces. This option replays the events stored in the trace sequentially in order, but uses more resources.

   ✔ **Replay Events Using Multiple Threads:** This option replays the events using multiple threads of execution, but does not ensure that events are replayed in sequential order.

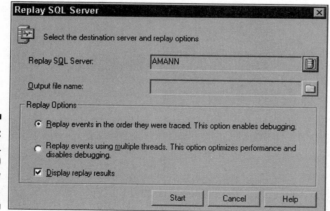

Figure 2-5:
The SQL
Server 2000
Replay
Options.

Creating a new trace

You can define your own traces. The traces that you define contain the events you want the Profiler to listen for. One thing that's new for SQL Server 2000 is that traces can be created from eight templates. A template allows you to preconfigure the events, columns, and filters that you want to use in the trace. You can also create your own templates. To create a new trace, follow these steps:

1. **Choose Start➪Programs➪Microsoft SQL Server➪Profiler to start the SQL Server Profiler (refer to Figure 2-3).**

2. **Create a Trace by clicking File➪New➪Trace.**

   In addition, you can click the New Trace toolbar icon. Or you can press the shortcut keys, CTRL+N.

   Each method brings up the Trace Properties dialog box, consisting of four tabs (General, Events, Data Columns, Filters), which allow you to configure the new trace (see Figure 2-6). The General tab is shown by default.

3. **Log into the server that you want to use with the new trace.**

   By default, the current server is shown.

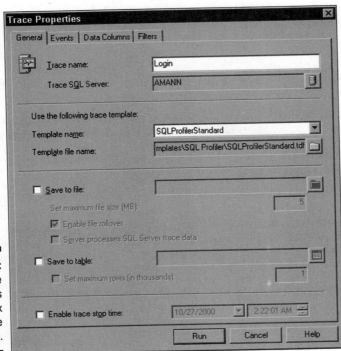

Figure 2-6:
The Trace
Properties
dialog box
showing the
General tab.

4. Fill in the desired data for the four tabs.

Create a new trace by filling in four tabs of data. The following four sections outline how to do this. Click OK when you are finished entering data to save the new trace.

Defining general information

Supply data that describes the trace as a whole in the General tab (see Figure 2-6). General data includes information such as the name and trace properties.

Click the General tab to make sure that it's selected. Then supply data for the following fields in the General tab:

- ✔ **Trace Name:** Give the trace a name, such as Login Trace. Use a name that describes the purpose of the trace.

- ✔ **Trace SQL Server:** Select the desired server. By default, the server that you logged into is presented.

- ✔ **Template Name:** Choose the drop-down list of templates. These templates come from the C:\Program Files\Microsoft SQL Server\80\Tools\Templates\SQL Profiler folder. To free you from having to choose from the list of templates every time, you can set the default template. Set the default template by clicking Tools⇨Options. Addition-ally, you do not have to choose a template name; you can create blank templates, which are not based on an existing template. If you choose a template name, the filename will appear in the Template file name field.

- ✔ **Template File Name:** By default, the filename is shown, based on the template name chosen. However, you can choose the template if you don't know the template name but know only the filename. If you change the filename (by using the button to the right), this will also change the name of the template.

- ✔ **Save To File:** Check this box if you want to store the results of the trace to a file for later analysis, in addition to displaying the results in the Profiler itself. Checking this box enables a button allowing you to select a file. Additionally, you can opt to limit the file size by checking the Set maximum file size option. If you do opt to limit the file size, you can also enable file rollover. File rollover indicates that if a file size is maxed out (based on the file size limit), a new file is created with the same name, appended with _1, _2, and so on as each of the previous files reaches the predetermined limit.

One final option is to determine where the processing for the trace takes place. If the Server Processes SQL Server Trace Data option is checked, processing for the trace takes place on the server. If it is not checked, processing takes place on the client, which is the default option. If processing takes place on the client computer, it is possible for events to be missed if the processor is very busy. However, client processing uses fewer server resources (obviously). If processing takes place on the server, more server resources are used but no events can be missed.

✔ **Save To Table:** Check this box if you want to store the results of the trace to a table, also in addition to displaying the results in the Profiler itself. Checking this box enables a button that allows you to select a table name within the database chosen in the SQL Server drop-down list. If this option is checked, you can opt to limit the number of rows captured to a table. This limitation prevents your disk from filling up.

✔ **Enable Trace Stop Time:** Check this box if you want your trace to stop after a certain time. You would want to use this option if you were concerned about capturing too much data and filling up your disk drive with a large file or table. This option is not checked by default.

Selecting events

Choose the events you want to trap with the trace. Events are stored in 14 different categories:

✔ Cursors

✔ Database

✔ Error and Warning

✔ Locks

✔ Objects

✔ Performance

✔ Scans

✔ Security Audit

✔ Server

✔ Sessions

✔ Stored Procedures

✔ Transactions

✔ TSQL

✔ User Configurable

Within the preceding categories are individual events, for a total of 98 events that can be monitored with the Profiler. To choose events, make sure that the Events tab is selected by clicking it (see Figure 2-7). Then select data for the following fields in the Events tab:

✔ **Available Event Classes:** The events listed in this list box are divided into categories. You can click the plus sign to expand a category to see the specific events under a category. You can select an entire category by selecting (highlighting) the name of the category and then clicking the Add button or double-clicking the item. You can also select an individual event by expanding the category (by clicking the + icon) in the Available event classes list box, selecting the individual event, and then clicking the Add button.

✔ **Selected Event Classes:** The events listed in this list box have been selected for use with your trace. To remove an event, highlight it and click the Remove button or double-click the item. You can remove an entire category by selecting (highlighting) the name of the category and then clicking the Remove button. You can also remove an individual event by expanding the category (by clicking the + icon) in the Selected event classes list box and then clicking the Remove button.

Selecting columns of data

After the event is trapped, you decide which data the trace needs to provide back to you. Click the Data Columns tab to make sure that it's selected (see Figure 2-8).

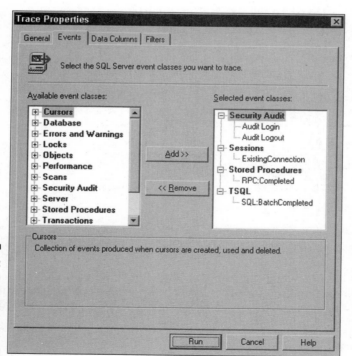

Figure 2-7:
The Trace
Properties
dialog box
showing the
Events tab.

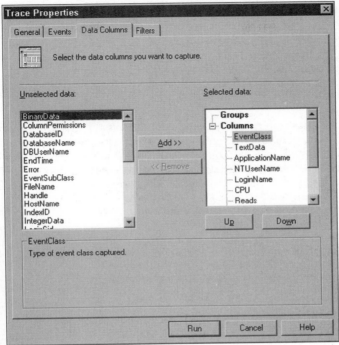

Figure 2-8:
The Trace
Properties
dialog box
showing the
Data
Columns
tab.

Then choose the data for the following fields in the Data Columns tab:

- ✔ **Unselected Data:** The data shown in this list box is a list of all possible data that can be captured by the event. To select the item, highlight it and click the Add button or double-click the item.

- ✔ **Selected Data:** The data shown in this list box has been selected from the Unselected data list box and is a list of all data items the event captures. To remove the item, highlight it and click the Remove button or double-click the item.

After the trace is run, the data will appear in columns, from left to right, according to the columns chosen in the Selected data list box. Therefore, if you want to reorder the columns, simply select an item in the list box and click the Up or Down button to relocate the item. Remember, the item that is shown on the top of the list box will appear in the leftmost column of data when the trace is run.

Entering filter data

Filter data is how you instruct the trace to determine the criteria for the events to capture. The trace will return data specified in the Data Columns tab only when all the criteria specified on this screen is matched. For example, if you want for the trace to return specific columns of data only when the value of the Windows NT User Name is amann (that's my username), you can indicate this.

This filter data is specified on (as you would expect) the Filters tab. This tab can look quite confusing when you first see it. However, it's not as bad as it looks. (Click the Filters tab to make sure that it's selected, as shown in Figure 2-9.) Then select and enter data for the Trace event criteria list. Select from the list of available events to monitor. These events, when the criteria is matched, generate the trace. The Trace event criteria box presents a tree that you can use to drill-down to see the individual events available.

When you click an individual event, you see the list of possible matching criteria below that event. However, not every event allows all these criteria:

- **Equals:** Tests for the exact equality of a value
- **Greater than:** Tests for any value greater than that supplied value, but not equal to it
- **Greater than or equal to:** Tests for the exact equality of a value, or anything greater than that value
- **Less than:** Tests for any value less than that supplied value, but not equal to it
- **Less than or equal to:** Tests for the exact equality of a value, or anything less than the value
- **Like:** Tests for values that are similar to the value entered
- **Not equal to:** Tests for the inequality of a value
- **Not like:** Tests for values that are not similar to the value entered

One final field that is available is the Exclude System IDs check box. Select this box if you do not want to monitor system objects. Checking this box will automatically add a criteria that limits the Object ID event to be greater than or equal to a value of 100. This box is unchecked by default.

When you are ready, click the Run button to run the trace. Clicking this button also saves it to a file or a table, if you've chosen to do so.

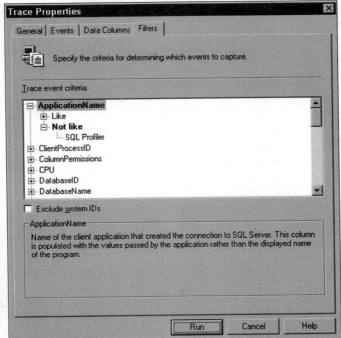

Figure 2-9:
The Trace
Properties
dialog box
showing the
Filters tab.

SQL Server Query Analyzer

The SQL Server Query Analyzer is a tool that comes with SQL Server 2000 to allow you to issue any SQL Statement to SQL Server. In addition, the results can be displayed in a tabular format or a grid format. To start the SQL Server Query Analyzer, choose Start⇨Programs⇨Microsoft SQL Server⇨Query Analyzer (see Figure 2-10). You can also launch the Query Analyzer from within the Enterprise Manager by choosing Tools⇨SQL Query Analyzer.

SQL Server Analyzer enables you to view an execution plan for a query, which is beneficial because you may be able to improve performance by constructing queries in a different way. See Chapter 9 for more of a discussion on the SQL Server Query Analyzer. One really cool new feature of the Query Analyzer for SQL Server 2000 is the addition of the object browser. Anybody who uses Microsoft Visual Studio knows all about the object browser. Jump to Chapter 9 if you can't wait to learn about the Query Analyzer.

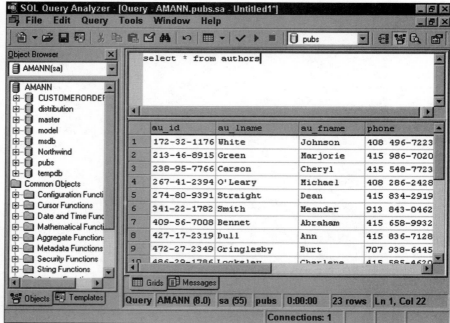

Figure 2-10:
The SQL
Server 2000
Query
Analyzer in
all its glory.

Microsoft English Query

Microsoft English Query is a tool that comes with SQL Server 2000 to allow you to issue queries by using English statements — instead of supplying SQL statements to SQL Server.

By specifying in English what you want SQL Server to do, Microsoft English Query applications that you write translate your English sentences into Transact-SQL and issue your requests to the server. This method is a great alternative to having to learn Transact-SQL. However, if you do want to take a look at SQL, I give you a great overview of the SQL language in Chapters 4, 5, and 8. I do not cover writing English Query applications in this book.

SQL Server Performance Monitor

The SQL Server Performance Monitor is a tool that allows you to monitor the performance of SQL Server, as the name suggests. This tool is available only if you are running SQL Server 7 or SQL Server 2000 on Windows NT 4.0 or Windows 2000. Performance Monitor isn't available for Windows 95/98 because the SQL Server Performance Monitor extends the ability of the performance monitor already built into Windows NT and Windows 2000.

The performance monitor allows for the graphical viewing of the performance of parameters that you specify. To start the SQL Server Performance Monitor, choose Start⇨Settings⇨Administrative Tools⇨Performance (see Figure 2-11).

When you install Microsoft SQL Server 2000 onto a Windows NT Server 4.0 or Windows 2000 computer, the Setup program automatically integrates SQL Server 2000 objects and counters into the Performance Monitor (PERFMON.EXE). The Performance Monitor is a tool that comes with Windows NT or Windows 2000 to allow you to view and monitor the performance of a specific process or application running on Windows NT or Windows 2000.

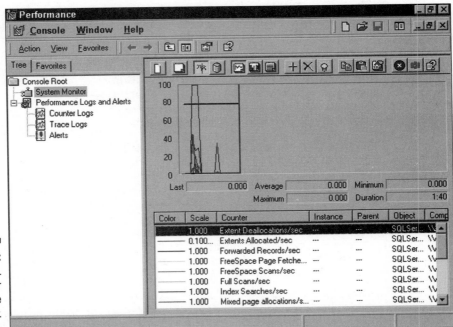

Figure 2-11: The SQL Server Performance Monitor.

Server Network Utility

The Server Network Utility allows you to configure a server to communicate using one or more network libraries. To start the Server Network Utility, choose Start⇨Programs⇨Microsoft SQL Server⇨Server Network Utility (see Figure 2-12).

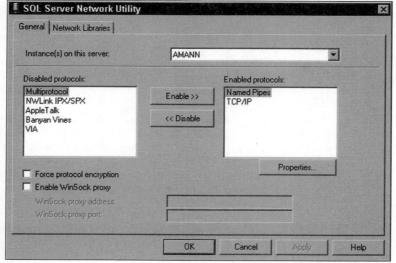

Figure 2-12:
The SQL
Server
Server
Network
Utility,
showing the
General tab.

There are two tabs (General and Network Libraries) that aid you in configuring the network libraries that are enabled on the server.

Entering general information

The General tab enables you to configure the network protocols that the server listens on (see Figure 2-12). Click the General tab to make sure that it's selected. Then supply data for the following fields in the General tab:

- ✔ **Instance(s) on This Server:** Lists all instances installed on the current server. Each instance can have its own protocols. Select from the drop-down list of instances that you want to configure. The default instance is listed automatically.

- ✔ **Disabled Protocols:** Lists all protocols that are not enabled for the instance shown in the Instance(s) on this server drop-down list. To enable a protocol shown in this list box, you can either select it and click the Enable button or double-click the desired protocol. It will move to the Enabled protocols list box.

- ✔ **Enabled Protocols:** Lists all protocols that are enabled for the instance shown in the Instance(s) on this server drop-down list. To disable a protocol shown in this list box, you can either select it and click the Disable button or double-click the desired protocol. It will move to the Disabled protocols list box.

Furthermore, for any selected enabled protocol, you can click the Properties button to configure properties for that protocol. Each protocol has its own properties that can be configured. For example, the TCP/IP protocol can have the port configured (which is 1433 by default).

✔ **Enable Protocol Encryption:** If this check box is selected, the protocol that is selected will automatically become encrypted, allowing for secure SSL communication between the client and the server.

✔ **Enable Winsock Proxy:** If this check box is selected, communication is allowed through a proxy server so that your network is secure from hackers. If this check box is selected, you can enter a Winsock proxy address and a Winsock proxy port. These values specify how the SQL Server connection will be made through the proxy server.

Viewing network libraries

The last tab allows you to view the network libraries that are installed on your system (see Figure 2-13). To view these options, use the Network Libraries tab. Click this tab to make sure that it's selected. You can view only the network libraries installed. You cannot add or change network libraries from this tab.

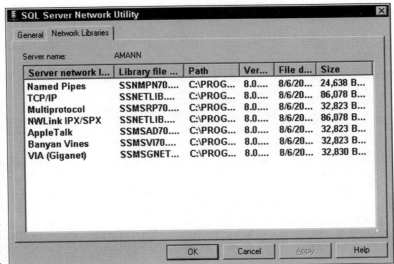

Figure 2-13: The SQL Server Server Network Utility, showing the Network Libraries tab.

Unless your client computer is set up to communicate with SQL Server using the same network libraries and parameters, a client cannot connect to SQL Server.

Client Network Utility

The Client Network Utility allows you to configure your client computer to communicate using one or more network protocols with SQL Server 2000 tools.

It is not necessary to use this utility for programs that you are writing to communicate with SQL Server 2000. It is used only for the tools that are installed with SQL Server 2000, such as the Query Analyzer. The only thing that you need for your own programs to communicate with SQL Server 2000 is to have the network libraries and database libraries installed.

To start the Client Network Utility, choose Start⇨Programs⇨Microsoft SQL Server⇨Client Network Utility (see Figure 2-14).

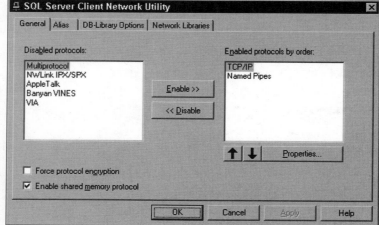

Figure 2-14:
The SQL
Server
Client
Network
Utility,
showing the
General tab.

There are four tabs (General, Alias, DB-Library Options, and Network Libraries) that aid you to configure the network protocols enabled on the client for communication with a similarly-configured server.

Selecting protocol information

Supply data that describes the protocol(s) that will be used in the General tab (see Figure 2-14). Click the General tab to make sure that it's selected. Then supply data for the following fields in the General tab:

✔ **Disabled Protocols:** Lists all protocols that are not enabled for the client. To enable a protocol shown in this list box, you can either select it and click the Enable button or double-click the desired protocol. It will move to the Enabled protocols list box.

✔ **Enabled Protocols by Order:** Lists all protocols that are enabled for the client. To disable a protocol shown in this list box, you can either select it and click the Disable button or double-click the desired protocol. It will move to the Disabled protocols list box.

SQL Server attempts connections using the protocols in the order shown. If you want to change the order, simply select the desired enabled protocol and click the up and down arrows, as desired.

Furthermore, for any selected enabled protocol, you can click the Properties button to configure properties for that protocol. Each protocol has its own properties that can be configured. For example, the TCP/IP protocol can have the port configured (which is 1433 by default).

✔ **Enable Protocol Encryption:** If this check box is selected, the protocol that is selected will automatically become encrypted, allowing for secure SSL communication between the client and the server.

✔ **Enable Shared Memory Protocol:** If this check box is selected, the shared memory protocol is used. Note that this works only if the client and the server are running on the same server. If so, this can be a very fast communications mechanism.

Defining aliases

An alias is another (usually shorter) name to refer to connection properties for SQL Server. The advantage is that an alias allows you to reference the alias name rather than supply the connection values again. To define an alias, use the Alias tab (see Figure 2-15). Click the Alias tab to make sure that it's selected.

Click the Add button, which brings up the dialog box shown in Figure 2-16.

Then supply data for the following fields in the dialog box:

✔ **Server Alias:** Enter the name that you will refer to after configuring the connection properties, such as LAB.

✔ **Network Libraries:** Select the desired network library through which communication will take place from the available option buttons. Named Pipes and TCP/IP are the most common communications protocols.

✔ **Connection Properties:** Enter the parameters for the selected network library. The properties shown in this section will depend on the network library chosen. Most often, the default values shown are the correct values to use in most cases.

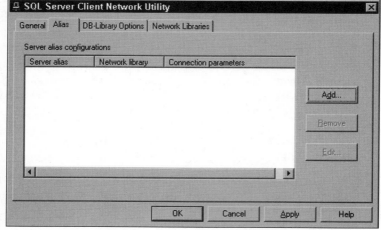

Figure 2-15:
The SQL
Server
Client
Network
Utility,
showing the
Alias tab.

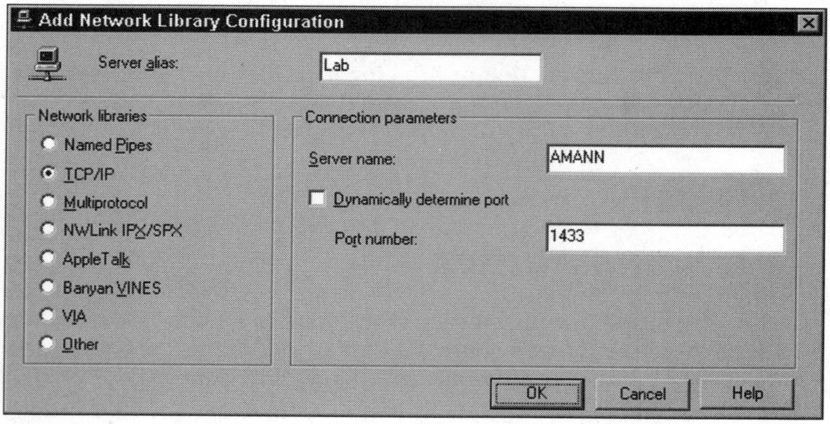

Figure 2-16:
The Add
Network
Library Con-
figuration
dialog box.

Selecting options

There are a couple of options available for the db-library on the client side. To define options, use the DB-Library Options tab. Click this tab to make sure that it's selected. You can choose from the following options:

- **Automatic ANSI to OEM Conversion:** Ensures that ANSI (American National Standards Institute) standards are being used when communicating from client to server and from server to client. This option is selected by default.

- **Use International Settings:** Ensures that date, time, and currency formats are retrieved from the system, based on locales. This option is selected by default.

Viewing network libraries

The last tab allows you to view the network libraries that are installed on your system. To view these options, use the Network Libraries tab. Click this tab to make sure that it's selected. You can view only the network libraries installed. You cannot add or change network libraries from this tab. Figure 2-13, which appears in the "Server Network Utility" section, shows the same image as that in the Client Network Utility.

Wonderful Wizards

Along with the great tools I show you in this chapter, some extremely helpful wizards come with SQL Server 2000. Most of the wizards are launched by first running the SQL Server Enterprise Manager. To start the SQL Server Enterprise Manager, choose Start➪Programs➪Microsoft SQL Server➪Enterprise Manager. After the Enterprise Manager is running, choose Tools➪Wizards from the Enterprise Manager toolbar. This command brings up the Select Wizard dialog box, which contains most of the wizards in SQL Server 2000.

I don't want to disappoint you too much, but in this book I don't cover every wizard. I cover a bunch of them, but I don't want this book to be 1,000 pages (and I'm sure you don't want to pay for 1,000 pages).

However, I do show a flowchart in Appendix A to show the flow of logic, based on the options that you choose for many of the following wizards, which are available in SQL Server 2000:

- ✔ Action
- ✔ Configure Publishing and Distribution
- ✔ Copy Database
- ✔ Create Database
- ✔ Create Database Backup
- ✔ Create Index
- ✔ Create Login
- ✔ Create Publication
- ✔ Create Pull Subscription
- ✔ Create Push Subscription
- ✔ Create View
- ✔ Cube
- ✔ Data Transformation Services

- Database Maintenance Plan
- Define Transformation of Published Data
- Dimension
- Disable Publishing and Distribution
- DTS Import/Export
- Full-Text Indexing
- Help topics
- Incremental Update
- Index Tuning
- Migrate Repository
- Mining Model
- OLAP Project
- Partition
- Project
- Replication
- SQL Project
- SQL Server Login
- Storage Design
- Usage Analysis
- Usage-Based Optimization
- Virtual Cube
- Web Assistant

Help Me, Help Me!

What if you need additional help beyond what I show you in the book? Well, fortunately, Microsoft thought of that. A very easy-to-use help system called Books Online is available. If you are new to Books Online, you'll find that you can't live without it.

To start Books Online, choose Start⇨Programs⇨Microsoft SQL Server⇨ Books Online.

Part II
Database Design

"We sort of have our own way of mentally preparing our people to take the MCSE NT workstation exam."

In this part . . .

I show you how to design your databases. I discuss all the main objects that relate to databases so that you can get up and running fast. I even show you how to use stored procedures and user-defined functions (which are new to SQL Server 2000). One other thing that Microsoft SQL Server 2000 gives you is lots of built-in functionality, and I tell you about this, too.

Chapter 3

Understanding the Relational Data Model

In This Chapter

▶ Discovering schema objects

▶ Defining a relational model

▶ Designing the model

▶ Documenting the model

Microsoft SQL Server is a relational database. A *relational database* is one that's organized in a series of two-dimensional tables. These tables relate to one another based on *fields* (or *columns*) in the tables. The fields between tables that relate to each other are known as *keys*. The *x*-axis (or horizontal) dimension of the table represents defined columns and the *y*-axis (or vertical) dimension of the table represents the data itself, stored as rows.

In this chapter, I describe the relational model, how it works, and what you need to know to design great databases. I don't go into great detail on the process of creating the database objects. If you are looking for detail about how to create these database objects (more than just a narrative and pretty pictures), see Chapters 4 and 5.

Schema Objects

The relational database is made up of objects. All the database objects that comprise the database are referred to as the *schema*. These objects include tables, indexes, and other types of objects that are discussed throughout this section. A database object, or schema object, is more commonly known as the database itself. The design of all the objects that make up the database schema is known as the data model. By design, I mean how you structure the tables and other objects to store data. An improper data design can severely affect performance of your database, so get a cup of coffee and let's dig in.

A schema starts with a database. That database contains one or more tables, which contains one or more columns (see Figure 3-1) with which to store rows of data in those tables.

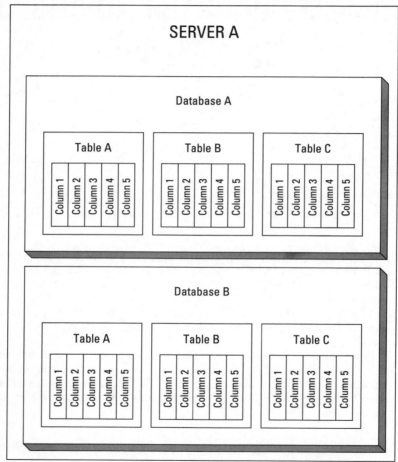

Figure 3-1:
Relationship
between
databases,
tables, and
columns.

Keys

A *key* identifies and defines a specific set of one or more columns in a table that serve a specific purpose. There are two main types of keys:

- Primary keys
- Foreign keys

Primary keys

A *primary key* refers to one or more columns in a table that uniquely identify how rows of data are stored in that table. You can think of a primary key as a way to locate specific data entries in a table. These data entries are called *records* or *rows*. The terms *records* and *rows* can be used interchangeably. A primary key is used by the database to enforce the uniqueness of rows within a table. You want to enforce uniqueness so that you don't store duplicate records. To help you understand primary keys, consider my example in Figure 3-2.

The Customer ID is the primary key.

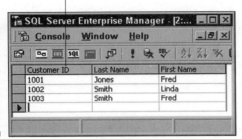

Figure 3-2: Customer ID as a candidate for the primary key.

Because the Customer ID column is unique per customer, the Customer ID column defines the primary key. You cannot define the Last Name column as the primary key because the last name of Smith appears more than once. This multiple listing would go against (or *violate*) the primary key definition. SQL Server does allow you to violate the primary key. You also cannot define the First Name column as the primary key because the first name of Fred appears more than once. Therefore, you must know how the data is stored in the table to define the primary key. The only possible way to define a primary key in this table is with the Customer ID column. However, in the following example, Customer ID no longer uniquely identifies a row (see Figure 3-3).

Figure 3-3: Customer ID and PO Num as the primary key, not just Customer ID.

The table shown in Figure 3-3 needs to have a primary key containing Customer ID and PO Num because the combination of these two columns uniquely identifies rows of data. In this example, the reason that the primary key is Customer ID and PO Num is because the values in the Customer ID column alone are not unique. Likewise, the values in the PO Num column alone are not unique. There are duplicate values in each of the columns. However, if the primary key is Customer ID and PO Num, the combination of these columns contains unique values.

Note: If the customer reused the same PO Numbers, doing so would violate the primary key.

Just because you know what the primary key is doesn't mean that SQL Server does. You need to actually define the primary key for SQL Server. You can define the primary key at one of two different times:

✔ When you create the table with SQL

✔ After you create the table with SQL or the Enterprise Manager

Foreign keys

A *foreign key* is one or more columns in a table whose values in those columns match the values in the primary key of another table. A foreign key is used by SQL Server to ensure that the value in the table containing the foreign key actually matches the value in the table containing the primary key. This match is known as referential integrity. *Referential integrity* maintains the integrity of data between one or more tables that relate to each other. If you use SQL Server to manage your relationships, this is called *declarative referential integrity,* or DRI. DRI allows SQL Server to enforce your relationships through foreign keys. Look at Figure 3-4 to see how the foreign key in the Orders table (Customer ID column) enforces the referential integrity in the Customers table (Customer ID column). In Figure 3-4, the primary keys are shown in bold. The foreign key relationship is defined by the line shown in the diagram. The symbols shown above the arrow indicate the type of relationship (one-to-many). For more information, see the section "Relationships" later in this chapter.

Figure 3-4:
Foreign keys enforce referential integrity.

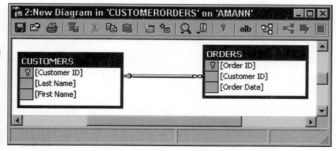

You need to define the foreign key to let SQL Server know how to enforce referential integrity. Much like a primary key, you define the foreign key at one of two different times:

- ✔ When you create the table with SQL
- ✔ After you create the table with SQL or the Enterprise Manager

For more information about creating a foreign key, see Chapter 5.

Rules

A *rule* is a database object that you attach, or *bind,* to a column in a table. A rule indicates to SQL Server what values are valid to be contained in one or more columns in a table. You can also apply a rule to a user-defined type. Rules are said to enforce domain integrity. This is just a fancy word to indicate that values in a column are validated before the data is allowed into the column.

Like any other database object, you define a rule with a name but rules also require a condition. This condition can be any expression that you enter in the WHERE clause of an SQL statement.

You can create a rule at one of two different times:

- ✔ By specifying when you create the table with SQL
- ✔ By specifying after you create the table with SQL or the Enterprise Manager

For more information about creating rules, see Chapter 5.

Rules are supported in Microsoft SQL Server 2000, but there is another, preferred method of defining valid values in a table. This method is by implementing a check constraint, which is also covered in Chapter 5.

Defaults

A *default* is a database object that indicates a value for a column so that if a value is omitted or null, a value is still inserted or updated for that column. Like rules and check constraints, defaults are said to enforce domain integrity.

You can create a default in one of three ways:

- ✔ By using the SQL Server Enterprise Manager
- ✔ By specifying when you create the table with SQL
- ✔ By specifying after you create the table with SQL or the Enterprise Manager

For more information about creating defaults, see Chapter 4.

Triggers

A *trigger* is a database object, made up entirely of Transact-SQL, which SQL Server automatically executes when you insert, update, or delete data from a table. When a trigger executes, it is said to *fire*. You define a trigger for a specific action or set of actions. For example, you can define a trigger that executes upon inserts and updates, but not deletes. You should know that if you define a trigger in this way, the exact same code will execute for inserts and updates. If insert code needs to be different from update code, you need to define two separate triggers. Likewise, if you need three different actions, you need to define three different triggers.

Triggers can be very useful for referential integrity. You can, for example, define a trigger so that every time you insert a value into table A, data is also inserted into table B.

The nice thing about triggers is that they're automatic. After an INSERT, UPDATE, or DELETE SQL statement successfully executes, your predefined triggers fire.

For more information about creating triggers, see Chapter 5.

Indexes

An *index* is a database object that helps speed queries by either instructing SQL Server to physically put the records in a table in order, or by providing an execution path so that SQL Server (actually the query optimizer) knows how to run the query.

Indexes can help or hurt query performance, depending on the situation. However, the query optimizer in SQL Server 2000 is very intelligent. This intelligence means that if the SQL Server optimizer determines that an index may adversely affect the performance of the query, SQL Server will do a table scan. A *table scan* occurs when SQL Server looks up all records by reading the table into memory and testing to discover which records match the specified criteria. In this case, SQL Server doesn't use an index to run a query.

There are two types of indexes:

- ✔ Clustered
- ✔ Nonclustered

A *clustered* index is an index that physically stores data in order, based on the fields in your primary key. This allows for greater access speed to your data because SQL Server can get right to the row(s) you need if they are stored in order. There can be a maximum of one clustered index on a table — the data in a table can be physically stored in only one way. Clustered indexes are particularly useful when the fields that make up the clustered index are integers.

You can equate a clustered index to entries in the white pages of a phone book. The way you look up an entry with the company name of "Mann Enterprises" is by knowing that "M" is physically laid out (or stored) after "A," "B," and so on, but before "N." You then traverse all letters in the name that you are looking for and, bingo, you've found the name. So, as you might imagine, if you add (or insert) an entry for a company, all companies that logically follow the newly added company have to be physically relocated to other pages so that subsequent retrievals work the way you expect.

A *nonclustered* index is one which is not physically stored in order of the primary key, but is stored in such a way that the index points to the location of the data in the table. This allows for fast retrieval, but not as fast as a clustered index.

A nonclustered index can be equated to the yellow pages of a phone book. Each entry is not listed by company name, but by category. All data entries (company names) are not physically laid out in order, but the index of categories helps you to quickly locate the entries.

If you had no indexes at all, you would have to scan each and every page in the phone book until you found the entry that you wanted. Obviously, this could take a very long time.

For more information about creating indexes, see Chapter 5.

What Is a Relational Model?

Notice how much data is repeated in the table in Figure 3-5. This data layout is referred to as *denormalized* data. The customer names, order numbers, and prices are all repeated. The design of the relational model affects how much (or how little) of your data is repeated. A relational model (sometimes called a data model or a relational data model) defines the way you design your database. In other words, this means that the way you lay out your databases, tables, and columns defines your relational model.

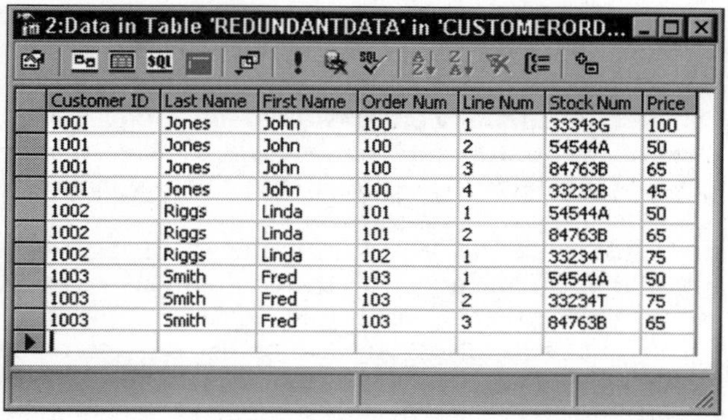

2:Data in Table 'REDUNDANTDATA' in 'CUSTOMERORD...

Customer ID	Last Name	First Name	Order Num	Line Num	Stock Num	Price
1001	Jones	John	100	1	33343G	100
1001	Jones	John	100	2	54544A	50
1001	Jones	John	100	3	84763B	65
1001	Jones	John	100	4	33232B	45
1002	Riggs	Linda	101	1	54544A	50
1002	Riggs	Linda	101	2	84763B	65
1002	Riggs	Linda	102	1	33234T	75
1003	Smith	Fred	103	1	54544A	50
1003	Smith	Fred	103	2	33234T	75
1003	Smith	Fred	103	3	84763B	65

Figure 3-5: Diagram showing redundant data.

Breaking this table into parts so that data is not repeated is called *normalization.* There are different levels of normalization called First, Second, and Third Normal Form. Technically, there is a Fourth Normal Form and a Fifth Normal Form, but these are rarely used in practice, so I don't cover them in this book. Depending on the level of normalization desired, you need to follow these rules:

- **Eliminate repeating groups:** This means that a separate table must be used for each set of related attributes. Each separate table must have a primary key. Primary keys are described earlier in this chapter. If this level of normalization is met, the database is said to be in *First Normal Form,* or 1NF.
- **Eliminate redundant data:** If an attribute depends on part of a multi-valued key, move it to a separate table. If this level of normalization is met, the database is said to be in *Second Normal Form,* or 2NF.
- **Eliminate columns not dependent on a key:** If attributes do not contribute to a description of a key, move them to a separate table. If this level of normalization is met, the database is said to be in *Third Normal Form,* or 3NF.

The level of normalization that you select can have a direct impact on performance. 1NF generally contains fewer tables but more data. 1NF helps in query performance, but the database is larger. 3NF contains more tables that can hurt query performance, but the database is smaller. As you might expect, 2NF is somewhere in the middle between 1NF and 3NF. It is typical that data warehouses and data marts are in 1NF (or possibly 2NF). It is typical that Online Transaction Processing (OLTP) systems are in 3NF (or possibly 2NF).

The table in Figure 3-6 shows the normalized table from Figure 3-5. To normalize the table in Figure 3-5, you would reconstruct it by creating three tables (`CUSTOMERS`, `ORDERS`, and `STOCK`) and enforcing these relationships:

CUSTOMERS.Customer ID -> ORDERS.Customer ID

ORDERS.Stock Num -> STOCK.Stock Num

In the preceding list of relationships, I show the relationships in the format of TABLE.COLUMN — the table name is followed by a period, followed by the column name.

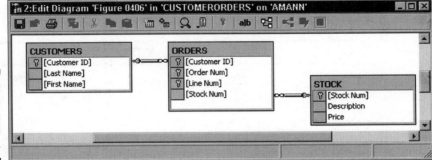

Figure 3-6:
Diagram
showing
normalized
tables.

You may think it is a good idea to always normalize the tables in a database. However, every time you split your data model from one table to two tables, a query will take longer to execute. This is called a *performance hit* — a very common term in database terminology. In the example in Figure 3-5, the database is large because so much data is repeated. On the other hand, in the example in Figure 3-6, the queries to access the data will take longer to execute, even though the database is smaller.

Designing the Model

The data model, sometimes referred to as the *schema,* is very important because it defines how your data is stored. Defining your data model can be a very difficult task because every situation is different and every project has its own level of complexity. However, I can show you some things to keep in mind, along with some tips and tricks.

There are two types of data models:

- ✔ Logical
- ✔ Physical

The logical data model refers to business concepts and table design without regard to how your data will be physically stored on the hard disk. Figure 3-6 can be considered a logical data model because it shows (albeit vaguely) how the business concepts are related to database tables. A logical data model is so named because the model shows how tables logically relate to each other and to business concepts.

Based on this logical design, you do not know (or even care) about, for example, what disk drive the index for the ORDERS table is stored on. That is where the physical data model comes in. A physical data model is not so much a visual model of the physical layout of the database(s) as it is a simple plan of how you will physically store your data. For example, a physical data model can be a spreadsheet, as shown in Table 3-1.

Table 3-1	Physical Data Model		
Object	*Object Type*	*Filegroup*	*Physical Path*
CUSTOMERS	Table	PRIMARY	C:\SQLDATA
IdxPK_Cust	Primary Key Index	PRIMARY	C:\SQLDATA
ORDERS	Table	PRIMARY	C:\SQLDATA
IdxPK_Orders	Primary Key Index	SECONDARY	D:\SQLDATA
STOCK	Table	PRIMARY	C:\SQLDATA
IdxPK_Stock	Primary Key Index	PRIMARY	C:\SQLDATA

Even though filegroups are covered in Chapter 4 (if you want to peek ahead), I wanted to make a point that in a physical data model, you simply map out the physical storage location of your database objects. Notice in Table 3-1 that the primary key index, named IdxPK_Orders, is stored on a separate physical disk drive than the other objects. Also notice that each of the table objects listed in Table 3-1 are also shown in the logical data model in Figure 3-6.

It is always a good idea to design your data model on paper first. If you design your data model as you are creating the tables, you will invariably have to change it.

Before designing the model, you must understand what your client needs. If you don't know, there's no way you can design the model. More often than not, you must first sit down with your client and document the user's requirements. It can also be helpful to create a prototype. A prototype is generally created using some tool that can create screens, but you'll have to use your own judgement as to when this is appropriate. Visual Basic is such a tool, used for fast prototyping.

One of the main reasons for prototyping your application is that it will show all fields on a screen to your users. Generally, every field on a screen corresponds to a column in a table in a database. Another reason for generating a prototype is that many times it will become apparent that you need to store data differently than you were originally thinking.

The diagram in Figure 3-7 shows a dialog box that I generated in Visual Basic. It simulates a dialog box similar to that which you may show to a customer to make sure that you are capturing the data that the customer wants. This example dialog box is used to present customer information.

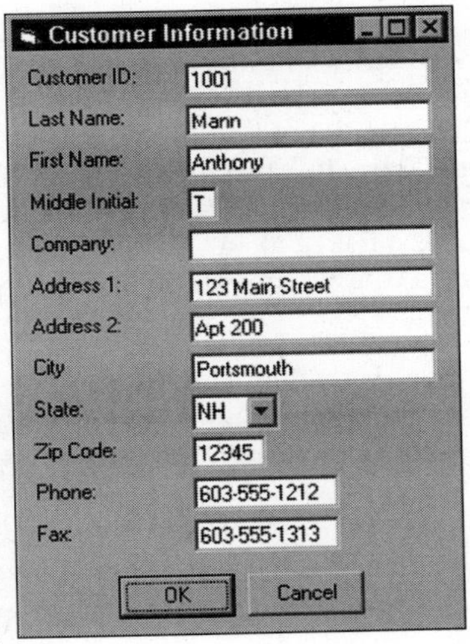

Figure 3-7:
A prototype
Customer
Information
dialog box.

Based on the dialog box shown in Figure 3-7, you know that you at least need one table — call it the Customer table — and you know that you need the following fields:

```
Customer ID
Last Name
First Name
Middle Initial
Company
Address 1
Address 2
City
State
Zip Code
Phone
Fax
```

Looking at these fields, it becomes obvious that Customer ID is the primary key to the table because the Customer ID uniquely identifies the customer. It doesn't make sense for any other field to be the primary key. For example, First Name doesn't make sense to be the primary key because many people in the database may have the same first name. The same theory applies to every other column in the table.

Although this model may seem easy so far, we're not finished with this dialog box. Notice that there is a drop-down list of states. Where does this list come from? It can't come from the Customer table because there may be customers in the database from only one state. If this were the case, the drop-down list of states would contain only one state. Therefore, it makes sense to create another table that contains only a list of all states. Creating a separate table that contains every state ensures that when you take an order, you can choose the correct state for a customer.

This type of table is called a look-up table. A *look-up table* is one whose sole purpose is to provide a valid list of values from which to choose your data. If the table were not used, it would not affect the ability of the data model to perform its function.

I'll call the look-up table States. The States table needs only one field:

    State

Alternatively, the States table could contain two fields: the state abbreviation and the state name. In addition to the two tables I've discussed so far, in an order-taking system, you need to have an Orders table to store the order information taken and to input into the dialog box shown in Figure 3-8. I constructed this dialog box, too, in Visual Basic.

Figure 3-8 shows a basic dialog box that contains many fields, most of which are read-only. A *read-only* field displays data on the dialog box but doesn't allow you to type any data into it. The following fields on the dialog box are read-only:

    Order Date
    Customer ID
    Name
    Description
    Unit Price
    Ext. Price
    Sub-Total

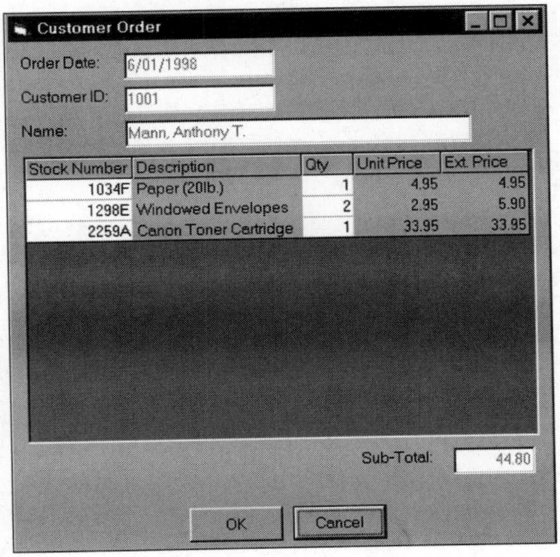

Customer Order

Order Date:	6/01/1998
Customer ID:	1001
Name:	Mann, Anthony T.

Stock Number	Description	Qty	Unit Price	Ext. Price
1034F	Paper (20lb.)	1	4.95	4.95
1298E	Windowed Envelopes	2	2.95	5.90
2259A	Canon Toner Cartridge	1	33.95	33.95

Sub-Total: 44.80

OK   Cancel

Figure 3-8:
A prototype
Customer
Order dialog
box.

The only two fields that are enterable, or known as *read-write,* are as follows:

    Stock Number

    Qty

Knowing which fields are read-only is important because these fields can come from the database or they can be derived. A *derived field* is one that can be calculated or formulated and not actually stored in the database. For example, notice that the value in the Name field in Figure 3-8 is my name, Anthony T. Mann, and is a derived field because my name is not stored in the database in one field. Names are stored in the Customer table under the three fields: Last Name, First Name, and Middle Initial.

Not all read-only fields are derived. The Customer ID field is read-only, not derived, and comes from the Customer table. The Order Date field is read-only and derived. It isn't derived from one or more database fields, but is derived from the computer's clock.

Now, look once again at Figure 3-8. The data stored from this dialog box needs to go into a table. Because it stores order information, I call the table Orders. The following columns are needed in the Orders table:

    Order Date

    Customer ID

    Stock Number

    Qty

These are the only columns needed in this table. Why, you may ask? Look at each of the other fields shown in Figure 3-8. Name is a derived field. Look up the Name by using a join in the Customer table. The Customer table contains the Customer ID, Last Name, First Name, and Middle Initial.

The Description field is not derived but is looked up in another table for stock information. Along with the stock information is the price of each unit. Therefore, when the user types a quantity, the system looks up the unit price and calculates, or derives, the Ext. (Extended) Price. Sub-Total is a derived field that is calculated based on all the Ext. Price values.

It's a good design tip to know that if a derived field can be derived every time from the values in the database, you probably don't want to store it in the database. Ext. Price is such a field. On the other hand, Order Date is not such a field. The client program written in Visual Basic automatically fills in the current date when the order is taken, but it needs to be stored so that reports can be generated based on date.

The stock information is stored in a separate table, mainly because if you follow rule number two in the three rules of data normalization described earlier (see "What Is a Relational Model?"), you'll see no repeating data. If the stock information is stored in the Orders table, much of the data may be repeated, such as Description, which greatly increases the size of the database. You may want to repeat this data (a concept known as denormalization), but you have to have a good reason! One such reason could be that you want to increase the speed of your queries at the expense of storing more data than you would if the table were normalized.

To normalize the design, I propose storing the stock information in a table called (what else?) Stock. The Stock table contains these columns:

    Stock Number

    Description

    Unit Price

The primary key for the table is Stock Number because it uniquely identifies a row in the Stock table.

To put it all together have a look at Figure 3-9, which shows the relationship between CUSTOMERS, ORDERS, and STATES tables I discuss in this section. It isn't possible to tell you about everything I've learned about database design over the years in one chapter, but I want to give you a good overview of the technique and show you the method to the madness as well.

The concepts that I discuss in this section, "Designing the Model," may prompt many questions in your mind. One question may be "Why don't you store the Unit Price in the Orders table?" The reason is that for my example, I have decided that there are no price overrides. If there were, the override price would need to be stored somewhere.

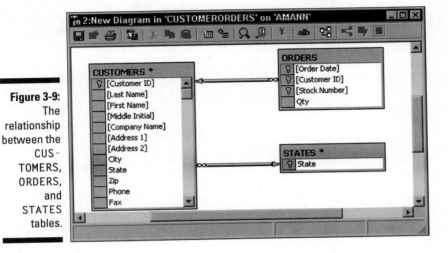

Figure 3-9:
The
relationship
between the
CUS-
TOMERS,
ORDERS,
and
STATES
tables.

Another question you may ask is "What about sales tax?" It's true that this example does not take sales tax into account. It isn't intended to be a real-world database but rather only serve as an example.

One final question may be "What happens if someone places an order outside the United States?" The example that I present takes into account orders only within the United States. You can easily expand it to take international orders into account.

Another way to design your data model is to design an entity relationship diagram based on data flow and the business process model. This way to design the data model generally works if your clients know exactly what they want. However, many times, your clients will need to see a screen prototype because they can't visualize the application based on an entity-relationship diagram or business definitions.

Datatypes

Every column in every table must be declared as a certain type of data, known as a *datatype*. A finite number of datatypes is available in SQL Server 2000. However, you can create your own. The next few pages outline both of these cases.

Standard datatypes

Microsoft SQL Server 2000 comes standard with many different datatypes. These almost always suit your needs. If they don't, however, refer to the next section, "User-defined datatypes."

Table 3-2 shows the standard datatypes available in SQL Server 2000. In the future, if you need a quick reference to these datatypes (as I know you will), you can find them on the Cheat Sheet at the front of the book.

Table 3-2	Suggested Database Object Prefixes
Datatype	*Explanation*
BigInt	New for SQL Server 2000, this datatype stores whole number integers in the range of -9,223,372,036,854,775,808 to +9,223,372,036,854,775,807. The BigInt datatype requires 8 bytes to store data.
Binary	Holds up to 8,000 bytes of binary data. Binary data is any data that is stored in a stream of 1s and 0s. The data stored in a Binary column must be fixed in length.
Bit	Used to hold either a 1 or a 0, commonly used as a True/False or Yes/No indicator, or a flag that indicates that something is "switched on or off." A Bit datatype takes 1 byte in storage.
Char	Holds up to 8,000 bytes (characters) of data. The data stored in a Char column must be fixed in length.
Cursor	Special datatype that holds a reference to a cursor. These variables are typically used in stored procedures.
Datetime	Stores a date and time value. A Datetime column takes two 4-byte integers of storage. The date range available in the 4-byte configurations is between 1/1/1753 and 12/31/9999. The time range spans the full range of the clock, accurate to within 3/100 of a second.
Decimal	Stores numeric data. The storage space required for the Decimal datatype range is from 2 to 17 bytes, depending on the precision and scale of the data. Precision indicates the number of digits required by the number. Scale indicates the number of decimal places required by the number.
Float	Stores numeric data with floating-point numbers. The range of data that can be stored is from -1.79E + 308 to 1.79E +308. The amount of space required to store a Float datatype is up to 8 bytes.
Image	Stores binary data represented by an image. The Image datatype can store more information than a Binary datatype but requires more space. An Image datatype holds variable-length binary data. The amount of space required varies, based on the amount of data. It can store more than 2GB (gigabytes) of binary data.

Datatype	Explanation
Int	Stores whole number integers in the range of -2,147,483,648 to +2,147,483,647. The Int datatype requires 4 bytes to store data.
Money	Stores monetary values in the range of -922,337,203,685,477.5808 to +922,337,203,685,477.5807. The Money datatype requires 8 bytes to store data.
nChar	Holds up to 4,000 bytes (characters) of Unicode data. The data stored in an nChar column must be fixed in length. Unicode data is used for international characters.
nText	Stores variable-length Unicode character data. The nText datatype can store up to 1,073,741,823 bytes (or characters).
Numeric	Same as the decimal datatype, but the Numeric datatype is preferred.
nVarchar	Holds up to 4,000 bytes (characters) of Unicode data. The data stored in an nVarchar column is variable-length. Unicode data is used for international characters.
Real	Stores numeric data with floating-point numbers. The range of data that can be stored is from -3.40E + 38 to 3.40E +38. The amount of space required to store a Real datatype is 4 bytes, which is half the size (and range) of the Float datatype.
Rowversion	New for SQL Server 2000, this datatype, formerly known as a Timestamp, stores binary data representing the current date and time. The data in a Rowversion column is automatically inserted or updated every time the data in a row is changed.
Smalldatetime	Stores a date and time value. A Smalldatetime column takes 4 bytes of storage. The date range available is between 1/1/1900 and 6/6/2079. The time range spans the full range of the clock, accurate to within one minute.
Smallint	Stores whole number integers in the range of -32,768 to 32,767. The Smallint datatype requires 2 bytes to store data.
Smallmoney	Stores monetary values in the range of @ms214,748.3648 to 214,748.3647. The Smallmoney datatype requires 4 bytes to store data. Decimal places are rounded to two places.

(continued)

Table 3-2 *(continued)*

Datatype	Explanation
SQL_Variant	New for SQL Server 2000, this datatype allows you to not specifically define a datatype when storing values. This is because any valid value of any datatype, except text, ntext, and rowversion can be used.
Sysname	Used to store the name of system tables. The Sysname datatype is automatically defined as being varchar(30) and therefore takes no more than 30 bytes to store.
Table	New for SQL Server 2000, this special datatype allows you to temporarily store result sets for later processing.
Text	Stores variable-length character data. The Text datatype can store up to 2,147,483,647 bytes (or characters).
Tinyint	Stores whole numbers in the range from 0 to 255 and requires only 1 byte to store.
Uniqueidentifier	Stores a globally unique identifier. The Uniqueidentifier datatype requires 16 bytes of storage.
Varbinary	Holds up to 8,000 bytes of binary data. Binary data is any data that is stored in a stream of 1s and 0s. The data stored in a Varbinary column is variable-length.
Varchar	Holds up to 8,000 bytes (characters) of data. The data stored in a Varchar column is variable-length.

User-defined datatypes

If one of the datatypes listed in the "Standard datatypes" section earlier in this chapter doesn't suit your needs, you can create your own. User-defined datatypes are also known as UDTs.

When I say *create your own,* I don't mean that you can create a datatype, such as extremelysmalldatetime, and have that built into SQL Server. You create your own datatype by using the SQL Server Enterprise Manager. The only thing that creating your own datatypes does is to configure the properties of a standard datatype. These configured datatypes can be wrapped into a new datatype so that you don't have to configure it again. The major advantage in creating UDTs is to enforce standards throughout your organization.

As an example, suppose that you wanted to create a new datatype called `Address`. The `Address` datatype would actually be a `varchar` datatype but with the length set to a value of `30`. After you create the datatype, you can then use it in the database where it was created.

To create a UDT, follow these simple steps:

1. **Choose Start⇨Programs⇨Microsoft SQL Server⇨Enterprise Manager to start the SQL Server Enterprise Manager.**

2. **Expand the tree so that you see the User Defined Data Types folder.**

   For more information about expanding the tree, see the Introduction of this book.

3. **Highlight the User Defined Data Types folder.**

   After highlighting the User Defined Data Types folder, notice the list of User Defined Data Types (UDTs) on the right part of the screen. If you have not created any UDTs, none will be listed (see Figure 3-10).

4. **Choose the Action⇨New User Defined Data Type menu option to bring up the User Defined Data Type Properties dialog box.**

   Alternatively, you can use the mouse to right-click anywhere on the right side of the screen and select the New User Defined Data Type menu. Also, you can right-click the User Defined Data Types folder in the tree and select the New User Defined Data Type menu.

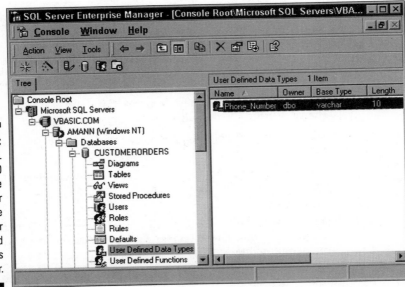

Figure 3-10: The SQL Server 2000 Enterprise Manager showing the User Defined Data Types folder.

Whatever method you choose to create a new User Defined Data Type, each brings up the User-Defined Data Type Properties dialog box (see Figure 3-11).

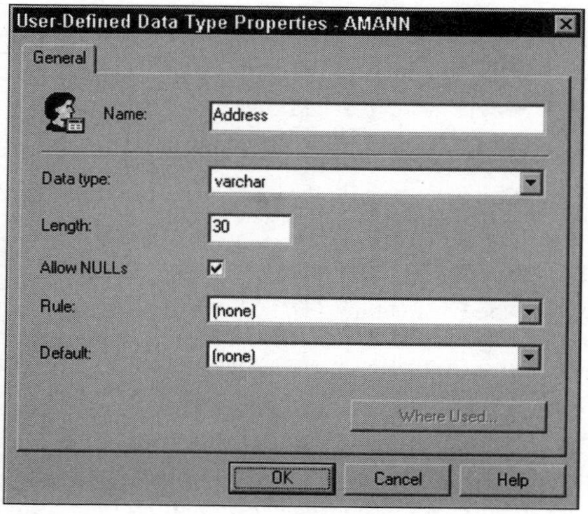

Figure 3-11:
Fill in the fields in the User-Defined Data Type Properties dialog box.

5. **Fill in the desired fields on the User-Defined Data Type Properties dialog box.**

   Fill in these fields:

   • **Name:** This is the name of your new datatype. Enter something like `Address`.

   • **Data Type:** Select from the drop-down list of available datatypes. These are all standard datatypes. For example, choose `varchar`.

   • **Length:** Type the length for you new datatype, if you want to change it from the default value. For example, enter `30`.

   • **Allow NULLs:** Check this box if your new datatype is to allow null values.

   • **Rule:** Select from the drop-down list of defined rules if the rule is to apply to your new datatype. This isn't mandatory, and `(none)` is the default value.

   • **Default:** Select from the drop-down list of defaults if the default is to apply to your new datatype. This isn't mandatory, and `(none)` is the default value.

6. **Click OK to save your new User Defined Data Type.**

The "Tier" Buzzword

You may have heard the term tier. A *tier* is a database term that indicates a specific level of business functionality that's encapsulated into a single object or set of objects. A tier is not created in SQL Server 2000, but it's important to understand the concept anyway because you can't be proficient with SQL Server 2000 and not know how tiers are related to it.

A very typical situation is what you may find in Figure 3-12. It shows a four-tier application. The client application written in a language such as Visual Basic is the first tier. The last tier is always the database itself. The middle tiers, for which there is no limit to the number, contain business logic. Figure 3-12 shows two middle tiers, one which calls the other. Such functionality can be customer-related functionality in one middle tier (tier 2), and order-related functionality in another middle tier (tier 3).

The main advantage to this four-tier application is that if the business rules change, a developer has only to change the object representing the tier, and not the database. An alternative representation of the four-tier application is not to have one object call another, but to have the client tier (tier 1) call either tier 2 or tier 3. There are no limits to the design, and I can't show them all to you. However, I give you a good overview of some of the concepts. This way, when your boss asks you, you can look like a smartie.

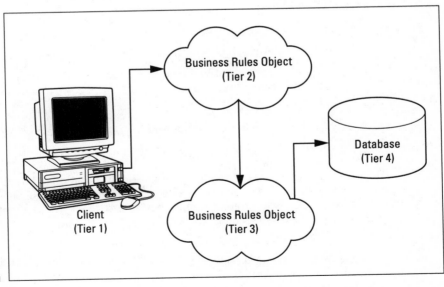

Figure 3-12:
A four-tier
application
architecture.

Business Rules Object
(Tier 2)

Database
(Tier 4)

Client
(Tier 1)

Business Rules Object
(Tier 3)

Naming Conventions

You need to take naming conventions into account when you design your database. A *naming convention* is a consistent way to name your database objects. Let's take a look at columns in a table. No specific convention exists that you need to use to name your columns. I present some possibilities shortly, but these aren't set in stone. Many organizations already publish a list of conventions that are acceptable. The main thing to keep in mind when defining naming conventions is that you should be consistent in your naming scheme.

Without a naming convention, if you ask people how they would name a table that contains customer information, you may get these six responses:

- CUSTOMER
- Customer
- Customer_Info
- CUSTOMERS
- TAB_CUSTOMER
- CustInfo

As you can see, it's important to have some type of convention so that all objects don't appear to have been named haphazardly. You need to keep these things in mind:

- Do your objects contain spaces?
- Do you prefix your objects with a code identifying the type of object?
- Are your objects written in mixed uppercase and lowercase, uppercase only, or lowercase only?
- Do you use plurals in your object names?
- Do you allow underscore characters in your object names?
- Do you limit the number of characters in an object name?

Because coming up with a naming convention is sometimes difficult, all I can do is let you know the naming convention that I use. Note that the naming conventions I show in the rest of this section are how I would construct a production database, which is many times different than the examples I show throughout the book.

Here are my own naming conventions:

- I do not use spaces in any of my object names (even though I show them for clarity in my examples in the book).
- I do prefix all my objects with the type of object it is. For example, I prefix all table names with TAB. Table 3-3 shows the prefixes I use.

Table 3-3	Suggested Database Object Prefixes
Prefix	*Database Object*
USP_	Custom Stored Procedure (User-Defined)
CXP_	Custom Extended Procedure
DEF_	Default
FK_	Foreign Key
IDX_	Index
PK_	Primary Key
RUL_	Rule
SCH_	Schema
TAB_	Table
TRG_	Trigger
UDT_	User-Defined Type
VW_	View

✔ All my table names are in uppercase, but all other objects can be in mixed case. For example, I may name a table TAB_CUSTOMER, but an index would be named IDX_PrimaryIndex.

✔ I rarely use plurals in my object names. For example, I may name a table ORDER, not ORDERS. I realize that ORDERS may make more sense, but by using the convention of no plural names, it's easier to create SQL statements. You don't need to remember which tables are plural and which ones are not.

✔ I do use underscore characters in my object names, but only after the prefix. After that, I use mixed case, where it makes sense. For example, a trigger used to update a customer's address would be named something like TRG_UpdateAddress.

✔ I don't limit the number of characters in an object name. I try to make the name as short as possible, but I don't abbreviate. SQL Server 2000 can handle very long names. Therefore, there's no need to truncate them if it isn't necessary. For example, I would name a column in a customer table LastName, not LstNme. I have seen many companies truncate names in this way. My feeling is, what's the point? In this example, truncating the name saves only two characters.

Relationships

A relationship defines how a column in one table relates to a column in another table. A relationship is defined within the database itself. If a relationship is defined, SQL Server can automatically enforce referential integrity with the definition.

The following types of relationships are available:

- One-to-one
- One-to-many
- Many-to-many

I outline these relationships in the next couple of pages.

One-to-one relationships

A one-to-one relationship indicates that a row in table A can have at most one matching row in table B. Also, a row in table B can have at most one matching row in table A. This type of relationship is not used very often. Primarily, a one-to-one relationship defines the relationship between primary keys in two tables.

So, how about an example? Suppose that you have two tables (with the columns shown in parentheses), as follows:

- `Employees` (`Employee ID, Last Name, First Name, Address, City, State, Zip, Phone`)
- `Salaries` (`Employee ID, Salary`)

The preceding tables each must have its primary key defined as `Employee ID`. This is because you cannot have more than one employee with the same ID.

If you define a relationship between the `Employee ID` column in the `Employees` table and the `Employee ID` column in the `Salaries` table, this would be a one-to-one relationship — one `Employee ID` in the `Employees` table can have at most one value in the `Employee ID` column in the `Salaries` table. Likewise, one `Employee ID` in the `Salaries` table can have at most one value in the `Employee ID` column in the `Employees` table.

Many times, as in the one-to-one relationship that I've shown, you can simply combine the tables. Because the primary key is the same in each table, you can decide which table you want to keep and transfer the non-primary key columns from the other table into that table. For example, if you want to keep the `Employees` table, you can simply add the `Salary` column to the `Employees` table and get rid of the `Salaries` table.

Unless you are going to employ cascading referential constraints, you need to make sure that you update the remaining table with the data from the table you are going to delete.

One-to-many relationships

A one-to-many relationship indicates that a row in table A can have many matching rows in table B. However, a row in table B can have only one matching row in table A. This type of relationship is extremely common.

An example of a one-to-many relationship is the example used in the earlier section, "Foreign keys," in this chapter (refer to Figure 3-4). A Customer ID column in the CUSTOMERS table can have at most one value and a Customer ID column in the ORDERS table can have many values. This is where the one-to-many comes in. Also, note in Figure 3-4 that there is a key symbol next to the Customer ID column in the CUSTOMERS table and an ∞ symbol (indicating infinite, or many) next to the Customer ID column in the ORDERS table. This identifies the relationship visually.

Many-to-many relationships

A many-to-many relationship indicates that a row in table A can have many matching rows in table B. Also, a row in table B can have many matching rows in table A. Generally, it is a good idea to stay away from many-to-many relationships. If you have this type of relationship on two tables, it can make enforcing referential integrity very difficult (if not impossible). It can also make the tables difficult or impossible to optimize for performance. A many-to-many relationship results in data that contains all possible combinations of all data in each of the tables. This type of data result is called a *Cartesian product.* Cartesian products are extremely slow.

An example of when you would have a many-to-many relationship is if you have the following two tables (with column names in parentheses):

- Computers (Manufacturer ID, Model)
- Vendors (Supplier ID, Manufacturer ID)

This is a many-to-many relationship because many manufacturers in the Computers table are supplied by the Manufacturer ID column in the Vendors table. Also, many manufacturers in the Vendors table supply computers in the Computers table.

You can turn two tables with many-to-many relationships into tables with one-to-many relationships by adding a third intermediate table, called a *resolution table.* You can name this resolution table something like `ComputerVendors` and add a couple of columns, like this:

- ✔ Computers (Manufacturer ID, Model ID)
- ✔ ComputerVendors (Model ID, Supplier ID)
- ✔ Vendors (Supplier ID, Manufacturer ID)

With the addition of the third table, one `Supplier ID` in the `Vendors` table can have many values in the `ComputerVendors` table. A `Model ID` in the `ComputerVendors` table can have many values in the `Computers` table. This is how the one-to-many relationships can be obtained, or resolved, from a many-to-many relationship.

Locking

Locking is a very complex topic. *Locking* is a mechanism by which SQL Server handles concurrent users trying to make changes (INSERTs, UPDATEs, or DELETEs) to the same row of data in a table simultaneously. The fact is that truly only one user can actually modify the row at a specific point in time, but it may seem as though the requests are submitted simultaneously. In other words, only one can be first. However, to ensure that other requests are handled properly, locks are created by the SQL Server 2000 Lock Manager. When certain types of locks are created, no further action can occur on a table or row until the lock is released. The Lock Manager can issue different modes of locking, depending on the SQL request. These modes are shown and described in Table 3-4.

Table 3-4	Lock Modes
Lock Mode	*Description*
SHARED	Sometimes called a select lock, a SHARED (S) lock is granted when a resource is selected from the database.
UPDATE	For statements that are not read-only, an UPDATE (U) is granted to avoid problems with deadlocks. This is an intermediate-level lock between a SHARED and an EXCLUSIVE (X) lock. If the update does not occur, the UPDATE lock is de-escalated to a SHARED lock. If the update does occur, the UPDATE lock is escalated to an EXCLUSIVE lock.

Lock Mode	Description
EXCLUSIVE	Anytime a data modification statement is executed, such as INSERT or an UPDATE statement, an EXCLUSIVE lock is needed. Therefore, if there are any other locks on the resource, the connection requesting the EXCLUSIVE lock must wait until the resource is free.
INTENT	An INTENT lock is used to establish a hierarchy of locks. Because SQL Server is a multi-user database, INTENT locks are needed to be able for SQL Server to determine which resources actually obtain specific locks. An INTENT lock is not a lock mode in and of itself. It is a modifier to a SHARED or EXCLUSIVE lock. That is, an INTENT SHARED (IS) lock can exist when a higher-level resource, such as a table, needs to read some of the resources within the table, such as a page. An INTENT EXCLUSIVE (IX) lock is the same as an INTENT SHARED lock, except that the higher-level resource needs to update a lower-level resource.
SCHEMA	There are two types of SCHEMA locks, as follows:
	1. SCH-S lock, which is granted when SQL Server compiles queries. This operation does not prevent any other locks from being granted.
	2. SCH-M lock, which is granted when the schema of a database is changing. For example, if you add a table to the database, a SCHEMA lock is granted on the database.
BULK UPDATE	Occurs when data is being bulk copied into or out of a table. However, this is the only lock for which an option needs to be set before it is granted. You are granted a BULK UPDATE lock under only two conditions:
	1. You have explicitly specified the TABLOCK hint for your INSERT, UPDATE, or DELETE query. This is not affected by a SELECT query. The TABLOCK hint is briefly shown in Chapter 8.
	2. The table lock on bulk load option for the sp_tableoption system stored procedure is set to 1. This option is presented here for completeness but is not covered further in this book.

For a given lock mode, the Lock Manager can issue a specific type of lock. The type of lock issued depends on the SQL request that SQL Server 2000 must process. The lock types are shown in Table 3-5.

Table 3-5	Types of Locks
Lock Type	*Description*
Database	Lock on the entire database.
Extent	Lock on an extent. An *extent* is 8 contiguous data or index pages. A page is 8KB in size, so an extent lock ties up 64KB of data. For more information about indexes, see Chapter 5.
Index Key	Lock on an individual row within an index.
Page	Lock on a single data or index page. A page is an 8KB block of storage used for data or indexes.
Row	RID stands for Row IDentifier. A row lock is placed on an individual row within a table if an index key lock is not used.
Table	Lock on a table. This type of lock places locks on all data and indexes associated with the table.

You may be wondering how locks affect you. Well, if you are having performance problems, such as queries timing out, locking issues may be the cause. You might be issuing SQL queries that SQL Server cannot execute because those queries are waiting for locks to be issued. Perhaps these locks cannot be issued because the Lock Manager has not yet released prior locks. You can view current locks in the Enterprise Manager.

To view the current locks in a database, follow these simple steps:

1. **Choose Start⇨Programs⇨Microsoft SQL Server⇨Enterprise Manager to start the SQL Server Enterprise Manager.**

2. **Expand the tree so that you see the Management folder.**

   For more information about expanding the tree, see the Introduction of this book.

3. **Expand the tree so that you see the Current Activity folder.**

4. **Expand the tree one last time to view either Locks / Process ID or Locks / Object.**

   Locks / Process ID shows all the locks that are placed on all databases in the current server, sorted by process. A *process* is usually related to a database connection, but in some cases multiple processes can be spawned by a single connection.

   Locks / Object shows all the locks that are placed on all databases in the current server, sorted by each object, such as tables or indexes.

Transactions

A *transaction* is a set of one or more SQL statements that are treated as a single unit of work. The individual statements that make up a transaction cannot be executed without 100 percent of the other statements in the transaction also being executed. SQL Server 2000 allows transactions to be nested. *Nested transactions* can be defined as transactions within transactions.

Transaction principles

For a transaction to be valid, it is said that the transaction must pass the ACID test. ACID is an acronym defined as follows:

- **Atomicity:** A transaction must be considered a complete unit of work, allowing all SQL statements to complete, or none of them. This unit of work is known as an atomic unit, hence the term *atomicity.*

- **Consistency:** Whether the transaction succeeds or fails, data must be left in a consistent state. In other words, no data can violate any rules or check constraints that are in place.

- **Isolation:** Concurrent users must be isolated from each other. Isolation is discussed later in this chapter.

- **Durability:** Data must be made durable (stored permanently) when the transaction completes either successfully or unsuccessfully.

Take a look at a common example of a transaction: banking. Suppose that you want to transfer $1,000 in funds from account A to account B. Two logical operations must be performed:

1. Remove $1,000 from account A.
2. Insert $1,000 into account B.

If these two logical units are not placed into a transaction, the funds can be correctly removed from account A, but the SQL statement to insert the transferred funds into account B fails. Now account A has $1,000 less than it did, but account B does *not* have $1,000 more. You just lost $1,000!

Now, if these two logical units are wrapped within a transaction, by definition, either both statements successfully complete or neither of them does. Therefore, you are guaranteed not to lose your money. However, you are *not* guaranteed that the transfer will take place. Either of the SQL statements that make up the transaction can fail, causing the funds not to be transferred — but at least you didn't lose the money!

Distributed transactions

Using the example that I presented in the last section, what if account A exists on a server in Boston, but account B exists on a server in Richmond? The transaction must be distributed across multiple servers in multiple locations. This is (not surprisingly) known as a *distributed transaction*.

A distributed transaction is handled and managed by the SQL Server 2000 Distributed Transaction Coordinator, or DTC. DTC is a service that is installed when you install Microsoft SQL Server 2000.

Distributed transactions work on a concept called a two-phase commit. In other words, two separate parts to the distributed transaction must occur for the distributed transaction to be successful. These two phases are as follows:

- ✔ **Prepare phase:** The DTC communicates with a resource manager on the other server(s) involved in the distributed transaction to alert it that a transaction is coming down the pike and to do whatever is necessary to prepare for it.
- ✔ **Commit phase:** The distributed transaction is committed.

Distributed transactions and queries are covered in Chapter 13.

Isolation

The *I* in ACID stands for Isolation. Isolation works with locking (discussed earlier in this chapter) to ensure that concurrent users can access the server. The level of locking depends on the isolation level set for the transaction. Table 3-6 describes each of the 4 isolation levels possible in SQL Server 2000. For each of the isolation levels shown in Table 3-6, consider that there are two connections, named C1 and C2, to the database.

Table 3-6	Isolation Levels
Isolation Level	*Description*
READ UNCOMMITTED	Transactions are barely isolated from each other. No locking takes place. READ UNCOMMITTED allows dirty reads, which means that C1 can start a transaction and write data, C2 reads the data, and C1 rolls back the transaction. With this isolation level, C2 read data that does not actually exist in the database. These records are known as phantoms. This can be a dangerous situation.

Isolation Level	Description
READ COMMITTED	This is the SQL Server 2000 default isolation level. READ COMMITTED does not allow dirty reads. If C1 starts a transaction and writes data, C2 cannot read the data until C1 commits or rolls back the transaction. The two problems with READ COMMITTED are the following:
	1. The same data may not be repeatable, thereby allowing for inconsistency.
	2. Phantom records may be present.
REPEATABLE READ	Similar to READ COMMITTED, REPEATABLE READ does not allow dirty reads but does promote consistency between reads. However, like READ COMMITTED, phantom records may be present when using the REPEATABLE READ isolation level.
SERIALIZABLE	Transactions are completely isolated from each other, but resource locks will make SQL Server slower because requests for resources will be waiting for locks to become free. With the SERIALIZABLE isolation level, no phantom records can be present.

Isolation levels can be set in SQL Server 2000 with the SET TRANSACTION ISLOATION LEVEL Transact-SQL statement. This statement is briefly covered in Chapter 13.

Chapter 4

Creating Base-Level SQL Server Objects

In This Chapter

▶ Building databases

▶ Designing tables

▶ Specifying default values

▶ Deleting objects

*I*n this chapter, I show you how to create base-level SQL Server objects. I use the term *base-level* because it describes the most elemental of all database objects — those that must exist for even the simplest database to function. SQL Server 2000 offers you multiple ways to create these objects, and I introduce you to most of them within this chapter.

To fully understand the concepts in this chapter, you may want to refer to Chapter 3 for an overview of databases, tables, indexes, and other database objects. Knowledge of relational databases can help you follow through the processes involved in creating base-level SQL Server objects. In this chapter, I don't show the SQL syntax of creating these objects; I show and explain examples only. To see the syntax of creating these objects, see Chapter 8.

Filegroups

Before we dive into SQL Server objects, it is important that you understand the concept of a filegroup. SQL Server 2000 stores databases and related objects in files within the operating system that you are using. By default, database objects and data are both stored in one file, whereas the transaction log is stored in another file. Therefore, a minimum of two files is needed to create a database. However, for performance reasons, you may want to spread the database file into multiple files. Perhaps these separate files are stored on separate disk drives with separate disk controllers.

If you decide to use multiple files, you group them into something called a *filegroup*. Then, some objects, such as indexes, can be placed in a specific filegroup. Doing so controls where the object is physically stored. You should note that the files that make up a filegroup can never be stored in more than one filegroup. A physical file is stored in one and only one filegroup. Also, note that log files cannot be stored in file groups. Only database files can be stored in filegroups.

SQL Server automatically creates a default filegroup when you create a database. This filegroup is called `Primary`. Therefore, if you don't explicitly specify a filegroup when you create databases and related objects, the `Primary` filegroup is used automatically.

Building Databases

A database, the most elemental of objects that you can have on a database server, acts as a container for other objects. You can create a database using any of three tools: the Create Database Wizard, SQL Server Enterprise Manager, or SQL.

To create a database, you must be a member of the `sysadmin` or `dbcreator` fixed server roles. For more information about roles and security, see "Security: Protecting Against Peeping Toms," on the Web site at `www.dummies.com/goto/ fd-0764507753.htm`.

Using the Create Database Wizard

SQL Server 2000 is equipped with many wizards, one of which is the Create Database Wizard. This handy utility guides you through a series of steps, prompting you for input along the way. (See Appendix A for a flowchart of the steps in the Create Database Wizard.) Here's how to create a database using the Create Database Wizard:

1. **To start the SQL Server Enterprise Manager, choose Start⇨Programs⇨ Microsoft SQL Server⇨Enterprise Manager.**

   The SQL Server Enterprise Manager opens, as shown in Figure 4-1.

2. **Click SQL Server Group so that you see the name of your server.**

   My server name is `AMANN`.

3. **From the Tools menu, click Wizards.**

   The Select Wizard dialog box appears (see Figure 4-2).

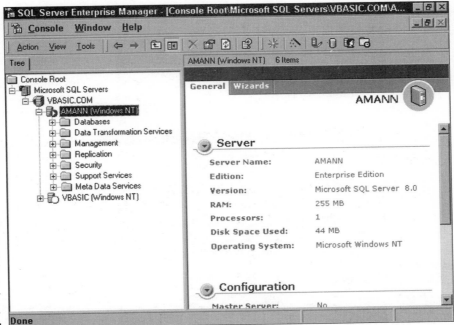

Figure 4-1:
The SQL
Server
Enterprise
Manager
screen.

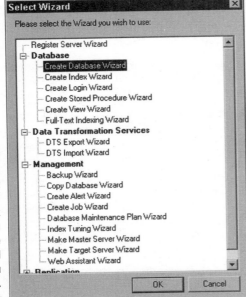

Figure 4-2:
The Select
Wizard
dialog box
enables you
to choose
the wizard
that you
want to use.

4. Click the Create Database Wizard (under the Database category) and then click the OK button.

The Create Database Wizard introductory dialog box appears. Just click Next and get ready to fill in some blanks!

5. Fill in the appropriate Database name and Location fields (see Figure 4-3); then click Next.

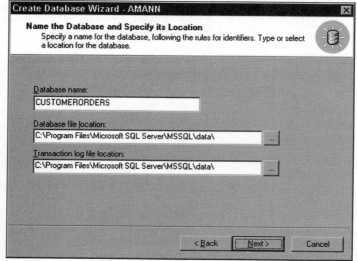

Figure 4-3:
Naming
your
database
and
specifying
its location.

- **Database Name:** The name that you give to your database is used when you connect to the server. If you are going to use the database to track orders, you may want to call it CUSTOMERORDERS.

- **Database File Location:** When you consider where you want your database to be stored, keep in mind that the default location is in the \data subdirectory of wherever you installed SQL Server 2000. The database file is used to store your actual data and database objects.

- **Transaction Log File Location:** When you consider where you want your transaction log to be stored, keep in mind that the default location is in the \data subdirectory of wherever you installed SQL Server 2000. The transaction log is used to by SQL Server to temporarily store data so that it can roll back changes if errors occur in your SQL statements.

6. Name the file(s) for the database and specify its initial size; then click Next.

Just like its own title suggests, the Name the Database Files window enables you to specify the filename and initial size of the database.

- **File Name:** By default, _Data is added to the end of the database name. For example, CUSTOMERORDERS_Data is the name of my file. You can change the filename by clicking it and typing a new name. The name of this file is not terribly significant, because all your SQL queries will refer to the database name (specified in the previous step), not the filename.

- **Initial Size (MB):** By default, the initial size is 1MB (megabyte). If you want to change the number, click the proposed size and type in a new size.

7. **In the Define the database file growth dialog box, choose one of the following option buttons (see Figure 4-4) and then click Next.**

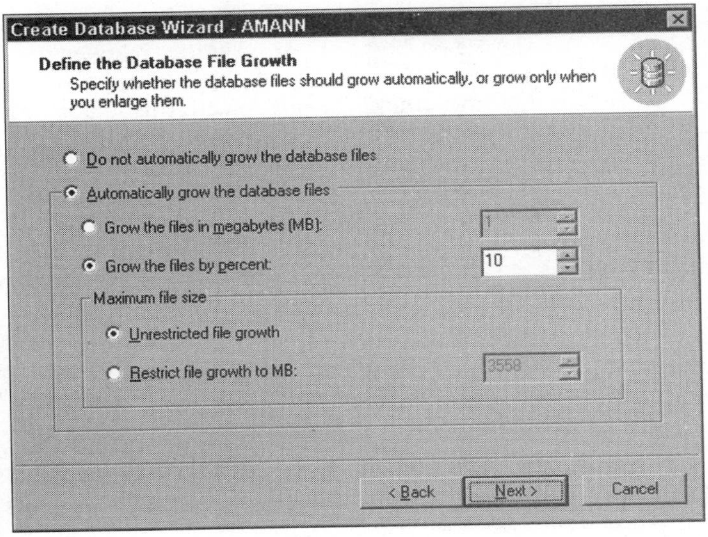

Figure 4-4:
Specify
database
growth
preferences.

- **Do Not Automatically Grow the Database Files:** This option indicates to SQL Server that you do not want SQL Server to automatically increase the size of the database files. You prefer to configure the size of your databases manually.

- **Automatically Grow the Database Files:** This default option indicates to SQL Server that you do not want to manually specify the size for a database as it grows; you want SQL Server to manage this automatically. If you choose this option, a few other options become available. These options are as follows:

  Grow the Files in Megabytes: You can tell SQL Server the increments of growth that you want each time the database needs to enlarge; 1MB is the default value. Unless you plan to add a tremendous amount of data at one time, the default setting is fine.

Grow the Files by Percent: This option indicates to SQL Server that you want the size of the database to grow by a certain percentage, enabling a bigger chunk to be allocated each time the database gets larger. For example, suppose that you set the size increase by 10 percent. If the database begins at 4MB, the next time it increases, it will enlarge by 400,000 bytes, or 10 percent in size. The next time it increases, it does so by 440,000 bytes. This is because of compounding (just like your bank statements).

Unrestricted File Growth: This option, chosen by default, specifies that the file is allowed to grow until you run out of disk space.

Restrict File Growth to (MB): This option specifies that the file is allowed to grow until it reaches the size that you specify in the box to the right. Because the option is very limiting, you're wise to go with the default setting instead.

8. **Name the transaction log file(s) and specify its initial size by filling in the fields and then click Next.**

   The transaction log is a file that SQL Server uses to list every change that has been made to a database within a transaction. This transaction log is how SQL Server recovers data if a transaction is not committed.

   - **File Name:** By default, your filename is your database name with _LOG at the end. For example, CUSTOMERORDERS_LOG is the name of my file. You can change the filename by clicking it and typing a new name. Again, the name of this file is not terribly significant. You will not be referring to this name in your SQL Queries.

   - **Initial Size (MB):** By default, the initial size of each file is 1MB. You can change the size by clicking the proposed size and typing your preference.

9. **Specify whether you want to automatically grow transaction log files or explicitly enlarge them by choosing an option button (similar to the dialog box already shown in Figure 4-4); then click Next.**

   - **Do Not Automatically Grow the Transaction Log Files:** With this option, you can indicate that you want to configure the size of your transaction logs manually.

   - **Automatically Grow the Transaction Log Files:** By default, this option indicates to SQL Server that you do not want to manually specify the size for a transaction log as it grows, but rather have SQL Server manage growth automatically. If you choose this option, a few other options become available. These options are as follows:

     Grow the Files in Megabytes: You can tell SQL Server the incremental size that you prefer for transaction log growth; 1MB is the default value. Unless you plan to add a tremendous amount of data at one time, the default setting is fine.

Grow the Files by Percent: This option indicates to SQL Server that you want the transaction to grow by a certain percentage, which means that a bigger chunk is allocated each time the transaction log gets larger. For example, if you choose this option and set the size increase to 10 percent, the transaction log file begins at 1MB and increases by 100,000 bytes. The next time the file increases, it does so by 110,000 bytes. Think of it as compounding — like the interest amounts on your bank statements.

Unrestricted File Growth: By default, this option specifies that the file is allowed to grow until you run out of disk space.

Restricted File Growth to (MB): This option specifies that the file is allowed to grow until it reaches the size that you specify in the box to the right. The option is too limiting for practical use.

Do Not Automatically Grow the Transaction Log Files: This option indicates to SQL Server that you do not want SQL Server to increase the size of the transaction log files automatically. You would like to configure the size of your transaction logs manually.

10. **Review the Completing the Create Database Wizard information and click the Finish button when you're satisfied with the criteria that the wizard will use to create the database.**

    If you want to change any of the criteria that you specified in earlier steps, you can click the Back button until you reach the dialog box that you want to change.

Relying on the SQL Server Enterprise Manager

You can use the SQL Server Enterprise Manager to create databases as well as many other objects. To use the SQL Server Enterprise Manager for creating a database, follow these steps:

1. **Start the SQL Server Enterprise Manager by choosing Start⊅Programs⊅ Microsoft SQL Server⊅Enterprise Manager.**

2. **Expand the tree by clicking your server name and then click Databases.**

    Notice the row of databases that appears on the right part of the screen (see Figure 4-5). If you don't see a list of databases, you may have clicked the wrong area of the tree.

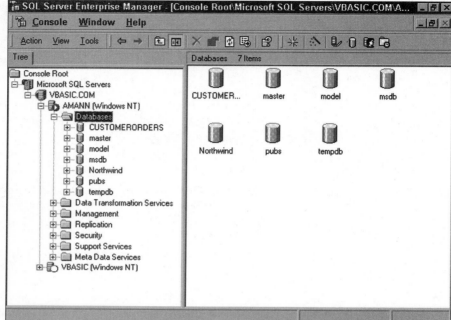

3. Click the New Database icon on the toolbar to bring up the Database Properties dialog box.

You can also right-click anywhere on the right side of the screen and select the `New Database` menu. Or you can right-click the `Databases` folder in the tree and select the `New Database` menu.

The Database Properties dialog box is used to specify properties of the new database; it consists of three tabs that enable you to type the new database's parameters and data (`General`, `Data Files`, and `Transaction Log`). The `General` tab shows by default.

The General tab

You can use the General tab (see Figure 4-6) to enter data that describes the properties of the database, including name, location, and size.

- **Name:** The name that you give to your database will be used each time you connect to the server. For example, if you're going to use the database to track orders, consider calling it `CUSTOMERORDERS`.

- **Collation Name:** Collations are new to SQL Server 2000. A *collation* is the way SQL Server stores strings for sorting and interprets character sets. This is used when you want to sort values using different character sets in different countries. Collation name used to be known as code pages and sort order in prior versions of SQL Server. `Server Default` is the default name shown. Generally, this option is correct in most cases.

The rest of the fields on the tab are read-only and not filled in because they are not known until the database is created.

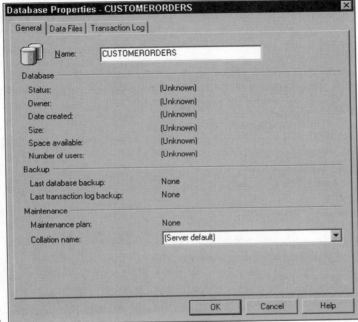

Figure 4-6:
Enter general database information on the General tab of the Database Properties dialog box.

The Data Files tab

The Data Files tab enables you to enter data that describes the database properties, such as name, location, and size (see Figure 4-7).

- ✔ **File Name:** Give your database file a filename. By default, _Data is appended to the name of your database.

- ✔ **Location:** Specify where your data file is to be stored. The default location is in the \DATA subdirectory of wherever you installed SQL Server 2000. Mine is C:\Program Files\Microsoft SQL Server\MSSQL\DATA.

- ✔ **Initial Size (MB):** Specify the initial size of the database. By default, this is 1MB. If you wish to change this, click the proposed size and type in the new size.

- ✔ **Automatically Grow File:** This option indicates to SQL Server that you do not want to manually specify the size for a transaction log as it grows. You would like SQL Server to manage this automatically. This is the default option.

✔ **In Megabytes:** This option indicates to SQL Server that every time the size of the transaction log needs to grow, you want it to grow in size increments specified here. One megabyte is the default value. Unless you plan to be adding a tremendous amount of data at one time, this setting is fine.

✔ **By Percent:** This option indicates to SQL Server that every time the size of the transaction log needs to grow, you want it to grow by a certain percentage. This option allows for a bigger chunk to be allocated every time the database gets larger. For example, suppose that you choose this option and set the size increase at 10 percent. If the transaction log file begins at 1MB, the next time it increases, it will increase by 100,000 bytes, or 10 percent in size. The next time it increases, it does so by 110,000 bytes. This increase occurs because of compounding.

✔ **Unrestricted Filegrowth:** This option specifies that the file is allowed to grow until you run out of disk space. This option is chosen by default.

✔ **Restrict Filegrowth (MB):** This option specifies that the file is allowed to grow until it reaches the size specified in the box to the right. This option is very limiting; you may want to avoid it.

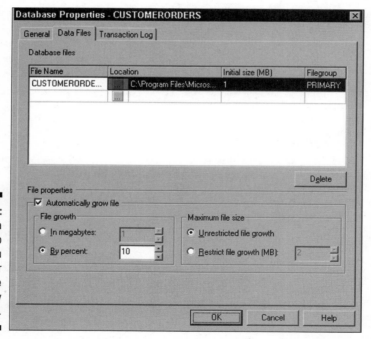

Figure 4-7:
The Data Files tab allows you to enter database property information.

The Transaction Log tab

The Transaction Log tab enables you to enter data that describes transaction properties, such as name, location, and size (see Figure 4-8), just as the Data Files tab did for the database.

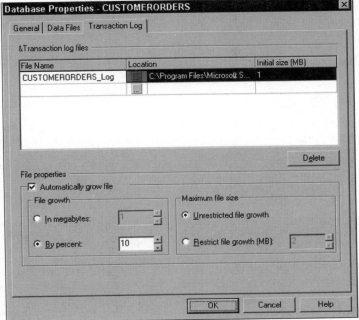

Figure 4-8:
The
Transaction
Log tab
presents
options
relating to
the
database
transaction
log.

✔ **File Name:** Give your transaction log a file name. By default, _Log is appended to the name of your transaction log.

✔ **Location:** Specify where your transaction log is to be stored. The default location is in the \DATA subdirectory of wherever you installed SQL Server 2000. Mine is C:\Program Files\Microsoft SQL Server\ MSSQL\DATA.

✔ **Initial Size (MB):** Specify the initial size of the database. By default, this is 1MB. If you want to change this, click the proposed size and type in the new size.

✔ **Automatically Grow File:** This option indicates to SQL Server that you do not want to manually specify the size for a transaction log as it grows. You would like SQL Server to manage this automatically. This is the default option.

✔ **In Megabytes:** This option indicates to SQL Server that every time the size of the transaction log needs to grow, you want it to grow in size increments specified here. One megabyte is the default value. Unless you plan to be adding a tremendous amount of data at one time, this setting is fine.

✔ **By Percent:** This option indicates to SQL Server that every time the size of the transaction log needs to grow, you want it to grow by a certain percentage. This option allows for a bigger chunk to be allocated every time the database gets larger. For example, suppose that you choose this option and set the size increase at 10 percent. If the transaction log file begins at 1MB, the next time it increases, it will increase by 100,000 bytes, or 10 percent in size. The next time it increases, it does so by 110,000 bytes. This increase occurs because of compounding.

✔ **Unrestricted Filegrowth:** This option specifies that the file is allowed to grow until you run out of disk space. This option is chosen by default.

✔ **Restrict Filegrowth (MB):** This option specifies that the file is allowed to grow until it reaches the size specified in the box to the right. This option is very limiting; you may want to avoid it.

Enlisting SQL Server Query Analyzer

You can use SQL Server Query Analyzer to create a new database by issuing SQL statements directly to the server. To issue the SQL statement to create a database, follow these steps:

1. **Start the SQL Server Query Analyzer by choosing Start⇨Programs⇨ Microsoft SQL Server⇨Query Analyzer.**

2. **Type the SQL statement needed to create a database.**

   To create a database through SQL, you must issue the CREATE DATA-BASE statement. For more information about the CREATE DATABASE statement, see Chapter 8 and follow this example:

   A database named CUSTOMERORDERS can be created with a statement that looks like this:

```
CREATE DATABASE CUSTOMERORDERS
ON
(NAME = CUSTOMERORDERS,
FILENAME = 'C:\PROGRAM FILES\MICROFOFT SQL
         SERVER\MSSQL\DATA\CUSTOMERORDERS_DATA.MDF',
SIZE = 4MB,
MAXSIZE = 100MB,
FILEGROWTH = 4MB)
LOG ON
(NAME = CUSTOMERORDERS_LOG,
FILENAME = 'C:\PROGRAM FILES\MICROFOFT SQL
         SERVER\MSSQL\DATA\CUSTOMERORDERS_LOG.LDF',
SIZE = 1MB,
MAXSIZE = UNLIMITIED)
```

This statement creates a database called CUSTOMERORDERS with an initial size of 4MB that can grow in 4MB increments up to a maximum of 100MB. Additionally, the logical name for the database is CUSTOMERORDERS_Data and is stored in a file called C:\PROGRAM FILES\MICROSOFT SQL SERVER\MSSQL \CUSTOMERORDERS_DATA.MDF.

A *logical name* is a name given to an object that you will use when you refer to that object after it is created. A logical name is different from a filename. A filename is sometimes referred to as a physical name. A *physical name* is the physical location given to an object. You generally do not refer to this physical name after the object is created. You refer to its corresponding logical name.

Also, this statement creates a transaction log with a logical name of CUSTOMERORDERS_Log. It begins with an initial size of 1MB and grows to an unlimited size. The transaction log is stored in a file named C:\PROGRAM FILES\MICROSOFT SQL SERVER\MSSQL\CUSTOMERORDERS _LOG.LDF.

You can also accept all the default values and create the database with this one line:

```
CREATE DATABASE CUSTOMERORDERS
```

Designing Tables

A table is a database object that actually stores and organizes your data. A database can contain one or more tables. Tables contain one or more attributes, known as *fields* or *columns*. Each of these fields must store a specific type of data, known as a *datatype*. In addition to the datatype, fields are also comprised of properties, many of which depend on the datatype that you assign to a field. You can create a table with either the SQL Server Enterprise Manager or by using SQL, as you can see in the next sections.

To create a table, you must be a member of the db_owner or db_ddladmin fixed database roles. For more information about roles and security, see "Security: Protecting Against Peeping Toms," on the Web site at www.dummies.com/goto/ fd-0764507753.htm.

Using the SQL Server Enterprise Manager

You can use the SQL Server Enterprise Manager to create and define tables with specified columns and column attributes. Here's how to accomplish this magic:

1. **To start the SQL Server Enterprise Manager, choose Start⇨Programs⇨ Microsoft SQL Server⇨Enterprise Manager.**

2. **Click the Tables folder in the Databases folder.**

   Notice the list of tables on the right side of the screen. If you just created the database, you see no tables, or only system tables that are automatically created and maintained by SQL Server, as shown in Figure 4-9. It is possible to configure any server shown in the Enterprise Manager to *not* show system objects. However, by default, system objects are shown.

3. **Choose New Table from the Action drop-down menu.**

   Alternatively, you can right-click anywhere on the right side of the screen or right-click the Tables folder and then click New Table to bring up the Choose Table dialog box.

   The Design Table screen appears (shown in Figure 4-10), allowing you to configure the properties of your new table. The screen is made up of rows and columns (a table unto itself). Now follow me on this one. Every row that you see in the Design Table screen represents a column in your new table. Every column in the Design Table screen represents attributes of that column in your new table.

4. **Fill in the following fields, according to your data model.**

   To refresh your understanding of data model design, you can review the relational data model discussion in Chapter 3.

   - **Column Name:** All the fields in this row are the names of the columns in the new table. If you have one column in your new table, there will be one row in this dialog box. Likewise, if you have five columns in your new table, there will be five rows in this dialog box. Well . . . you get the picture.

   - **Datatype:** This column specifies the type of data that will appear in your new table. SQL Server has 28 different datatypes that you can choose from. For a description of these datatypes, see Chapter 3. You do not have to physically type the datatype. You select it from a drop-down list of available datatypes. Char is the datatype chosen by default. If you specify a formula (shown below), you cannot choose a datatype.

If you use a text, ntext, or image datatype, SQL Server does not, by default, actually store the data in the same space, called a *page,* as the rest of the data in the table. It stores the data on a different page, which can take longer to retrieve.

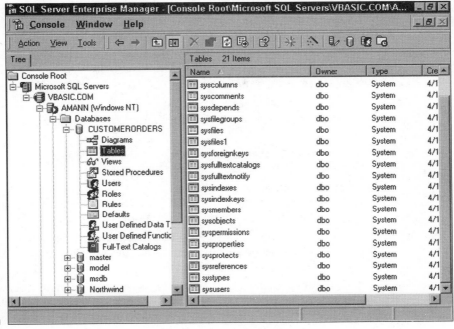

Figure 4-9:
SQL Server
Enterprise
Manager,
showing
system
tables.

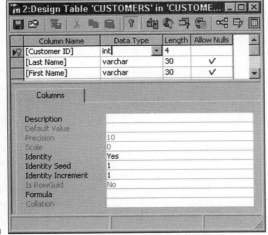

Figure 4-10:
Configure
table
properties
with the
Design
Table
screen.

New with SQL Server 2000, however, is the capability to turn on an option that forces SQL Server to store the text, ntext, or image data on the same page as the rest of the table data. To do this, you must issue the following Transact-SQL statement (substituting your table name for the *table_name* placeholder in the following line):

```
sp_tableoption 'table_name', 'text in row', '1'
```

- **Length:** This column specifies the length of data for the datatype chosen. You can change this value only for a datatype of binary, varbinary, char, or varchar.

- **Allow Nulls:** Placing a check in this box enables you to omit null values when you insert data into the table.

- **Description:** You can add a description of the selected column to make the purpose more understandable if the column name alone is not sufficient. The description property is new for SQL Server 2000.

- **Default Value:** If you want to use a default value (a value that is entered automatically if one is not supplied), enter that value in this field.

- **Precision:** This column indicates the maximum number of digits used for the chosen datatype. By default, this value is zero, except for decimal and numeric datatypes, whose Precision is 18.

- **Scale:** Here, you find the number of decimal places to the right of the decimal. By default, this value is zero.

- **Identity:** You can check this box if you want the column of data to be an identity column. An *identity* column is one whose value is automatically increased by one every time a row is added. An identity column is often used as part of a primary key. A *primary key* is a term used to describe the columns whose values uniquely identify a row in a table. An identity column is useful when each value needs to be unique, such as with a Customer ID column. For more information about primary keys, refer to Chapter 3.

- **Identity Seed:** A check in the Identity box enables you to alter the number that SQL Server uses as its start value. By default, a seed value of 1 is used. This means that when the first record is inserted into the new table, a value of 1 appears in this column. Every row after is incremented by the value that you specify in the Identity Increment field. Change this seed value if you want the number to begin at any value other than 1.

- **Identity Increment:** If you place a check in the Identity box, you can alter the number that SQL Server uses when it increments the value in the Identity column. The default increment value is 1. This means that when the second and subsequent records are inserted into the new table, the value entered will be the prior value plus the increment value placed in this field.

- **Is RowGuid:** Place a check in this box if you want this column to be a row global unique identifier. Only one column in a table can be identified as a global unique identifier column.

- **Formula:** Enter a formula used in the calculation of value to be placed in this field. This field is optional. An example would be if you wanted to have a FullName field, but you already have a FirstName and a LastName field, you could enter a formula of LastName + ', ' + FirstName. This way the formula is calculated automatically by SQL Server and placed into the field. If you specify a formula, you cannot specify any other properties. The formula property is new for SQL Server 2000.

- **Collation:** Select from the list of collations on the server for the column. Collation is the sort order for strings for a specific language. Database default is chosen automatically, but only when you choose a character-based datatype. The collation property is new for SQL Server 2000.

5. **Click the Save icon on the toolbar after you finish filling in rows for every column that you want to create in your new table.**

6. **Type the name of your new table; then click OK.**

You must carefully consider the datatype and length of your columns. For example, if you're going to store character data, decide whether you need a char or varchar datatype. A char datatype appends spaces after your data, up until the maximum number of characters that you specify. In other words, if you define a First Name column as a datatype of char(20) and you store only the value of Fred, your data will be returned as Fred, followed by 16 spaces (20 allocated, minus 4 for Fred). Therefore, you don't want to make a First Name column a char datatype because it's not always going to be the same size. On the other hand, a State column will always be two characters (if you're abbreviating). Therefore, it makes sense to use the char datatype.

Turning to the SQL Server Query Analyzer

With the SQL Server Query Analyzer, you can issue SQL statements directly to the server to create a new table rather than use the Enterprise Manager. Here's how to issue the SQL statement to create a table:

1. **Choose Start➪Programs➪Microsoft SQL Server➪Query Analyzer.**

2. **Type the SQL needed to create a database.**

   To create a table through SQL, you must issue a CREATE TABLE statement. For a complete review of the CREATE TABLE statement, see Chapter 8.

New tables require the following basic information: number of columns in the table, their datatypes, and any properties for the columns. These properties can include determination of whether the column allows null values, whether the column is an identity column, and so on. For a more thorough understanding of this, see the preceding section on using the Enterprise Manager to create tables.

To create a table named CUSTOMER in the CUSTOMERORDERS database, you issue a statement such as this:

```
CREATE TABLE CUSTOMER
([Customer ID] numeric IDENTITY (1001,1),
[Last Name] varchar (30) NULL,
[First Name] varchar (30) NULL,
[Middle Initial] char (1) NULL,
[Company Name] varchar (30) NULL,
[Address 1] varchar (30) NULL,
[Address 2] varchar (30) NULL,
[City] varchar (30) NULL,
[State] char(2) NULL,
[Zip] char (5) NULL,
[Phone] char (10) NULL,
[Fax] char (10) NULL)
```

Square brackets ([ ]) around column names indicate the entire column name to SQL Server — significant when you use spaces in the column name. Without the brackets, SQL Server would have a bit of trouble knowing where the column begins and ends. You don't need square brackets for column names that don't use spaces, but they can't do any damage, either. I use brackets for consistency. Many software developers and database administrators advise against using spaces in column names (or any other database object). The main reason for this is that some SQL Server add-on tools might have a problem with spaces in the object names, even though SQL Server 2000 supports them.

This SQL statement is all that's required to create the table, but it doesn't specify anything about primary. In the CUSTOMER table, the Customer ID column is the primary key. Usually, any column that's defined as an Identity column is the primary key (or at least part of the primary key). For more information about primary keys, refer to Chapter 3.

You can define the primary key at the same time you issue the CREATE TABLE statement. The same statement example can create a primary key like this:

```
CREATE TABLE CUSTOMER
([Customer ID] numeric IDENTITY (1001,1) PRIMARY KEY,
[Last Name] varchar (30) NULL,
[First Name] varchar (30) NULL,
[Middle Initial] char (1) NULL,
[Company Name] varchar (30) NULL,
[Address 1] varchar (30) NULL,
[Address 2] varchar (30) NULL,
[City] varchar (30) NULL,
[State] char(2) NULL,
[Zip] char (5) NULL,
[Phone] char (10) NULL,
[Fax] char (10) NULL)
```

Falling Back on Default Values

If you have a column in a table that requires a value (not null) and one is not specified in a SQL query when you insert data, what happens? Does your INSERT query fail? The answer is, "Yes, the INSERT query fails." That is, unless you create a default.

A *default* is a way to indicate to SQL Server 2000 what value to use for a column in a table when the value is omitted from a SQL statement. Having a default ensures that a value is always inserted into a table. A default does not affect SELECT, UPDATE, or DELETE statements.

The steps for creating a default in SQL Server 2000 are the following:

1. Create the default.

2. Bind the default to one or more columns in a table to put the default in effect.

You can create a default in one of two ways. You can use the SQL Server Enterprise Manager or SQL. I outline both ways in the next few pages.

You can also specify a default value when you create a table. Refer to Chapter 8 for more information on doing this.

To create a default, you must be a member of the sysadmin fixed server role or the db_owner or db_ddladmin fixed database roles. For more information about roles and security, see "Security: Protecting Against Peeping Toms," on the Web site at www.dummies.com/goto/fd-0764507753.htm.

DEFAULTing with the SQL Server Enterprise Manager

To use the SQL Server Enterprise Manager to create a default, follow these steps:

1. **Start the SQL Server Enterprise Manager by choosing Start⇨Programs⇨ Microsoft SQL Server⇨Enterprise Manager.**

2. **Expand the tree so that you can see the Defaults folder within the desired database under the Databases folder.**

   For more information about expanding the tree, see the Introduction.

3. **Highlight the Defaults folder by clicking Defaults.**

   When you highlight the Defaults folder, the list of defaults appears on the right part of the screen. If this is your first time to create a default, the right part of the screen is blank.

4. **Choose Action⇨New Default to bring up the Default Properties dialog box.**

   Alternatively, you can use the mouse to right-click anywhere on the right part of the screen and choose the New Default menu. Also, you can right-click the Defaults folder in the tree and choose the New Default menu. Whatever method you choose to create a new default, each brings up a dialog box in which you can specify the properties of your new default (see Figure 4-11).

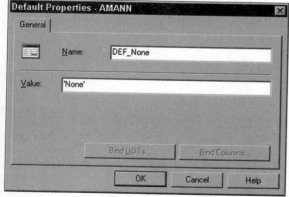

Figure 4-11:
The Default
Properties
dialog box
with a
default that
I've entered.

To use the Default Properties dialog box, you simply fill in the fields.

- **Name:** Give your default a name.

   You should use a name that is germane to the purpose of your default. For example, if your default specifies to use a value of "None," you could use the name DEF_None.

- **Value:** Specify the value for your default.

  Because the value you enter here must be a string literal, you must enclose your value inside *ticks* (single quotation marks). A *string literal* is a series of characters that is to be used literally — that is, exactly as you see it (without the quotation marks). It will not be substituted or interpreted in any way by SQL Server. An example would be me saying, "Hello." It means the same as "Hi," but I did not say "Hi." My string literal is "Hello."

- **Bind UDTs:** Click this button to specify how to bind your default to a user-defined type.

- **Bind Columns:** Click this button to specify how to bind your default to one or more columns in a table.

5. **Click the OK button to create your default.**

Maintaining control over defaults with SQL

You can use the SQL Server Query Analyzer to issue SQL statements directly to the server to create a new default and to bind that default to a column in a database. To issue the SQL statement to create a default, follow these steps:

1. **Start the SQL Server Query Analyzer by choosing Start⇨Programs⇨ Microsoft SQL Server⇨Query Analyzer.**

2. **Type the SQL needed to create a default.**

   You create a view through SQL by issuing the CREATE DEFAULT statement. For more information about the CREATE DEFAULT statement, see Chapter 8.

   To create a default named DEF_None that specifies a default value of "none," for example, you issue a statement like this:

```
CREATE DEFAULT DEF_None
AS
'None'
```

   Everything after the AS clause is the actual default. A default is a string literal, but you can enclose it in either double or single quotation marks (ticks). This string literal corresponds to the text that you enter in the Value field if you use the SQL Server Enterprise Manager to create your default (see Step 4 in the preceding section).

3. **Bind the default to a column in a table.**

   It would be nice if a clause in the CREATE DEFAULT statement allowed you to bind the default to a column, but no such luck. You need to use the sp_bindefault system stored procedure to bind a default to a column. For more information about system stored procedures, see Chapter 7.

The system procedure is not called *sp_binddefault,* as if the two words *bind* and *default* were simply joined. Microsoft chose to leave one of the *d*s out.

The sp_bindefault system stored procedure follows this general syntax:

```
sp_bindefault {'default'} [,'object_name' [,
          futureonly_flag]
```

where default is the name of the default you created with the CREATE DEFAULT statement, and object_name is the name of the object to bind the default to. This object can be either a column, in the form of table.column, or a user-defined type. Futureonly_flag is a flag that can contain only one value, called futureonly. If this flag is set, then the default is bound only to columns in the user-defined type that do not already have a default bound to them.

Therefore, to bind the DEF_None default to the Address column in the EMPLOYEES table, use this statement:

```
sp_bindefault 'DEF_None', 'EMPLOYEES.Address'
```

Deleting Database Objects

Any of the database objects discussed in this chapter can be deleted, or dropped, by using the DROP SQL keyword.

The same security that applies to creating specific database objects also applies to deleting those objects. For more information about roles and security, see "Security: Protecting Against Peeping Toms," on the Web site at www.dummies.com/goto/fd-0764507753.htm.

The SQL Server Query Analyzer enables you to issue SQL statements directly to the server to drop a database object. To issue the SQL statement to delete an index, follow these steps:

1. **Choose Start⇨Programs⇨Microsoft SQL Server⇨Query Analyzer from the Windows menu to start the SQL Server Query Analyzer.**

2. **Type the SQL needed to drop the database object.**

   Dropping a database object follows this basic format:

   ```
   DROP ObjectType [Database.]Object
   ```

   - `ObjectType` is the type of object, either database, table, or index.
   - `Database` is the name of the database in which the object that you're dropping resides.
   - `Object` is what you named the object when the object was initially created.

   Therefore, if you want to drop the table CUSTOMER in the CUS-TOMERORDERS database, you issue this statement:

   ```
   DROP TABLE CUSTOMERORDERS.CUSTOMER
   ```

   If you want to drop the index Index1 on the CUSTOMER table, you issue this statement:

   ```
   DROP INDEX CUSTOMER.Index1
   ```

   If you want to drop the database named CUSTOMERORDERS database, you issue this statement:

   ```
   DROP DATABASE CUSTOMERORDERS
   ```

Security on Database Objects

Most database objects can have security permissions set on them. These security permissions control which users and/or groups can access, create, edit, or delete the objects.

In the Enterprise Manager, you can usually right-click an object and choose the Properties menu. This brings up a Properties dialog box that has a Permissions button on it. Figure 4-12 shows a Table Properties dialog box for the author's table in the pubs database with the Permissions button.

If you click the Permissions button, you see a dialog box containing a grid of permissions per user or role, as shown in Figure 4-13. You manipulate the permissions for the selected object by simply clicking in the desired box to give the appropriate permissions.

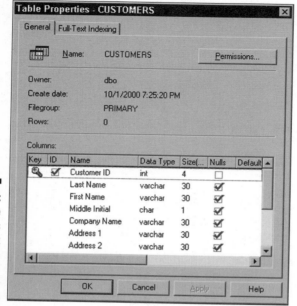

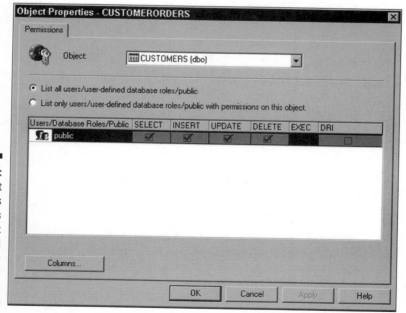

Figure 4-12:
The Table
Properties
dialog box
showing the
Permissions
button.

Figure 4-13:
The Object
Properties
Permissions
dialog box
showing
database
table
permissions.

Chapter 5

Creating Advanced SQL Server Objects

● ●

In This Chapter

▶ Establishing house rules for Microsoft SQL Server 2000

▶ Making your queries fast with indexes

▶ Teaching SQL Server 2000 to react to triggers

▶ Full-text cataloging

● ●

*I*n Chapter 4, I show you how to create base-level objects in Microsoft SQL Server 2000. These base-level objects are most likely used in every SQL Server database that you create. In this chapter, I expand on the basic objects in Chapter 4 and show you more advanced objects that are often used in a well-designed database.

Because SQL Server 2000 gives you multiple ways to create these advanced objects, I show all those methods to you throughout this chapter, as I did in Chapter 4. Again, I don't show the SQL syntax of creating these objects; I show and explain only examples. To see the syntax of creating these objects, see Chapter 8.

Laying Down the Law: Setting Up Rules in SQL Server 2000

A *rule* is a way to indicate to SQL Server 2000 what values are valid for the insertion or updating of data. The following list shows some examples of rules:

- Allow all values from A to Z, but in uppercase only.
- Allow only values from the CUSTOMER_ID column of the CUSTOMER table.
- Social Security numbers must be in the ###-##-#### format.
- Values must be a multiple of 5.
- Values must be greater than 100.

Another way to create a rule is to use a special type of constraint, called a CHECK constraint. CHECK constraints can apply multiple rules to a column, whereas only one rule can be applied to a column. CHECK constraints are specified as part of the CREATE TABLE statement. For more information about creating constraints, see the section, "An Alternative to Creating Rules: Check Constraints," later in this chapter and also Chapter 8.

As you would expect, you can't establish these rules just by saying them out loud to your computer, the way you set rules for your kids or your dogs (although my dogs don't understand rules no matter what I say). You have to jump through a few hoops to get SQL Server 2000 to know the rules.

The steps for creating a rule in SQL Server 2000 are to create the rule and then bind the rule to one or more columns in a table in order to put the rule in effect. You can create a rule in one of two ways. You can use the SQL Server Enterprise Manager or simply use Transact-SQL (sometimes just referred to as SQL). I outline both ways in the next few pages.

When you create rules, you use a variable to serve as a placeholder for the actual value of a column. It's important to note that you can't use more than one variable in a rule because only one value at a time can be substituted when SQL Server tests the rule. You'll see what I mean later in this chapter.

To create a rule, you must be a member of the sysadmin fixed server role or the db_owner or db_ddladmin fixed database roles. For more information about roles and security, see "Security: Protecting Against Peeping Toms," on the Web site at www.dummies.com/goto/fd-0764507753.htm.

Creating rules with SQL Server Enterprise Manager

To use the SQL Server Enterprise Manager to create a rule, follow these steps:

1. **Start the SQL Server Enterprise Manager by choosing Start⇨Programs⇨ Microsoft SQL Server⇨Enterprise Manager.**

2. **Expand the tree so that you can see the** `Rules` **folder within the desired database under the Databases folder.**

   For more information about expanding the tree, see the Introduction of this book.

3. **Highlight the Rules folder by clicking** `Rules`.

   When you highlight the Rules folder, notice the list of rules that appears on the right part of the screen (see Figure 5-1). If this is your first time to create a rule, the right part of the screen is blank.

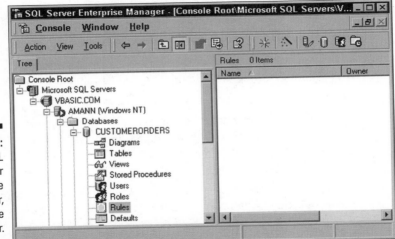

Figure 5-1:
The SQL
Server
Enterprise
Manager,
showing the
Rules folder.

4. **Choose Action⇨New Rule to bring up the Rule Properties dialog box.**

   Alternatively, you can use the mouse to right-click anywhere on the right part of the screen and choose the New Rule menu. Also, you can right-click the Rules folder in the tree and select the New Rule menu.

   Whatever method you choose to create a new rule, the Rule Properties dialog box appears, allowing you to specify the properties of your new rule (see Figure 5-2).

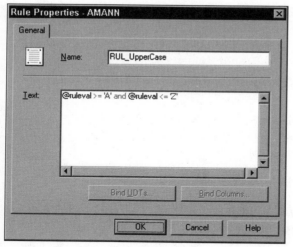

Figure 5-2:
The Rule
Properties
dialog box,
with a rule
I've already
entered.

To use the Rule Properties dialog box, you simply fill in the fields.

- **Name:** Give your rule a name in the Name field.

  You should use a name that is germane to the purpose of your rule. For example, if your rule specifies that the only values allowed are uppercase letters, you could enter the name Rul_UpperCase.

- **Text:** Specify your rule.

  Any valid SQL WHERE clause is valid here. For more information about the SQL language or a WHERE clause specifically, see Chapter 8.

  For your rule that allows only uppercase letters, the following text is valid:

```
@ruleval >= 'A' and @ruleval <= 'Z'
```

Notice the @ruleval variable. All SQL Server variables are preceded by the @ sign. Because there is no value to test at the time you create the rule, you insert a variable in its place. When the queries are run, the values that are inserted or updated in the columns that are bound to the rule are tested against the rule, using the variable placeholder. You can name this variable anything you want except @value. The @value variable name is reserved, so I use @ruleval. SQL Server substitutes the value that is attempting to be inserted or updated into the column (after you bind it) and substitutes that value for @ruleval.

- **Bind UDTs:** Click this button to bind your rule to a user-defined datatype.
- **Bind Columns:** Click this button to specify how to bind your rule to one or more columns in a table.

The Bind UDTs and Bind Columns buttons are disabled at the time you first create a rule. This is because before you click the OK button, the rule doesn't actually exist in the database. Therefore, to bind the rule, you need to click OK and open the Rule Properties dialog box again. This second time, the buttons become enabled.

5. **Click the OK button to create your rule.**

Creating rules with SQL

You can use the SQL Server Query Analyzer to issue SQL statements directly to the server to create a new rule and to bind that rule to a column in a database. Using SQL to create the rule can be advantageous in a case in which you have a friend who wants to create a rule but doesn't know how (because he or she doesn't have this wonderful book). You can write the rule, send it, and the friend can execute the SQL statement.

Another reason for you to know how to create rules with SQL: If you want to create a script that recreates all your database objects (in case of a disaster), this SQL will go into the script.

To issue the SQL statement to create a rule, follow these steps:

1. **Start the SQL Server Query Analyzer by choosing Start⇨Programs⇨ Microsoft SQL Server⇨Query Analyzer.**

2. **Type the SQL needed to create a rule.**

   You create a view through SQL by issuing the CREATE RULE statement. For more information about the CREATE RULE statement, see Chapter 8.

   To create a rule named Rul_UpperCase that allows only uppercase letters in values, you type a statement like this:

   ```
   CREATE RULE rul_UpperCase
   AS
   @ruleval >= 'Z' and @ruleval <= 'Z'
   ```

   Everything after the AS clause is the actual rule. This rule corresponds to the text that you type in the Text field if you use the SQL Server Enterprise Manager to create your rule (see the preceding section).

3. **Bind the rule to a column in a table.**

   It would be nice if a clause in the CREATE RULE statement allowed you to bind the rule to a column. However, things are not always a one-step process, and this is one of those times. You need to use the sp_bindrule system stored procedure to bind a rule to a column. For more information about system stored procedures, see Chapter 7.

   The sp_bindrule system stored procedure follows this general syntax:

   ```
   sp_bindrule {'rule'} [,'object_name' [, futureonly_flag]
   ```

   where rule is the name of the rule you created with the CREATE RULE statement, and object_name is the name of the object to bind the rule to. This object can be either a column, in the form of table.column, or a user-defined type. Futureonly_flag is a flag that can contain only one value, and that value is futureonly. If this flag is set, the rule is bound only to columns in the user-defined type that do not already have a rule bound to them.

   To bind the Rul_UpperCase rule to the State column in the CUSTOMERS table, use this statement:

   ```
   sp_bindrule 'Rul_UpperCase', 'CUSTOMERS.[State]'
   ```

An Alternative to Creating Rules: Check Constraints

As I mentioned earlier, you can create a check constraint instead of creating a rule. In fact, this is the preferred method of enforcing rules and they are easier to create because you don't have to explicitly bind them to columns or user-defined datatypes. You can create a rule in one of two ways. You can use the SQL Server Enterprise Manager or simply use SQL. Coming up . . . I outline both ways.

To create a check constraint, you must be a member of the db_owner or db_ddladmin fixed database roles. For more information about roles and security, see "Security: Protecting Against Peeping Toms," on the Web site at www.dummies.com/goto/fd-0764507753.htm.

Creating check constraints with SQL Server Enterprise Manager

To use the SQL Server Enterprise Manager to create a check constraint, follow these steps:

1. **Start the SQL Server Enterprise Manager by choosing Start⇨Programs⇨ Microsoft SQL Server⇨Enterprise Manager.**

2. **Expand the tree so that you can see the Tables folder within the desired database under the Databases folder.**

   For more information about expanding the tree, see the Introduction of this book.

3. **Click the desired table.**

4. **Choose Action⇨Design Table to bring up the screen that allows you to design your table.**

   Alternatively, you can use the mouse to right-click anywhere on the right part of the screen and choose the Design Table menu. Also, you can right-click the Tables folder in the tree and select the Design Table menu.

   Whatever method you choose to create the check constraint, each shows the screen that allows you to design your table.

5. **Right-click anywhere in the screen and choose Check Constraints to bring up the Properties dialog box showing the Check Constraints tab (see Figure 5-3).**

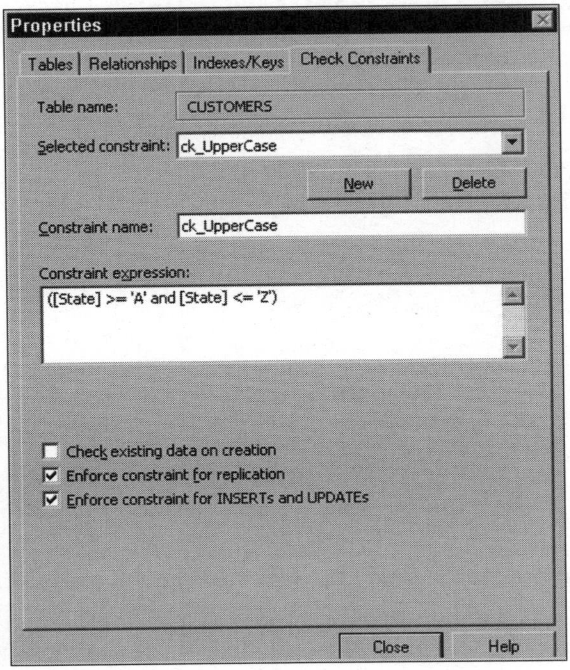

Figure 5-3: Configuring Check Constraint properties.

To configure your check constraint, click the New button and fill in the fields.

- **Constraint Name:** Give your constraint a name.

  You should enter a name that is germane to the purpose of your constraint, such as ck_UpperCase. However, by default, the constraint name shown is ck_, followed by the name of the table.

- **Constraint Expression:** Specify your constraint.

  The constraint expression is similar to the format you would specify in a SQL WHERE clause. For example, if you are going to create a check constraint that enforces the requirement that all characters entered be in uppercase on the State column, you enter:

```
(State >= 'A' and State <= 'Z')
```

- **Check Existing Data on Creation:** Check this box if you want not only new data but also existing data to conform to the rules of the check constraint. By default, this box is not checked.

- **Enforce Constraint for Replication:** Check this box if you want data that is replicated into another database to conform to the rules of the check constraint. By default, this box is checked.

- **Enforce Constraint for INSERTs and UPDATEs:** Check this box if you want data that is inserted or updated in the table to conform to the rules of the check constraint. By default, this box is checked. After all, this is the main reason for creating the constraint.

6. **Click the Close button to create your check constraint.**

   SQL Server 2000 will test the validity of your constraint when you click the Close button. If all goes well, your constraint will be created.

Creating check constraints with SQL

You can use the SQL Server Query Analyzer to issue SQL statements directly to the server to create check constraints. However, you must do this at the time you create a table. To issue the SQL statement to create a rule, follow these steps:

1. **Start the SQL Server Query Analyzer by choosing Start⇨Programs⇨ Microsoft SQL Server⇨Query Analyzer.**

2. **Type the SQL needed to create the table and check constraint.**

   You create a new check constraint through SQL by issuing the CREATE TABLE Transact-SQL statement. For more information about the CREATE TABLE statement, see Chapter 8.

To create the same constraint shown in the previous section when you create the CUSTOMERS table, you type a statement like this:

```
CREATE TABLE CUSTOMER
([Customer ID] numeric IDENTITY (1001,1),
[Last Name] varchar (30) NULL,
[First Name] varchar (30) NULL,
[Middle Initial] char (1) NULL,
[Company Name] varchar (30) NULL,
[Address 1] varchar (30) NULL,
[Address 2] varchar (30) NULL,
[City] varchar (30) NULL,
[State] char(2) NULL constraint ck_UpperCase CHECK (State
          >= 'A' and State <= 'Z'),
[Zip] char (5) NULL,
[Phone] char (10) NULL,
[Fax] char (10) NULL)
```

Defining Foreign Key Relationships

In Chapter 3, I tell you all about foreign keys and give you examples of what a foreign key is. Now I show you how to create foreign key relationships by using the Enterprise Manager. To use the SQL Server Enterprise Manager to create a check constraint, follow these steps:

1. **Start the SQL Server Enterprise Manager by choosing Start⇨Programs⇨ Microsoft SQL Server⇨Enterprise Manager.**

2. **Expand the tree so that you can see the Tables folder within the desired database under the Databases folder.**

   For more information about expanding the tree, see the Introduction of this book.

3. **Click the desired table.**

4. **Choose <u>A</u>ction⇨Design Table to bring up the screen that allows you to design your table.**

   Alternatively, you can use the mouse to right-click the desired table on which you define the foreign key relationship; then choose the Design Table menu. Whatever method you choose to define the foreign key relationship, each shows the screen that allows you to design your table.

5. **Right-click anywhere in the screen and choose Relationships to bring up the Properties dialog box, showing the Relationships tab.**

   To define the new relationship, click the New button and fill in the fields:

   • **Relationship Name:** Give your relationship a name or select the default name presented. The name of the relationship is not very critical because you generally don't refer to this name in code.

- **Primary Key Table:** Select from the list of available tables in the database that represents where the foreign key data comes from. A foreign key always needs to reference a primary or unique key in another table. In the unlabeled grid below this drop-down list, select the column(s) in the specified primary key table that represent the primary key that the foreign key will reference.

- **Foreign Key Table:** Select from the list of available tables in the database that is to have the foreign key defined on it. This foreign key will always reference a primary or unique key in another table. Again, in the unlabeled grid below this drop-down list, select the column(s) in the foreign key table that will have a foreign key relationship with the selected column(s) in the primary key table.

- **Check Existing Data on Creation:** Check this box if the data already in the database must conform to the new foreign key relationship that you are defining.

- **Enforce Relationship for Replication:** Check this box if data in a replicated table must conform to the new foreign key relationship.

- **Enforce Relationship for INSERTs and UPDATEs:** Check this box if data that is inserted or updated in a table must conform to the new foreign key relationship. If you check this option, two more options become enabled, as follows:

- **Cascade Update Related Fields:** Check this box if you want the foreign key values to automatically be updated when you update a primary key value.

- **Cascade Delete Related Records:** Check this box if you want the foreign key row, or record, to automatically be deleted when you delete a primary key value.

6. **Click the Close button to create your foreign key relationship.**

Creating Indexes

An index is a database object that helps speed queries. There are two types of indexes, clustered and nonclustered. A *clustered* index physically orders data. For example, the last name of Mann is physically stored before Taber. This way SQL Server knows how to retrieve the values very fast. Clustered indexes are especially useful when storing numerical values.

A *nonclustered* index stores a pointer to where the data is. This is similar to the index in this book. If you are looking for the page that contains information on creating indexes, you will have to thumb through all the pages unless you look it up in the index at the back of the book. If I had organized this book to cover topics physically in the order of the alphabet (that is, alphabet-ically), you wouldn't need the index.

The alphabetic storage of data is the way a clustered index stores data. If I organized this book in the manner that I suggested earlier, creating rules would be covered after creating indexes, which you can tell by this chapter is not the case. Therefore, you could say that this book has a nonclustered index. For more information about indexes, see Chapter 3.

You can create an index by using either the Create Index Wizard or SQL in the SQL Server Query Analyzer. The next sections outline both methods.

To create an index, you must be a member of the `sysadmin` fixed server role or the `db_owner` or `db_ddladmin` fixed database roles. For more information about roles and security, see "Security: Protecting Against Peeping Toms," on the Web site at `www.dummies.com/goto/fd-0764507753.htm`.

Discovering the Create Index Wizard

SQL Server 2000 features many handy utilities, including the Create Index Wizard. This wizard guides you through a series of steps, prompting you for input along the way (see Appendix A for a flowchart of the steps in the Create Index Wizard). To create a database using the Create Index Wizard, follow these steps:

1. **Start the SQL Server Enterprise Manager by choosing Start⊅Programs⊅ Microsoft SQL Server⊅Enterprise Manager.**

2. **Expand the tree so that you see the name of your server.**

   For more information about expanding the tree, see the Introduction of this book.

3. **Choose Tools⊅Wizards.**

   The Select Wizard dialog box appears.

4. **Click Create Index Wizard (under the Database category) and then click OK to start the Create Index Wizard.**

   The Welcome dialog box sums up everything the wizard can do for you (select the database and the table that you want to index, view informa-tion about current indexes, and select one or more columns to include in the index). When you're properly impressed, click Next to continue.

5. **Specify the database and table name by filling in the following fields, and then click Next:**

- **Database Name:** Select the database from the drop-down list of existing databases that contains the object that you want to create an index for.

- **Object Name:** From the drop-down list, select the table or view that you want to create an index on. The tables and views presented are those that belong to the name selected in the Database name field.

  In versions of SQL Server prior to SQL Server 2000, you could create indexes only on tables. SQL Server 2000 allows you to create indexes on views.

6. **View the indexes that are currently defined on the selected object, as shown in Figure 5-4 for the** Authors **table in the** pubs **database; then click Next.**

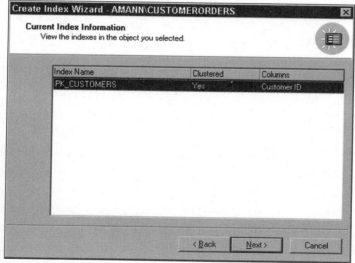

Figure 5-4:
Viewing current indexes on a table.

7. **Select any column(s) that you want to include in the index by clicking the check box in the** Include in Index **column to communicate your intent to the wizard, as shown in Figure 5-5; then click Next.**

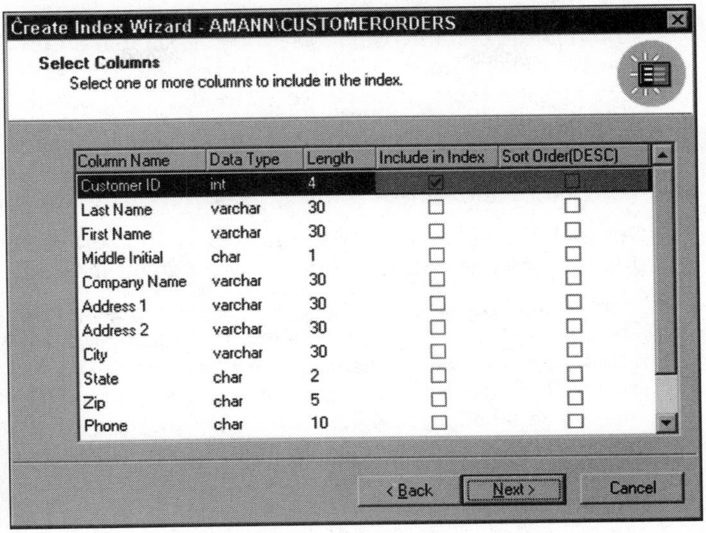

Figure 5-5:
You can
choose one
or more
columns for
your index.

If you see an X icon in the Include in Index column, this means that an index is not allowed for the data type shown in the Data Type column. Indexes are not allowed on bit, text, ntext, or image data. If you want to create an index for a text or ntext column, you must use Full-Text cataloging, which is discussed later in this chapter.

8. **In the dialog box that appears (see Figure 5-6), specify the index options that you prefer by filling in the following fields; then click Next.**

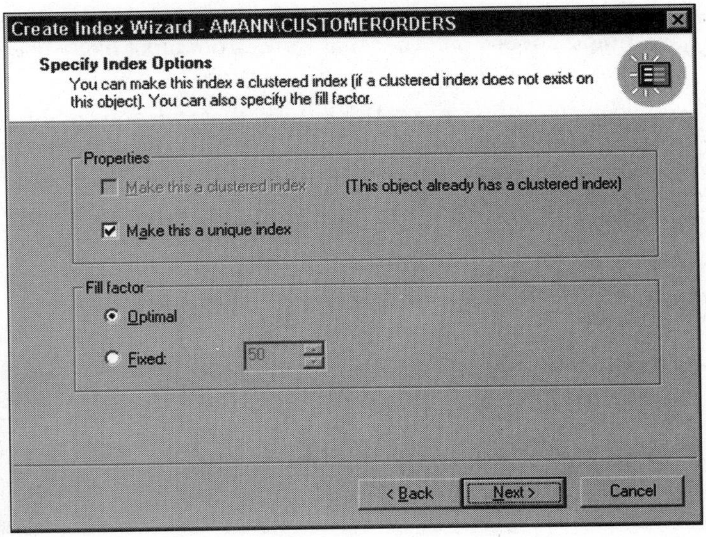

Figure 5-6:
Specify your
index
options.

- **Make This a Clustered Index:** Click this box if you want data to be stored in the column order that you specified in Step 7. The order that the data is stored is from top to bottom, as chosen in Step 7. For more information on clustered indexes, see Chapter 3.

- **Make This a Unique Index:** Check this box if you want the columns specified in the earlier step to be the primary key. For more information about primary keys, refer to Chapter 3.

- **Optimal:** This default option indicates to SQL Server that you prefer automatic configuration of page size for indexes.

- **Fixed:** This option indicates to SQL Server that you want to manually identify index page fullness before creating a new page. I don't recommend choosing this option for beginners. For you beginners, it's not that I don't trust you — I just don't want you to waste disk space. If you specify a value that is too low, your index pages will not be very full and will take up more space. The term used to describe how full an index page is before a new one is created is known as a *fill factor*.

9. **Now change or accept the index name and column order through the following options:**

   - **Index Name:** By default, an `index name` is already entered. You can replace this name with one of your choosing, although a change isn't likely to be beneficial because you don't use the `index name` on a daily basis.

   - **Columns Included:** The columns that you specified in Step 7 are listed in this box. If you want to change the order of the columns, click the column name and then click the Move Up or Move Down buttons to position the column name where you want it. The order of the columns in the index can be significant on performance. You should choose an order that ranks from most likely used to least likely used in your queries.

If you want to change any of the criteria that you specified in earlier steps, click the Back button until you reach the desired dialog box. When you're satisfied with your creation, click Finish. Voilà — your index awaits!

Using SQL Server Query Analyzer

With the SQL Server Query Analyzer, you can issue SQL statements directly to the server to create an index without using a wizard. Here's how it works:

1. **To Start the SQL Server Query Analyzer, choose Start⇨Programs⇨ Microsoft SQL Server⇨Query Analyzer.**

2. **Type the SQL needed to create an index.**

   Creating an index through SQL requires issuing the CREATE INDEX statement — and Chapter 8 is a resource for review of the CREATE INDEX statement.

   When you create an index, you must specify the index name, the table that contains the index, and the columns that make up the index. As an example, suppose that you want to create a basic index on the Customer ID column of the CUSTOMER table, and you want to call the index Index1. Your statement would look like this:

   ```
   CREATE INDEX Index1 ON CUSTOMER ([Customer ID])
   ```

   To create a unique clustered index using this same criteria, you would issue this statement:

   ```
   CREATE UNIQUE CLUSTERED INDEX Index1 ON CUSTOMER
           ([Customer ID])
   ```

   For more information on clustered indexes, see Chapter 3.

The Safe Way to Pull the Trigger

A *trigger* is a very powerful feature that allows SQL statements to execute, or *fire,* when a certain event happens. These events are the following:

   ✔ Insert

   ✔ Update

   ✔ Delete

Using a trigger is a great way to enforce data integrity because everything happens automatically. A trigger is also a great way to have any process occur automatically when specific conditions exist. For example, the HR Manager can be notified by e-mail when a new employee's salary is entered for more than $100,000 annually.

SQL Server 2000 introduced two new options for creating triggers. They are the INSTEAD OF and AFTER keywords. An INSTEAD OF trigger is fired, just as you would expect, instead of the actual SQL statement that fired the trigger. An AFTER trigger fires after the actual SQL statement that fired the trigger is executed. An AFTER trigger will be used by default if you don't specify any keywords. In case this is confusing, Figure 5-7 illustrates these concepts.

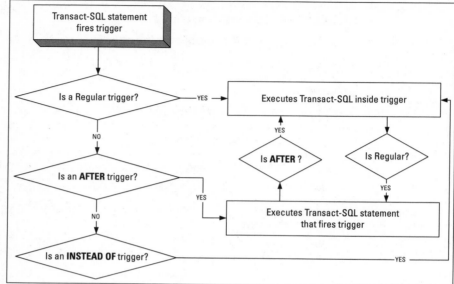

Figure 5-7:
Illustration
showing the
flow of
different
trigger
types.

You can create a trigger in one of two ways. You can use the SQL Server Enterprise Manager or SQL. I outline both ways in the next few pages.

To create a default, you must be a member of the `sysadmin` fixed server role or the `db_owner` or `db_ddladmin` fixed database roles, or you must be the table owner. For more information about roles and security, see "Security: Protecting Against Peeping Toms," on the Web site at `www.dummies.com/goto/fd-0764507753.htm`.

Creating triggers with the SQL Server Enterprise Manager

To use the SQL Server Enterprise Manager to create a trigger, follow these steps:

1. **Start the SQL Server Enterprise Manager by choosing Start➪Programs➪ Microsoft SQL Server➪Enterprise Manager.**

2. **Expand the tree so that you can see the Tables folder within the desired database under the Databases folder.**

   For more information about expanding the tree, see the Introduction of this book.

3. **Highlight the Tables folder by clicking Tables; then click the table on which a trigger will be created.**

   When you highlight the SQL Server Tables folder, notice the list of tables that appears in the right part of the screen (see Figure 5-8). Click the table that you want to create the trigger on.

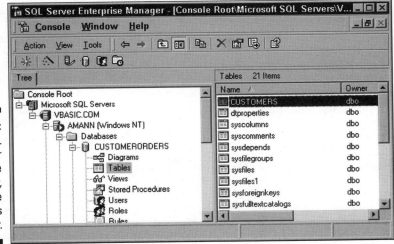

Figure 5-8:
The SQL
Server
Enterprise
Manager,
showing the
Tables
folder.

4. **Choose Action⇨All Tasks⇨Manage Triggers to bring up the Trigger Properties dialog box.**

   The Trigger Properties dialog box appears (see Figure 5-9).

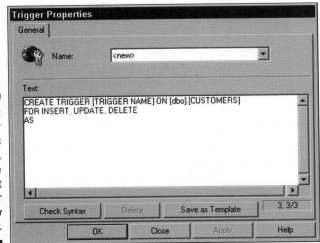

Figure 5-9:
The Trigger
Properties
dialog box,
showing the
default
template for
a new
trigger.

5. **Type the Trigger SQL in the Text field.**

   Type in the SQL necessary to create your trigger. For more information about the SQL needed to create a trigger, see the next section and Chapter 8.

6. **Check the syntax of your SQL by clicking the Check Syntax button.**

   SQL Server 2000 also includes another button on the Trigger Properties dialog box. This button, labeled Save as Template, allows you to save the current text in the text box provided as a template. A template allows you to base other triggers on the trigger text that you define here. Even though each trigger will be different, you can use the template to enforce coding standards within your triggers. For example, you can create a template that contains the format of a header used to indicate the author, date, time, and purpose of the trigger.

7. **Click the OK button to create the trigger.**

Creating triggers with SQL

You can use the SQL Server Query Analyzer to issue SQL statements directly to the server to create a trigger. Almost all SQL statements can be used within a trigger. The exceptions are any statements that affect database objects. The following list shows the SQL statements that are *not* allowed within a trigger:

```
ALTER DATABASE
CREATE DATABASE
DISK INIT
DISK RESIZE
DROP DATABASE
LOAD DATABASE
LOAD LOG
RECONFIGURE
RESTORE DATABASE
RESTORE LOG
```

In SQL Server 7, 34 statements were not allowed to be in triggers. SQL Server 2000 has only the ten shown in the preceding list. Therefore, your triggers can be much more powerful then they were before.

To issue the SQL statement to create a trigger, follow these steps:

1. **Start the SQL Server Query Analyzer by choosing Start➪Programs➪ Microsoft SQL Server➪Query Analyzer.**

2. **Type the SQL needed to create the trigger.**

   Guess what statement you use to create a trigger. As you may expect, it's the CREATE TRIGGER statement. For more information about the CREATE TRIGGER statement, see Chapter 8.

Before you can construct your trigger, you need to break the trigger into logical questions, such as these:

- What type of trigger will you use?
- What are the conditions of the trigger?
- What are the action(s) of the trigger?
- Should the trigger fire after or instead of the SQL statement that fired the trigger?
- How will you execute the action(s) of the trigger?

Consider the scenario that I mention earlier: Suppose that you want to create a trigger to notify automatically the HR Manager when a salary entered for a new employee is greater than $100,000. Here's how I answered the preceding questions:

- I'll use an INSERT trigger.
- The condition of the trigger is for the Salary column in the EMPLOYEES table to exceed 100,000.
- The action of the trigger is to e-mail tmann@vbasic.com, the HR Manager.
- Because the timing of the trigger firing is not critical, I won't specify the INSTEAD OF or AFTER keywords. Alternatively, I could specify the AFTER keyword, as it is the default. It doesn't matter. I just need to be notified. However, I could not specify the INSTEAD OF keyword because then the SQL statement that enters the salary information would never be executed.
- I'll execute the trigger action by using the xp_sendmail extended stored procedure.

Now, use the answers to the questions and apply the CREATE TRIGGER SQL statement.

```
 1: CREATE TRIGGER TRG_NotifySalary
 2: ON EMPLOYEES
 3: FOR INSERT,UPDATE
 4: AS
 5:
 6: declare @tempsalary money
 7: declare @tempemployee varchar(30)
 8: declare @tempstring varchar(50)
 9:
10: IF UPDATE (Salary)
11: BEGIN
12:    select @tempsalary = (select Salary FROM Inserted)
13:    if @tempsalary > 100000
```

```
14:    BEGIN
15:    select @tempemployee = (select name FROM Inserted)
16:    select @tempstring = 'Salary for ' + @tempemployee + '
           Exceeds $100,000'
17:    exec master.dbo.xp_sendmail
           'tmann@vbasic.com',@tempstring
18:    END
19: END
```

The preceding statement is quite complicated, so I explain what it does. This statement follows the CREATE TRIGGER syntax:

Line 1 names the trigger TRG_NotifySalary.

Line 2 indicates that the table in which the trigger is created is called EMPLOYEES.

Line 3 specifies that the trigger will fire when data is either inserted or updated.

Line 4 indicates that every statement after the one in Line 4 defines the actions of the trigger.

Lines 6, 7, and 8 declare variables that are used later in the trigger.

Line 10 is an IF structure that executes the code within the structure only if a value is inserted or updated into the Salary column.

Line 11 starts the code block for the condition of the Salary column being updated with a value.

Line 12 inserts a value into the @tempsalary variable. This value is based on a small query from the Inserted virtual table. SQL Server maintains this table automatically and holds the values that are inserted into the table. The Salary value that has been inserted (from the Inserted table) is assigned to the @tempsalary variable.

Line 13 tests to see whether the value inserted into the table is greater than 100,000. If it is, the code block between Lines 14 and 18 is executed.

Line 14 marks the beginning of this code block. Line 18 marks the end of this code block.

Line 15 assigns the name of the employee that is inserted to the @tempemployee variable. The reason for this variable is to allow a string to be built in Line 16.

Line 16 builds a string and assigns it to the @tempstring variable. This string is then used in Line 17.

Line 17 executes an extended stored procedure that sends a mail message. Notice that in this line, the xp_sendmail command is preceded by master.dbo. This is because the xp_sendmail extended procedure exists in the master database. The mail message that is sent is the string that was built in Line 16. Line 19 marks the end of the first code block.

Every time a value is inserted or updated into the EMPLOYEES table, this trigger is automatically run. That's the beauty of triggers. You do nothing. Everything happens automatically.

Full-Text Catalogs

Indexes are not efficient for text or ntext fields. This is because they simply store too much text, or data that is not character-based. The way around this is to create a full-text catalog. A full-text catalog is a special file that is populated with all the significant words in one or more character-based or image fields that you define for the catalog. These significant words are referred to as *non-noise* words.

Population of the full-text catalog can be scheduled when you create the full-text catalog. For example, you might want to repopulate the catalog with the values from the defined fields every morning at 2:00 a.m. Doing so ensures that queries against the full-text catalog will yield the proper results.

Although it takes more server resources, population can also take place using a new feature called change tracking. *Change tracking* enables full-text catalogs to be updated in near real-time.

Speaking of queries, you can access the data in the full-text catalog by using the traditional SELECT Transact-SQL statement. However, you must use some explicit keywords to access the catalog. They are CONTAINS, FREETEXT, CONTAINSTABLE, and FREETEXTTABLE. Querying full-text data is discussed in Chapter 8.

To define a full-text catalog, all the following conditions must exist:

- The Microsoft Search service must be started. Ensure this is started by choosing Start⇨Programs⇨Microsoft SQL Server⇨Service Manager. Select Microsoft Search from the Services drop-down list. Click the Start/Continue button if it is enabled.

- A unique index must be created in the table on a single column. Most often this will be a primary key. You cannot have a primary key that spans multiple columns.

- The unique index cannot allow NULL values. If you are using a column with a primary key, you don't have to worry about this because primary keys, by definition, don't allow null values.

To create a full-text catalog, you must be a member of the sysadmin fixed server role or the db_owner fixed database roles. Alternatively, you can also create a full-text catalog if you are a member of a fixed database role that has more privileges than the db_owner fixed database role. For more information about roles and security, see "Security: Protecting Against Peeping Toms," on the Web site at www.dummies.com/goto/fd-0764507753.htm.

Creating a full-text catalog with the SQL Server Enterprise Manager

To use the SQL Server Enterprise Manager to create a full-text catalog, follow these steps:

1. **Start the SQL Server Enterprise Manager by choosing Start⇨Programs⇨ Microsoft SQL Server⇨Enterprise Manager.**

2. **Expand the tree so that you can see the Tables folder within the desired database under the Databases folder.**

   For more information about expanding the tree, see the Introduction of this book.

3. **Highlight the Tables folder by clicking Tables; then click the table on which the full-text catalog will be created.**

   When you highlight the SQL Server Tables folder, notice the list of tables that appears in the right part of the screen (refer back to Figure 5-8). Click the table that you want to create the full-text catalog on.

4. **Choose Action⇨All Tasks⇨Full-Text Index Table⇨Define Full-Text Indexing on a Table to bring up the Full-Text Indexing Wizard.**

   Alternatively, you can use the mouse to right-click the desired table and choose Full-Text Index Table⇨Define Full-Text Indexing on a Table.

   Whatever method you choose, the Full-Text Indexing Wizard welcome screen appears. When you're ready, click Next to begin.

5. **Select an index from the Unique index drop-down list (see Figure 5-10).**

   A list of all unique indexes and primary keys is presented in the drop-down list. This index is used in creating joins with other tables when you select data from the full-text catalog. Click Next when you are ready to continue to select full-text columns.

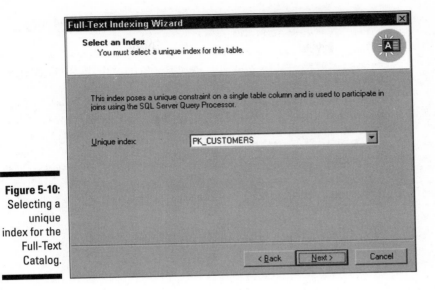

Figure 5-10:
Selecting a
unique
index for the
Full-Text
Catalog.

6. **Select the column(s) that you want to use in the full-text catalog (see Figure 5-11); then click Next.**

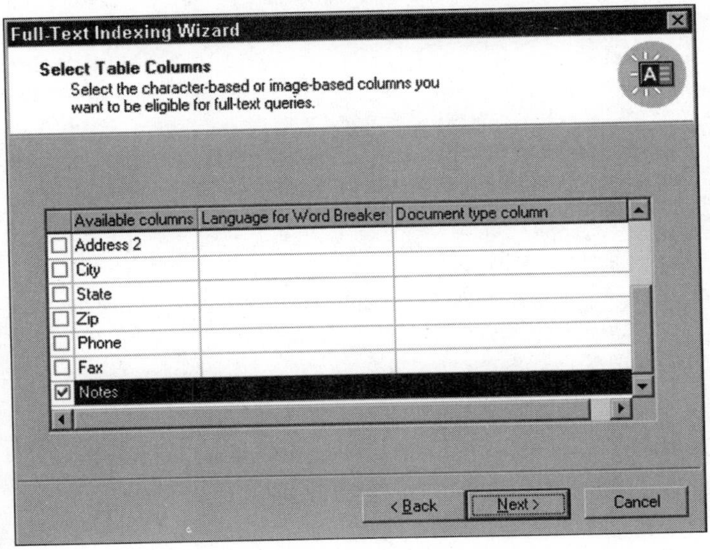

Figure 5-11:
Select the
columns to
be used in
the Full-Text
Catalog.

You are presented with a grid allowing for three bits of information to be selected for each column in the table:

- **Available Columns:** Check the column(s), represented one on each row in the table, that you want to participate in the full-text catalog.

- **Language for Word Breaker:** Select the desired language used to determine where the words are broken up when determining what the non-noise words are. If you choose nothing, the default language on the server will be used.

- **Document Type Column:** This field is valid only for image datatypes. Because an image datatype can store any binary data, that binary data can be a document or other type of file, such as a Microsoft Word document. The document type column shows a drop-down list of the available types of documents so that SQL Server knows how to encode the binary data. If this field is left blank, the document will be treated as a text document.

Click Next when you are ready to continue to select a catalog.

7. **Select or create that catalog that will contain the populated data (see Figure 5-12); then click Next.**

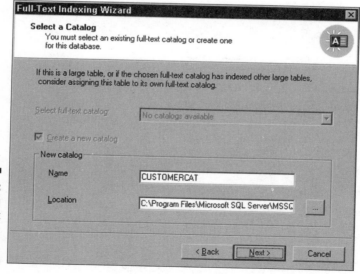

Figure 5-12: Entering Full-Text Catalog properties.

Enter the desired name of the new catalog, as well as the data location if you don't want to accept the default. You generally don't need to refer to this name in the future.

8. **Select or create a population schedule for the catalog; then click Next.**

   If you want to schedule full-text population, click one or both of the following buttons and enter the desired schedule data:

   - **New Table Schedule:** Creates a schedule to repopulate a single table.

   - **New Catalog Schedule:** Creates a schedule to repopulate the entire catalog.

   Click the Next button to show a review screen of your choices.

9. **Click the Finish button to create and optionally populate the full-text catalog.**

Chapter 6

Programming SQL Server 2000

● ●

In This Chapter

▶ Understanding SQL Server 2000 control-of-flow programming constructs

▶ Using SQL Server 2000 functions

▶ Creating your own functions

● ●

*T*o use SQL Server 2000, you need to know Structured Query Language, or SQL. I cover SQL in Chapter 8. This chapter discusses how you program SQL Server 2000 so that you can structure your Transact-SQL statements. *Transact-SQL* is Microsoft's version of the SQL language for use with Microsoft SQL Server. All programming languages allow for statements that control the flow of logic; Transact-SQL is no different. Controlling the flow of logic means that you test for specific conditions and react according to the results of those tests. You'll see what I mean throughout this chapter. Within your control-of-flow logic, you will also benefit from using both SQL Server 2000 functions and creating your own functions.

Declaring Variables

A *variable* is a programmatic placeholder that can hold values. These values are assigned and also referenced in your Transact-SQL statements. In other words, variables are a way to temporarily store values so that they can be used later.

Before you can use any variable in your Transact-SQL statements, you first must declare it. *Declaring* a variable is the act of instructing SQL Server 2000 as to the name of your variable, its datatype, and its scope. I cover SQL Server datatypes in Chapter 3. The *scope* of a variable refers to the lifetime of the variable — in other words, how long can you use it. Generally, a variable is declared within a Transact-SQL statement and is available only within the procedure where the variable is declared.

Variables are declared with the DECLARE keyword. The DECLARE keyword has three separate uses. Each is outlined in the following sections.

Declaring local variables

To declare a local variable, use this syntax:

```
DECLARE @local_variable datatype
```

where you substitute the following:

> @local_variable is the name that you give your variable that is germane to its purpose. All local variables begin with the @ sign.
>
> datatype is any valid SQL Server 2000 datatype (see Chapter 3).

An example is to declare a local variable, called @UserName, using the datatype of char, with a length of 10:

```
DECLARE @UserName char(10)
```

Declaring cursors

Cursors are covered in Chapter 9, but here is a brief description of the syntax:

```
DECLARE @cursor_variable CURSOR
```

where you substitute the following:

> @cursor_variable is the name that you give the variable that is to represent and hold a cursor. This cursor variable is a local variable. Again, all local variables begin with the @ sign.

The following example serves to declare a local cursor variable, called @curAuthors:

```
DECLARE @curAuthors CURSOR
```

To learn how to use the cursor, refer to Chapter 9.

Declaring table definition variables

SQL Server 2000 allows you to declare a variable that represents and holds tables. To declare a local variable, use this syntax:

```
DECLARE @table_variable TABLE (table_definition)
```

where you substitute the following:

> @table_variable is the name that you give the variable that is to represent and hold a table definition. This cursor variable is a local variable. Once again, all local variables begin with the @ sign.

> @table_definition is the definition that you give your table. The table definition is specified the same way as it is with the CREATE TABLE statement. I discuss the CREATE TABLE statement in Chapter 8.

As an example, you can declare a local table definition variable, called @TempUser, like this:

```
DECLARE @TempUser TABLE
(
UserName varchar(10),
UserPassword varchar(10)
)
```

Then, you can use the @TempUser variable, just as if it were a regular table name. This can be used instead of a temporary table. Check Chapter 8 to see how you can use SQL with tables.

Going with the Flow

Your Transact-SQL statements can contain control-of-flow logic. If you are familiar with any programming language, such as Visual Basic, Visual C++, or Java, you already understand control-of-flow logic. Transact-SQL uses its own constructs for these types of statements, but you'll be up-to-speed in no time at all.

Nine separate sets of control-of-flow statements are available in SQL Server 2000. Some of these statements must be used in pairs so that SQL Server knows where the construct begins and ends. Table 6-1 shows these control-of-flow statements. I've ranked them in the order that I use them, from most often to least often.

Table 6-1	SQL Server 2000 Control-of-Flow Statements
Statement	**Description**
IF...ELSE	Tests for specific conditions that you specify. The results of these conditions always return values of TRUE or FALSE As such, they are known as Boolean expressions.
BEGIN...END	Defines a block of Transact-SQL code.
RETURN	Immediately exits the current procedure, query, or code.
CASE...WHEN...ELSE...END	Tests for multiple conditions. This is more powerful than the IF...ELSE construct.
WHILE	Loops until a specific condition exists.
GOTO	Instructs SQL Server to jump immediately to a specific place in the code.
BREAK	Unconditionally exits a WHILE loop.
WAITFOR	Delays the execution of a statement until a specific condition exists.
CONTINUE	Restarts a WHILE loop.

The best way to show you how to use these statements is to dive into some examples. The next few pages show some examples of using these statements.

IF...ELSE

The IF...ELSE statements are used very often. They are used to test for specific conditions, like this

```
IF @Department = 'A'
          PRINT 'ACCOUNTING DEPARTMENT'
ELSE
          PRINT 'UNKNOWN DEPARTMENT'
```

In the preceding code, if the @Department variable contains the value of A, then SQL Server prints a message indicating that this is the accounting department. If the value of the @Department variable is anything else, SQL Server prints the default message indicating that the department is not known. However, what if you also wanted to test for the marketing department? You can either add a condition to the construct or use the CASE...WHEN statement. If you want to continue with the preceding example, you can alter the construct like this:

```
IF @Department = 'A'
        PRINT 'ACCOUNTING DEPARTMENT'
ELSE IF @Department = 'M'
        PRINT 'MARKETING DEPARTMENT'
ELSE
        PRINT 'UNKNOWN DEPARTMENT'
```

BEGIN...END

The BEGIN...END statements are also used very often. These statements mark the beginning and ending of a Transact-SQL block of code. To explain this, first consider this example:

```
IF @Department = 'A'
        PRINT 'ACCOUNTING DEPARTMENT'
ELSE
        PRINT 'UNKNOWN DEPARTMENT'
        PRINT 'CONTACT YOUR ADMINISTRATOR'
```

Under which condition will you see the CONTACT YOUR ADMINISTRATOR message printed? Okay, time's up. The answer is . . . all conditions. Every time the preceding code is executed, this message is displayed. The reason for this is that in each section of the IF...ELSE construct, only the very next Transact-SQL statement applies. Therefore, the ELSE condition does not contain the CONTACT YOUR ADMINISTRATOR message, but only the UNKNOWN DEPARTMENT message. To be sure that you explicitly mark your blocks of code, it is a good idea to use the BEGIN. . .END statements around all blocks of code, even if the blocks contain a single line of code. This can help to avoid confusion.

To include the CONTACT YOUR ADMINISTRATOR message in the ELSE condition, you would use a BEGIN. . .END construct, like this:

```
IF @Department = 'A'
        PRINT 'ACCOUNTING DEPARTMENT'
ELSE IF @Department = 'M'
        PRINT 'MARKETING DEPARTMENT'
ELSE
        BEGIN
            PRINT 'UNKNOWN DEPARTMENT'
            PRINT 'CONTACT YOUR ADMINISTRATOR'
        END
```

RETURN

The RETURN statement exits unconditionally from the current procedure. To illustrate this point, look at this Transact-SQL code:

```
IF @Department = 'A'
          PRINT 'ACCOUNTING DEPARTMENT'
ELSE IF @Department = 'M'
PRINT 'MARKETING DEPARTMENT'
ELSE
          BEGIN
                PRINT 'UNKNOWN DEPARTMENT'
                RETURN
          END
PRINT 'DEPARTMENT FOUND'
```

In the preceding code, the DEPARTMENT FOUND message is printed only when the @Department variable contains a value of A or M. This is because the DEPARTMENT FOUND message is outside the IF...THEN construct. However, after the ELSE condition is executed and the UNKNOWN DEPARTMENT message is printed, the RETURN statement is executed. It immediately exits the code.

CASE...WHEN...ELSE...END

The CASE...WHEN...ELSE...END statements are very powerful. They are similar to the IF...ELSE statements, except that they can be used in conjunction with a SELECT statement. This is not possible with the IF...ELSE construct. Here's how a CASE...WHEN...ELSE...END statement works:

```
SELECT @Result =
          CASE @Department
                WHEN 'A' THEN 'ACCOUNTING DEPARTMENT'
                WHEN 'E' THEN 'EXECUTIVE MANAGEMENT'
                WHEN 'M' THEN 'MARKETING DEPARTMENT'
                WHEN 'S' THEN 'SALES DEPARTMENT'
                WHEN 'I' THEN 'IS DEPARTMENT'
                ELSE 'UNKNOWN DEPARTMENT'
          END
```

When you use the CASE...WHEN...ELSE...END statement inside a SELECT statement, you can compare only with the equal sign. In the preceding code, tests are made on each WHEN line as to the value of @Department. If there is a match, the value after the THEN keyword is assigned to @Result. If all tests fail, UNKNOWN DEPARTMENT is assigned to @Result. When you are finished with all your tests, encapsulate the entire construct by placing an END keyword after all statements.

WHILE

The WHILE statement creates a loop that continually executes the same set of Transact-SQL statements until a specific condition exists. One of the most popular ways to use the WHILE statement is when you are using a cursor (as you can see in Chapter 9), like this:

```
WHILE @@FETCH_STATUS = 0
BEGIN
    FETCH NEXT
    FROM CUR_Temp INTO @LastName
END
```

In the preceding code, the condition being tested for is that the @@FETCH_ STATUS system function returns a value of 0. As long as this value is 0, all Transact-SQL statements between the BEGIN and END statements are executed repeatedly. Fortunately, if there are no more records in the cursor, the FETCH NEXT function will return a nonzero number, thereby exiting the WHILE loop.

If you don't properly write your WHILE constructs, the code can become stuck in an endless loop. Therefore, make sure that it is possible for a condition to exist that will exit the WHILE loop.

GOTO

The GOTO statement is used to immediately jump to a specific point in your Transact-SQL code. This point must contain a label that you specify. You should specify a label that means something to you or makes sense in the code. Here's an example of a GOTO construct:

```
WHILE @@FETCH_STATUS = 0
BEGIN
    FETCH NEXT
    FROM CUR_Temp INTO @LastName

    IF @LastName = 'Smith'
        GOTO FoundLastName

END

FoundLastName:
        print @LastName
```

In the programming world, a GOTO statement is generally thought of as poor code. This is because the code can be considered to be sloppy, even though it is functional. The same code can be rewritten to avoid the use of the GOTO statement, like this:

```
WHILE (@@FETCH_STATUS = 0) and (@LastName <> 'Smith')
BEGIN
    FETCH NEXT
    FROM CUR_Temp INTO @LastName

END
```

As you can see, the code looks cleaner. The WHILE loop executes as long as the @@FETCH_STATUS system function returns 0 and the @LastName value is not Smith. If either of these conditions is not met, the loop is exited. Therefore, it doesn't matter whether the cursor runs out of records or the last name is Smith.

BREAK

The BREAK statement is not used very often. It can be used to unconditionally exit a WHILE loop if a specific condition exists. It is my opinion that if you need a BREAK statement, then you probably should reconstruct your WHILE construct to eliminate the BREAK statement. This is the same school of thought that says you shouldn't use GOTO statements in BASIC because they promote poor code structure. Here's an example of how the BREAK statement can be used:

```
SET @index= 1
WHILE @index < 10
BEGIN
            IF @index = 5
                    BREAK
            ELSE
                    SET @index = @index + 1
END
```

The preceding example shows a WHILE loop that continually executes as long as the value of @index is less than 10. As long as the value of @index is not equal to the value of 5, @index will be incremented by one. Therefore, the WHILE loop will never be exited normally. It will always be exited with the BREAK statement, because the value of 5 will always be reached before the WHILE condition of less than 10.

Again, in my opinion, the preceding code should be rewritten to avoid using the BREAK statement, like this:

```
SET @index= 1
WHILE @index < 5
BEGIN
            SET @index = @index + 1
END
```

The preceding code is considerably cleaner and easier to read than the earlier code using the BREAK statement.

WAITFOR

The WAITFOR statement gives you some very interesting possibilities. The WAITFOR statement basically pauses execution until either a specific clock time or elapsed time. The clock time refers to the actual time on the clock, like an alarm clock. Elapsed time is the amount of time that you specify to elapse from the moment you execute your query. Here's an example of how you can use the WAITFOR statement to execute a user-defined stored procedure called usp_GenerateReport at exactly 11 p.m.:

```
WAITFOR TIME '23:00'
BEGIN
            Execute usp_GenerateReport
END
```

The time specified in the preceding code is contained within single quotation marks and is specified in 24-hour mode (also known as military time). Anything within the BEGIN...END construct will be executed at the specified time.

Likewise, using the elapsed time option, here is how you would execute the same stored procedure at exactly five minutes from now:

```
WAITFOR DELAY '000:05:00'
BEGIN
            Execute usp_GenerateReport
END
```

You'll notice that the format for the DELAY option is different than the TIME option. The DELAY option accepts time in the hours:minutes:seconds format.

CONTINUE

The CONTINUE statement is used to restart a WHILE loop if a specific condition exists. Restarting the loop means that the code immediately moves to the statement immediately after the BEGIN keyword that starts the beginning of the loop:

```
set @MatchedItems = 0
set @UnmatchedItems = 0
FETCH NEXT
FROM CUR_Temp INTO @LastName
WHILE @@FETCH_STATUS = 0
BEGIN
    FETCH NEXT
    FROM CUR_Temp INTO @LastName

    IF @LastName = 'Smith'
            BEGIN
                SET @MatchedItems = @MatchedItems + 1
                CONTINUE
            END
    SET @UnmatchedItems = @UnmatchedItems + 1
END
```

Okay, so how about a little explanation? Sure, no problem. The main thing to know is that when the CONTINUE statement is reached, nothing is executed after the CONTINUE statement. Instead, the code immediately jumps to the statement immediately after the BEGIN statement that starts the loop. Therefore, if the @LastName variable equals Smith, after the @MatchedItems variable is incremented by one, the next iteration of the loop is started immediately. This bypasses the incrementing of the @UnmatchedItems variable. On the other hand, if the value of @LastName is not Smith, then the @UnmatchedItems variable is incremented. This is not an elegant solution at all, but only a functional one to illustrate the use of the CONTINUE statement.

Additional Transact-SQL Programming Statements

So now that you are an expert at control-of-flow statements, you should know about some other programming features that might help you in programming SQL Server 2000.

Comments

Many times, you want to leave yourself or others comments in your SQL Server code. Comments help to describe complex functions or those that are not obvious. There are two ways to mark your Transact-SQL code with comments.

The first is to mark a block of comments with the following syntax:

```
/*
Comments
*/
```

where `Comments` is any number of lines of comments buried within your Transact-SQL code. The /* and */ tags are placed to encapsulate your text to denote it as being commented.

The other way to comment code is to use the following syntax:

```
--Comment
```

where `Comment` is your desired comment. The difference in this syntax is that the -- tag comments only from the point immediately following the tag to the end of the line only. If you need to comment multiple lines, you must either use multiple -- tags, or the /* and */ tags.

An example of using both types of comments follows:

```
/*
This is a sample comment
*/
--This line selects the data
SELECT * FROM Authors
```

Displaying information

You find out how to use the Query Analyzer in Chapter 9. However, what I don't explicitly show you in Chapter 9 is that you can display information in the Query Analyzer from within your Transact-SQL code. You do this with the `PRINT` statement.

To use the `PRINT` statement, simply specify the `PRINT` statement followed by the data that you want to return to the Query Analyzer, like this:

```
PRINT 'DATA SELECTED FROM AUTHORS'
```

The PRINT statement has little or no effect on any program other than the Query Analyzer. It does not create a recordset or actually return data back to your Web pages or Visual Basic, Visual C++, or JAVA programs.

Executing Transact-SQL code

There are times when you need to execute Transact-SQL code from within your Transact-SQL code. A very common reason for doing this is that you might have a stored procedure (discussed in Chapter 7) that builds a Transact-SQL statement dynamically. That is, depending on the conditions specified in the stored procedure, a Transact-SQL statement may need to be built. This is all done with the EXECUTE statement.

Here is how I sometimes use the EXECUTE statement:

```
--declare a variable to hold the Transact-SQL string
declare @cmd varchar(100)
--build the Transact-SQL string
SET @cmd = 'SELECT * FROM Authors'
--execute the Transact-SQL string
EXECUTE (@cmd)
```

I included comments in the code here so that you can understand what is happening. Basically, I am building a valid Transact-SQL string that selects all data from the Authors table and executes it at run time. Why not just execute this line of code rather than build a command string?

```
SELECT * FROM Authors
```

The answer is, "You could." However, what if you wanted to do something like this:

```
declare @cmd varchar(100)
declare @tablename varchar(20)

SET @tablename = 'Authors'
SET @cmd = 'SELECT * FROM ' + @tablename
EXECUTE (@cmd)
```

Notice that the Authors table is stored in a variable named @tablename. Storing the Authors table in this variable allows for the @cmd string to be built, substituting the value for the @tablename variable at run time. That's when the real power of the EXECUTE statement comes into play.

What about errors?

You can do many things to cause an error to occur. For example, you can have a syntax error in your Transact-SQL statements. However, what if your Transact-SQL statements are constructed correctly, but you want some user-defined condition to generate an error? No problem: Use the RAISERROR statement.

The RAISERROR statement allows client programs to handle errors known as *exceptions* and to have SQL Server 2000 flag that an error has happened. For example, Visual Basic has an Error object that stores errors that occur. The RAISERROR function works in conjunction with the Visual Basic Error object.

The RAISERROR statement follows this general syntax:

```
RAISERROR ({msg_id | msg_str}, severity, state
   [, argument [,....n]])
   [WITH options]
```

where you can substitute the following parameters:

msg_id is the message number stored in the sysmessages system table. Generally 50000 and below is reserved for SQL Server messages. Your user-defined messages should have a number greater than 50000. Alternatively, you can specify the msg_str argument.

msg_str is the string containing the desired message to raise. You use this option if the message is not stored in the sysmessages system table.

severity is the number representing how serious the error is. A number of 10 is to be used for informational purposes. You can use levels 11 through 16 to define your own severity levels. Levels 17 through 25 are reserved for system problems.

state is used to give additional information about the state of the error, beyond the severity argument. You can use any number that you want from 1 to 127. It is very common to always use a state value of 1.

argument is used to specify formatting arguments. I don't cover these possibilities in this book, but they do follow general C- or C++-style formatting.

options can be one of three possible keywords:

- LOG: Logs the error in the error and application event log.
- NOWAIT: Immediately raises the error to the client program.
- SETERROR: Unconditionally sets the error to a value of 50000.

An example of using the RAISERROR statement follows:

```
RAISERROR ('No Database Users Exist', 10, 1) WITH NOWAIT
```

The preceding statement immediately raises the error (because of the WITH NOWAIT keywords) and sends the informational message No Database Users Exist. You know it's an informational message because of the severity level of 10.

Conjunction-Junction, What's Your Function?

I must give Schoolhouse Rock credit for the fabulous song. A function is one or more Transact-SQL statement(s) that are encapsulated to serve a specific purpose. For example, you can have a function that adds a user to the database. Obviously, the function would need to know which user to add, so functions can (but don't have to) accept parameters, known as arguments.

SQL Server 2000 gives you some functions that are built-in to help you with everyday tasks, such as mathematical or administrative functions. Also, you can write your own. The next two sections tell you all about system and user-defined functions.

System functions

System functions are defined by Microsoft and are built into SQL Server 2000. A system function can have a logical name, such as DAY, which returns the specific day for a date. Other functions, formerly known as global variables, begin with the @@ prefix. An example is @@ROWCOUNT, which returns the number of rows affected by the last executed Transact-SQL statement.

Another very useful system function is @@Error. This function can be called directly after a Transact-SQL statement to see whether it produced an error. This function returns 0 if the last Transact-SQL statement is successful; otherwise, the error number is returned. Here's an example of how you would use the @@Error function:

```
INSERT INTO Employees(EmployeeID, LastName, FirstName)
VALUES(1, 'Mann', 'Anthony')
IF (@@Error <> 0)
PRINT 'Error Occurred'
```

It is impossible to list all the system functions available in SQL Server 2000 because there are just too many. However, here are the categories of functions that are available for you to use:

- Configuration
- Cursor
- Date and Time
- Mathematical
- Metadata
- Security
- Statistical
- String
- System
- Text and Image

For more information on any of the functions available in these categories, refer to Books Online.

User-defined functions

SQL Server 2000 introduced the ability to include user-defined functions. If you know anything about stored procedures (which you can learn about in Chapter 7), you may wonder what a user-defined function can do for you that a stored procedure can't. Suppose, for example, that you created a stored procedure whose sole purpose in life was to take a string value as a parameter and remove all carriage returns from it? How would you call this stored procedure and return the data from within a SELECT statement? You can't! If the stored procedure that you're using is called usp_RemoveCR, you cannot use it in this context:

```
INSERT INTO Comments (UserID, Comment)
VALUES (1, usp_RemoveCR(@Comment))
```

The preceding statement would result in a syntax error because stored procedures cannot be called from within a Transact-SQL statement. A stored procedure can be called only as a single Transact-SQL statement in itself.

The answer is to create a user-defined function. User-defined functions are created with the CREATE FUNCTION Transact-SQL statement. This statement can be specified by typing the required syntax into the Query Analyzer or by using the Enterprise Manager. To use the Enterprise Manager, follow these simple steps:

1. **To start the SQL Server Enterprise Manager, choose Start⇨Programs⇨ Microsoft SQL Server⇨Enterprise Manager.**

2. **Click the** User Defined Functions **folder under the desired** Database **folder.**

   Notice the list of user-defined functions on the right side of the screen. If you have never created a user-defined function, you see nothing on the right side.

3. **Choose New User Defined Function from the <u>A</u>ction drop-down menu.**

   Alternatively, you can right-click anywhere on the right side of the screen, or right-click the User Defined Functions folder and then click New User Defined Function to bring up the User-defined Function Properties screen.

   The User-defined Function Properties screen appears (shown in Figure 6-1), allowing you to enter the required text to define your new user-defined function.

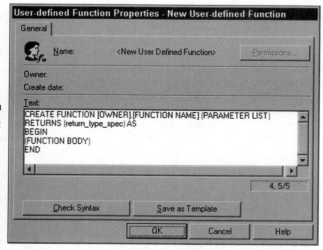

Figure 6-1:
Creating a new user-defined function with the Enterprise Manager.

Whether you use the Enterprise Manager or Query Analyzer, the CREATE FUNCTION syntax is needed to create the user-defined function, like this:

```
CREATE FUNCTION [owner.] function_name
        ([@parameter datatype [=default][,...n]])
        RETURNS datatype
BEGIN
        statements
        RETURN datatype
END
```

where you can substitute the following parameters:

owner is the desired owner name for the function. If this is not specified, dbo or the current user is the default owner, depending on the roles that the user is a member of.

function_name is the name of your function, such as RemoveCR.

@parameter is the name of a parameter used for input. Multiple parameters can be specified. If you create a function to remove carriage returns, you need to take a string as an input parameter, from which carriage returns will be removed.

datatype is one of the valid SQL Server datatypes. These are covered in Chapter 3.

default is the value that should be used if the parameter is not specified when the function is called.

statements are the valid Transact-SQL statements that make up the body of your function.

As hinted previously, suppose that you want to create a user-defined function to remove carriage returns (just like with the stored procedure). You can do that like this:

```
CREATE FUNCTION RemoveCR
        (@InputString varchar(1000))
        RETURNS varchar(1000)
BEGIN
        DECLARE @ReturnStr varchar(1000)
        DECLARE @CharLoop int
        DECLARE @CurrentChar char(1)

        --initialize
        SET @ReturnStr = ''
        SET @CharLoop = 1

        --loop through all characters
        WHILE @CharLoop <= len(@InputString)
                BEGIN
                        --get the current character
                        SET @CurrentChar =
```

```
        SUBSTRING(@InputString, @CharLoop, 1)
                    --test to see if this character is a
carriage return
            IF @CurrentChar <> CHAR(13)
                    --This is NOT a carriage return
- use it
                SET @ReturnStr = @ReturnStr +
@CurrentChar
                --increment character position
            SET @CharLoop = @CharLoop + 1
        END
    --all characters were iterated - returned cleansed
string
    RETURN @ReturnStr
END
```

You can read the comments in the code to determine what it is doing. I don't think you want me to reiterate the same thing here. The main point is to show you how your Transact-SQL statements come together to become a function and return a value. This function can then be called by sending a string as a parameter, like this:

```
SELECT dbo.RemoveCR ('test' + char(13) + 'THIS')
```

I make sure to include a carriage return for my test, which is the ASCII value of 13.

You must specify the owner of the function or SQL Server 2000 will not be able to find it.

The result of running this Transact-SQL statement is as follows:

```
TestTHIS
```

Chapter 7

Fun with Stored Procedures

- -

In This Chapter

▶ Taking advantage of system procedures

▶ Thinking outside the box with extended procedures

▶ Unleashing your creative side with user-defined procedures

- -

A *stored procedure* is a package of SQL code that is compiled and stored within SQL Server as a single module. This module can then be called up and executed easily. After you create the stored procedure, you no longer have to worry about the SQL that made up the procedure, unless it needs modification.

There are two major advantages of calling stored procedures over issuing SQL statements directly to SQL Server:

✔ You almost always send less information over the network when calling stored procedures.

✔ The query plan that SQL Server uses to execute a stored procedure is cached in memory on the server the first time the stored procedure is called. A *query plan* is the path that SQL Server will take when executing SQL statements. In this context, the path refers to the index(es) used to speed-up query performance. Query plans can dramatically increase performance because otherwise, the SQL statements that make up the stored procedure have to be parsed every time they are executed. Parsing takes time.

Stored procedures are classified in three different ways, some of which you can create and some you can't. The classifications are as follows:

✔ System Procedures (Execute Only)

✔ Extended Procedures (Create and Execute)

✔ User-Defined Procedures (Create and Execute)

Throughout this chapter, I show you how to create and use stored procedures. Let the fun begin.

System Procedures

A system procedure is a stored procedure that Microsoft created for you and included in Microsoft SQL Server 2000 to provide administrative and informational tasks. To find out certain system information, you ordinarily need to know which tables Microsoft stores the data in. With a system procedure, you don't have to know the tables. You simply call the system procedure from the SQL Server Query Analyzer or from any other program that has a connection to the database.

One convention to be aware of is that a system procedure always begins with the prefix sp, followed by an underscore character. Therefore, if you see a procedure named sp_help, you know that it's a system procedure provided by Microsoft and not a procedure a coworker created.

System procedures are automatically included when you install SQL Server. You don't have to purchase anything or install anything separately. What a deal!

Discovering available system procedures

In versions of Microsoft SQL Server prior to 7.0, you had to query system tables to find out what system procedures were available. However, since that version, it has become very easy to find this out. To know what system procedures are available, follow these steps:

1. **Choose Start➪Programs➪Microsoft SQL Server➪Enterprise Manager to start the SQL Server Enterprise Manager.**

2. **Expand the tree so that you see the** Stored Procedures **folder within the desired database under the** Databases **folder.**

   For more information about expanding the tree, see the Introduction of this book.

3. **Select the** Stored Procedures **folder.**

   After selecting the Stored Procedures folder, notice the list of stored procedures on the right part of the screen (see Figure 7-1). Some system procedures are located in each database; others are located only in the master database. System stored procedures are contained only within system databases.

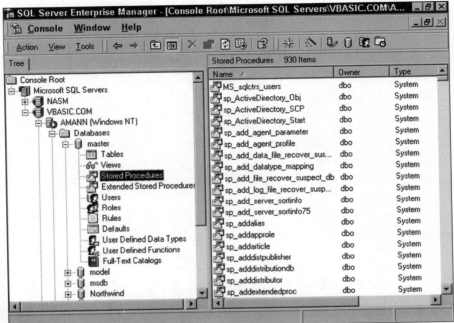

Figure 7-1:
The SQL
Server
Enterprise
Manager
screen,
showing
system
procedures.

Viewing the SQL for a system procedure

All stored procedures, including system procedures, are made up of
Transact-SQL. You may often like to view the SQL to understand or edit how a
stored procedure works. For more information about Transact-SQL, see
Chapter 8. To view the SQL for a system procedure, follow these few steps:

1. **Select the system procedure in the right pane of the SQL Server
   Enterprise Manager.**

2. **Double-click the system procedure to view.**

   For example, double-click `sp_addalias`, which brings up the Stored
   Procedure Properties dialog box (see Figure 7-2). These properties not
   only show the SQL for the system procedure but also allow you to click
   Permissions to view the security settings for the system procedure.

   One final thing about this dialog box that's new for SQL Server 2000 is
   the ability to indicate that this system procedure should automatically
   run when SQL Server starts. This feature can be very useful for performing initial system or administrative functions. To use this option, ensure
   that the Execute whenever SQL Server Starts check box is selected.

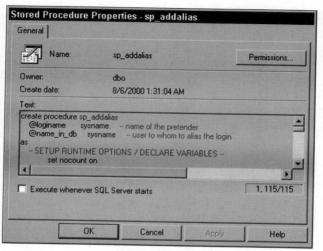

Figure 7-2: The Stored Procedure Properties dialog box, showing the sp_add-alias system procedure.

Executing a system procedure

Execute a system procedure as though you were executing any SQL command by using the SQL Server Query Analyzer (see Chapter 9). To execute a system procedure, follow these steps:

1. **Choose Start➪Programs➪Microsoft SQL Server➪Query Analyzer to start the SQL Server Query Analyzer.**

   You're then prompted to log into SQL Server. Type your ID and password in the Login Name and Password boxes.

2. **Type your query.**

   A query can consist of multiple statements or a single statement containing the name of a system procedure. For example, type **sp_helpdb**. Choose Query➪ Execute (or press F5) to execute the query. Sp_helpdb is a system procedure that returns information about the database you specify. If you don't specify a database when using this system procedure, information about all databases is returned (see Figure 7-3).

Extended Procedures

An extended procedure is similar to a system procedure or a user-defined stored procedure, except that the procedure is not stored in SQL Server but rather in a DLL. Likewise, it is not made up of SQL statements but rather programming code. Extended procedures greatly expand the capabilities of SQL Server 2000. An example of an extended procedure is an interface with SQL Server from your e-mail system.

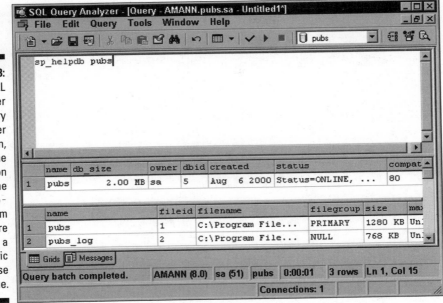

Figure 7-3:
The SQL
Server
Query
Analyzer
screen,
showing the
execution
of the
sp_help-
db system
procedure
passing a
specific
database
name.

A convention to be aware of is that an extended procedure usually begins with the prefix xp, followed by an underscore character. Therefore, if you see a procedure named xp_fileexist, you know this is an extended procedure. However, with every rule there are exceptions. Some extended procedures begin with the prefix sp, followed by an underscore character.

Unveiling available extended procedures

Just as with system procedures, Microsoft makes it easy to find out which extended procedures are available. To find out what extended procedures are available, follow these steps:

1. **Choose Start⇨Programs⇨Microsoft SQL Server⇨Enterprise Manager to start the SQL Server Enterprise Manager.**

2. **Expand the tree so that you see the Extended Stored Procedures folder within the** master **database under the Databases folder.**

   For more information about expanding the tree, see the Introduction of this book.

3. **Select the Extended Stored Procedures folder.**

   After selecting the Extended Stored Procedures folder, notice the list of stored procedures on the right part of the screen (see Figure 7-4). Unlike system procedures, which can exist in all databases, extended procedures are always located in only the master database.

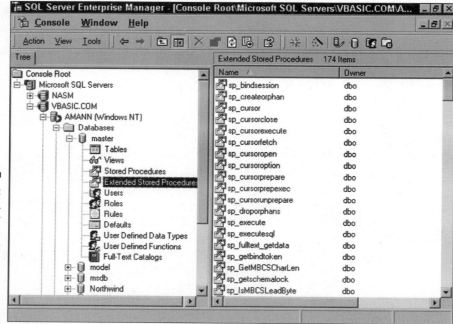

Figure 7-4:
The SQL
Server
Enterprise
Manager
screen,
showing
extended
procedures.

Viewing the properties for an extended procedure

All extended procedures have properties that list the procedure name and path of the library (DLL) when the procedure name is stored. *DLL* stands for Dynamically Linked Library. Windows is based on these types of libraries. Within these libraries, there are one or more functions that your extended stored procedures can call to achieve some function or purpose. Such a purpose can be something like logging someone off of your network (not mischievously, but for administrative reasons). This type of functionality is not built into SQL Server 2000, so your extended procedures must call external functions in DLLs. This gives almost unlimited extensibility.

You probably want to view properties for extended stored procedures so that you can see what the path is for the DLL library. To view the properties for an extended procedure, follow these few steps:

1. **Select the extended procedure in the right pane of the SQL Server Enterprise Manager.**

   See the section "Unveiling available extended procedures," earlier in this chapter, to see how to select the extended procedure.

2. Double-click the extended procedure to view it.

For example, double-click xp_cmdshell, which brings up the Extended Stored Procedure Properties dialog box (see Figure 7-5). These properties not only show the properties for the extended procedure but also enable you to click Permissions to view the security settings for the extended procedure.

Figure 7-5:
The
Extended
Stored
Procedure
Properties
dialog box,
showing the
xp_cmd-
shell
extended
procedure.

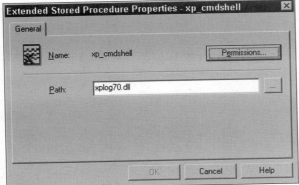

Executing an extended procedure

Execute an extended procedure as though you were executing any SQL command; do so by using the SQL Server Query Analyzer (see Chapter 9).

Many of the extended procedures installed with Microsoft SQL Server 2000 run only on Windows NT, version 4.0 and higher — they can't run on Windows 95 or Windows 98. Also, there are some extended procedures that may run only on Windows 2000.

To execute an extended procedure, follow these steps:

1. Choose Start⇨Programs⇨Microsoft SQL Server⇨Query Analyzer to start the SQL Server Query Analyzer.

You're prompted to log into SQL Server. Type your ID and password in the Login Name and Password boxes.

2. Type your query.

A query can consist of multiple statements or a single statement containing the name of an extended procedure. For example, type xp_enumgroups. Choose Query⇨Execute (or press F5) to execute the query. Xp_enum-groups is a system procedure that returns all the groups available on a local NT Server or within a domain. If you don't specify a domain name, information about groups on the local server is returned (see Figure 7-6).

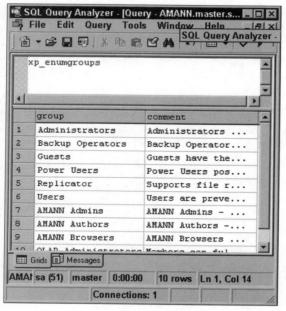

Figure 7-6:
The SQL
Query
Analyzer
screen,
showing the
execution of
the
xp_enum-
groups
extended
procedure.

Creating extended procedures

Creating an extended procedure isn't as glorious as it sounds. You must create and encapsulate some functionality into a DLL by using another programming language. Visual C++ is one such language. At the time of this writing, Visual Basic 6 is the current version of Visual Basic, but Visual Studio 7 is coming out shortly. The next version of Visual Basic (version 7?) included in Visual Studio 7 may be able to create extended stored procedures. Although Visual Basic 6 has the capability to create DLLs, it does not support the interface required by SQL Server for extended procedures. Writing these DLLs is outside the scope of this book, but if you do have a DLL that already supports the SQL Server interface, you must add the functions exposed in the DLL to SQL Server.

To create a new extended procedure in SQL Server, follow these steps:

1. **Choose Start⇨Programs⇨Microsoft SQL Server⇨Enterprise Manager to start the SQL Server Enterprise Manager.**

2. **Expand the tree so that you see the Extended Stored Procedures folder within the** master **database under the Databases folder.**

   For more information about expanding the tree, see the Introduction of this book.

3. Select the Extended Stored Procedures folder.

After selecting the Extended Stored Procedures folder, notice the list of stored procedures on the right part of the screen (refer to earlier Figure 7-4). Extended stored procedures are always located in the master database.

4. Create a new extended stored procedure by clicking Action⇔New Extended Stored Procedure.

Clicking Action⇔New Extended Stored Procedure brings up a dialog box containing properties for the extended procedure (see Figure 7-7). Again, remember that you aren't actually creating the extended procedure — you're only indicating to SQL Server where the procedure is inside the DLL that you've created in another language. Alternatively, you can right-click the Extended Stored Procedures tree folder and choose the New Extended Stored Procedure menu option.

Figure 7-7:
The Extended Stored Procedure Properties dialog box, showing fields that you can use to enter new parameters.

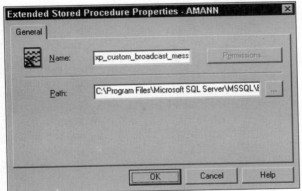

5. Type data in the Name and Path fields.

Type the name of the procedure that resides in the DLL and the path of the DLL. For example, if you write a DLL function that sends a broadcast message to all users in the company 10 minutes before you take the server down, you can type **xp_custom_broadcast_message** in the Name field, and **C:\Program Files\Microsoft SQL Server\MSSQL \Binn\ custom.dll** in the Path field.

Of course, for the extended procedure to work, you have to create a DLL named custom.dll and place it in the C:\Program Files\Microsoft SQL Server\MSSQL\Binn directory. Also, it needs to contain the xp_custom_broadcast_message function. If it doesn't, you receive an error while trying to execute the extended procedure.

You may want to differentiate your custom extended procedures from the ones that Microsoft provides when you install SQL Server 2000 because that way you'll know where to turn if there are errors. You can't be upset with Microsoft if the extended procedure is your own. I suggest you use the prefix xp_custom_. You can, of course, come up with your own convention if you don't like mine. The main point is to differentiate your extended procedures from the Microsoft procedures.

6. **Click OK to save your changes.**

   After you click OK to save your changes, notice that the name of your new extended procedure is now listed in the Enterprise Manager.

If you want to change permissions on the extended procedure, you can't do it at the same time that you create the extended procedure. You have to save your changes and bring up the Properties dialog box again by double-clicking the extended procedure you want in the Enterprise Manager. The Extended Stored Procedure Properties dialog box returns, but this time the Permissions button is enabled.

Creating User-Defined Stored Procedures

You can create your own user-defined stored procedures. Like system procedures, your own stored procedures can exist in any database. It's very common for a client/server application to use many stored procedures. Stored procedures are made up of SQL, utilizing control statements (such as IF, THEN, and ELSE) and variables. Stored procedures allow for the abstraction of Transact-SQL code whose purpose is to provide a specific function.

For example, you can have a stored procedure that creates a customer record in all the appropriate tables in the database. In this example, the person who is executing the stored procedure doesn't even have to know which tables are being populated with customer information. This concept is called *abstraction* because all the functionality that happens at a lower level is abstracted from the person who calls the procedure. All he/she knows is that a stored procedure is called, a few parameters are passed, and, magically, the correct tables are populated with the correct data.

To create a user-defined stored procedure, follow these steps:

1. **Choose Start➪Programs➪Microsoft SQL Server➪Enterprise Manager to start the SQL Server Enterprise Manager.**

2. **Expand the tree so that you see the Stored Procedures folder within the desired database under the Databases folder.**

   For more information about expanding the tree, see the Introduction of this book.

3. Select the Stored Procedures folder by clicking it.

After selecting the Stored Procedures folder, notice the list of stored procedures on the right part of the screen.

4. Create a new Stored Procedure by clicking Action⇨New Stored Procedure.

Clicking Action⇨New Stored Procedure brings up the Stored Procedures Properties dialog box, allowing you to create your stored procedure (see Figure 7-8). Alternatively, you can right-click the Stored Procedures tree folder and choose the New Stored Procedure menu option.

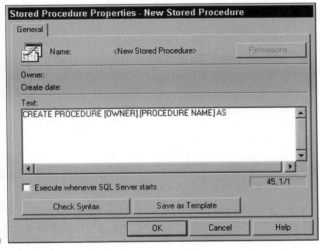

Figure 7-8: The SQL Server Enterprise Manager screen, showing the Stored Procedure Properties dialog box.

Creating a stored procedure involves typing in the CREATE PROCEDURE SQL statement, which the Enterprise Manager does for you. What you type in next is totally up to you. Deciding what to type next is dependent on the functionality you desire from your stored procedure.

5. Type the SQL that makes up your stored procedure.

Here I show you a specific example that you can use for a variety of possibilities. Say that you want to create a user-defined stored procedure called usp_NewCustomer, a simple stored procedure that accepts five arguments. The arguments will be used to insert data into a table, called Customer. The arguments are the following:

- Name
- Address
- City
- State
- Zip

The SQL syntax for creating a stored procedure is as follows:

```
CREATE PROC[EDURE] procedure_name [;number]
    [({@parameter_name | parameter} data_type [ VARYING]
        [= default]
    [OUTPUT])] [,...n]
    [WITH {RECOMPILE | ENCRYPTION ]
    [FOR REPLICATION]
    AS
    sql_statement [...n]
```

The following lists the arguments available for substitution in the preceding statement:

- *procedure_name* is the name of your stored procedure, which is the name you use when you execute your stored procedure.

- *;number* is an optional parameter that allows you to group multiple stored procedures together.

- *@parameter_name | parameter* is an optional parameter that's the name of a parameter to be used as an argument in the stored procedure.

- *data_type* is the type of data that is represented by the parameter. The data_type must be a valid SQL Server 2000 datatype. You must specify this argument if you specify a @parameter_name.

- VARYING is an optional keyword that indicates that an output parameter's result set can vary.

- *default* is an optional keyword that can be specified for each @parameter_name. The default keyword is assigned to a value via an equal (=) sign. The default keyword indicates that when the stored procedure is called, this value will be used if the value for @parameter_name is not explicitly specified.

- OUTPUT is an optional keyword that indicates that the @parameter_name is used for output.

- *n* indicates that multiple parameters can be specified.

- WITH RECOMPILE is an optional set of keywords that instructs SQL Server to recompile the stored procedure every time it's run.

- WITH ENCRYPTION is an optional set of keywords that instructs SQL Server to encrypt the text of the stored procedure in the syscomments system table.

- FOR REPLICATION is an optional set of keywords that indicates that the stored procedure will be used for replication. For more information about replication, see Chapter 12.

- *sql_statement* is any valid SQL statement that you have permission to execute.

- n indicates that more than one sql_statement can be executed.

To understand how to use this syntax, see the following:

```
CREATE PROCEDURE sp_NewCustomer (
@name varchar(30),
@address varchar(30),
@city varchar(30),
@state char(2),
@zip char(5))
AS
INSERT INTO Customer (
cust_name,
cust_address,
cust_city,
cust_state,
cust_zip)
VALUES (
@name,
@address,
@city,
@state.
@zip)
```

As you can see, as long as you know how to write SQL statements, you can write user-defined stored procedures. Good luck in your stored procedure writing.

Stored Procedure Security

Like most objects in SQL Server, you must be concerned with security on those objects. Security refers to the granting or restricting access to those objects. In the case of stored procedures, security is granted through the use of the Permissions button in any of the dialog boxes presented in this chapter. You can assign specific permissions to specific users or roles.

Part III
Interface Design

The 5th Wave · By Rich Tennant

"For further thoughts on that subject, I'm going to download Leviticus and go through the menu to Job, chapter 2, verse 6, file 'J.' It reads..."

In this part . . .

I give you an overview into using Structured Query Language, or SQL. SQL is the "language" of databases. I also show you how to use SQL with Microsoft SQL Server 2000 — with the tool provided by Microsoft, called the Query Analyzer. One final thing that I cover in this part is to show you how to import and export data.

Chapter 8

Making Microsoft SQL Server 2000 Work by Using SQL

In This Chapter

▶ Creating database objects with DDL

▶ Manipulating data with DML

▶ Creating SQL constructs with DCL

The term SQL stands for *Structured Query Language*. It is the language from which most databases, or database management systems (DBMS), allow manipulation of data and much more. SQL Server is no exception. A SQL statement is a bit of text containing clauses in a particular structure. I know this conjures up visions of Christmas time, but a *clause* is actually a part of a SQL statement that starts with a SQL keyword. I show you how to use clauses in your SQL statements throughout this chapter. Also in this chapter, I show you the Microsoft-specific SQL syntax and examples, known as Transact-SQL. Transact-SQL is sometimes also known as *T-SQL*.

The rest of this chapter is dedicated to showing you how to use SQL with SQL Server 2000. However, bear in mind that I can't show in this chapter the full range of SQL supported in SQL Server 2000. It is just too expansive. For more information about SQL as an entire topic, refer to *SQL For Dummies,* 2nd Edition, by Allen G. Taylor (from IDG Books Worldwide, Inc.). So why do I show you SQL at all in this chapter if you can refer to this book? Actually, because SQL is the basis of SQL Server (quite literally), the book would be incomplete if I didn't at least show you the basics.

You can execute any of the statements that I show you in this chapter using the SQL Server Query Analyzer or any other tool that allows the execution of SQL statements (see Chapter 9). The same functionality achieved by the SQL statements that I show you in this chapter can be achieved graphically by using the SQL Server Enterprise Manager (see Chapters 4 and 5). However, if you want to create a program that accesses Microsoft SQL Server and issues queries, you will not have the Enterprise Manager at your disposal. Therefore, you need this chapter to construct your queries. So buckle up and here we go.

SQL-92 and you

A SQL statement is defined by the SQL standard, named SQL-92. This standard basically identifies the version of SQL to which a DBMS conforms. The standard defines things like syntax and keywords that are to be used. The main purpose for the standard is so that it can be used in databases other than Microsoft SQL Server (not that you would ever do that). Each database vendor develops its own extensions to the SQL-92 language to allow you to take advantage of specific database features. This is why Transact-SQL, the SQL language used in Microsoft SQL Server 2000, is a subset of the SQL-92 standard set. Transact-SQL is proprietary to Microsoft SQL Server but must be used to get the full benefit of the specific database features.

The Categories of SQL

SQL is a language that is divided into a series of *categories*. It can be confusing because these categories are also called "languages," but they really are not. These categories are all part of the SQL language. The categories are as follows:

- ✔ Data Definition Language (DDL)
- ✔ Data Manipulation Language (DML)
- ✔ Data Control Language (DCL)

In each one of these categories, the SQL statements are made up of a series of clauses, just as the English language is. To make a SQL statement readable, each clause is usually specified on a separate code line.

In this chapter, I show you how to use all these categories of SQL statements.

Using Data Definition Language (DDL) Statements

A *Data Definition Language,* or DDL, is a SQL statement that is designed to specifically manipulate database objects, such as databases, tables, indexes, views, defaults, rules, and triggers. (For more information about database objects, see Chapters 4 and 5.) This section shows you how to create a database, a table, and an index. Generally, a DDL consists of using CREATE, ALTER, or DROP Transact-SQL statements.

Creating a database: The mother of all containers

A database serves as a big container to hold other objects such as tables, indexes, views, and even data. However, to contain these objects, you must first create the database itself with the CREATE DATABASE statement. The CREATE DATABASE statement follows this general syntax:

```
CREATE DATABASE database_name
[ ON [PRIMARY]
[ <filespec> [,...n] ]
[, <filegroup> [,...n] ]
]
[ LOG ON { <filespec> } ]
[ COLLATE collation_name ]
[ FOR LOAD | FOR ATTACH ]
```

The following keywords are used in the preceding syntax:

database_name is the name that you will give when you refer to your database in Transact-SQL.

ON indicates that you will specify the files to be created in the creation of the database.

PRIMARY indicates that the files are stored in the primary filegroup.

filespec is a group of properties that indicates attributes of the files that make up a database. A filespec contains these arguments:

```
[ NAME = logical_file_name, ]
FILENAME = 'os_file_name'
[, SIZE = size]
[, MAXSIZE = { max_size | UNLIMITED } ]
[, FILEGROWTH = growth_increment]
```

logical_file_name is the name that you will use in your Transact-SQL statements.

os_file_name is the filename as it appears to the operating system.

size is the size of the initial file in megabytes.

max_size is the maximum size of the operating system file that is allowed. If UNLIMITED is specified, the file can grow until the operating system runs out of room on the hard disk.

growth_increment is the amount of space that is reserved and incremented by the operating system every time more space is needed. You can specify a percentage or a specific number of megabytes.

filegroup is an administrative grouping of filespecs. A filegroup contains these arguments (note that *filespec* refers to the same filespec attributes shown you previously):

```
FILEGROUP filegroup_name <filespec>
```

LOG ON specifies the filespec attributes for the transaction log.

COLLATE specifies the name of the collation that you want to use. A collation is new for SQL Server 2000 and specifies the ordering and storage for strings, as well as the code page used to translate ASCII characters. If no collation is specified, the default collation for the server is used.

FOR LOAD is used only for older version of SQL Server. This clause is not discussed in this book.

FOR ATTACH attaches existing files to a database. This clause is not discussed in this book.

Suppose that you want to create a database to hold all your customer information, such as contact information, orders, and invoices. To create a database named Customer using all the defaults, issue this SQL statement:

```
CREATE DATABASE Customer
```

If you don't want to use all the default values, you can specify your own with this example:

```
CREATE DATABASE Customer
ON PRIMARY
( NAME = Customer_dat,
  FILENAME = 'c:\Program Files\Microsoft SQL
           Server\mssql\Data\Customer.mdf',
  SIZE = 1,
  MAXSIZE = 10)
LOG ON
( NAME = Customer_Log,
  FILENAME = 'c:\Program Files\Microsoft SQL
           Server\mssql\Data\CustomerLog.ldf',
  SIZE = 1,
  MAXSIZE = 10)
```

The preceding example creates a data file called Customer_dat in the default data directory with a file named Customer.mdf. This file is allocated a size of 1 megabyte and allowed to grow up to 10 megabytes. The same parameters are specified for the log file, except that it is called Customer_Log with a file named CustomerLog.ldf.

Where do I put all my data?

After you create a database (see the preceding section), you can create one or more tables to stuff your data into. A *table* is a database object that logically looks like a spreadsheet, containing rows and columns. Each row is sometimes referred to as a *record* in the table. Each column is sometimes referred to as a *field* in the table.

A table is created inside a database, so the database must exist first. Because more than one database can be on the server, you must instruct SQL Server as to which database the table is to be created into. To indicate which database to use, you must "switch" to the desired database with the USE statement. To switch to the Customer database, use this statement:

```
USE Customer
```

After you have switched to the desired database, nothing is standing in your way of creating a table to store your data into. To create a table, you use the CREATE TABLE statement. This statement is one of the most complex in Transact-SQL, so I'm going to limit the information that I present to you here. Within the CREATE TABLE statement, you specify the name of your table, the columns your table is to contain, and the type of data each column represents. The CREATE TABLE statement follows this general syntax (which I show as being simplified from the advanced syntax):

```
CREATE TABLE
[database_name].[owner].table_name
(
{ <column_definition>
| column_name AS computed_column_expression
| <table_constraint> } [,...n]
)
```

The following keywords are used in the preceding syntax:

> *database_name* is the name of the database in which the table will be created. If the database is not the current one, you need to specify the name of the database.

> *owner* is the individual or role that is to own the table that you are creating. If no owner is specified, dbo is used as the owner.

> *table_name* is the name of the table that you want to create.

> *column_definition* is a group of properties that indicates the attributes of a single column. A *column_definition* contains these arguments:

```
{ column_name data_type }
    [ [ DEFAULT constant_expression ]
        | [ IDENTITY [ ( seed , increment ) [ NOT FOR
            REPLICATION ] ] ]
    ]
    [ ROWGUIDCOL ]
    [ COLLATE < collation_name > ]
    [ < column_constraint > ] [ ...n ]
```

column_name is the name of an individual column.

data_type is any valid datatype that is allowed in SQL Server 2000. See Chapter 3 for more information about valid datatypes.

constant_expression is any hard-coded value that you want to give to a column if no value is specified when data is inserted into the column.

seed and increment are values used to identify where to start (seed) and how many numbers to increment every time a row of data is inserted into this table.

collation_name is the name of the collation to use if you are not going to use the default collation.

column_constraint is a set of properties used to define how a column will be constrained. For an understanding of the concepts relating to the table_constraint, see Chapter 3. A column_constraint contains these arguments:

```
[ CONSTRAINT constraint_name ]
    { [ NULL | NOT NULL ]
        | [ { PRIMARY KEY | UNIQUE }
            [ CLUSTERED | NONCLUSTERED ]
            [ WITH FILLFACTOR = fillfactor ]
            [ON {filegroup | DEFAULT} ] ]
    ]
```

table_constraint is a group of properties that indicates how the table will be constrained. For an understanding of the concepts relating to the table_constraint, see Chapter 3. A table_constraint contains these arguments:

```
[ CONSTRAINT constraint_name ]
    { [ { PRIMARY KEY | UNIQUE }
        [ CLUSTERED | NONCLUSTERED ]
        { ( column [ ASC | DESC ] [ ,...n ] ) }
        [ WITH FILLFACTOR = fillfactor ]
        [ ON { filegroup | DEFAULT } ]
    ]
```

Okay, so what does all of this mean? Take a look at some examples. If you want to create a table named `Contact` (for customer contact information), you probably need to store things such as `ContactID`, `LastName`, `FirstName`, `Address`, `City`, `State`, `Zip`, and `Phone`. You'll probably need more than that, but I want to keep it simple for now. Believe it or not, I've just identified the columns in the table. The only other thing you need to do is to define the types of data (referred to as a *datatypes*) that each column represents. (For more information about datatypes, see Chapter 3 or the Cheat Sheet at the front of this book.) I take the liberty of showing you the `CREATE TABLE` statement with datatypes:

```
CREATE TABLE Contact
(ContactID integer,
LastName varchar (30),
FirstName varchar (30),
Address varchar (30),
City varchar (30),
State char (2),
Zip varchar (10),
Phone char (10))
```

The `ContactID` field is defined as an integer because it will store number data. The `LastName`, `FirstName`, `Address`, and `City` fields are created with the `varchar` datatype. The `varchar` datatype allows for variable character data. Here, I define each of these with a maximum length of 30. The State field allows for character data with a maximum length of 2. The `Zip` field is also a `varchar` datatype but with the maximum length of 10. The length is decreased (from the other fields) because a United States ZIP Code will never have more than 10 characters. The `Phone` field is defined as `char` with a maximum length of 10. The field is not defined as a `varchar` because the phone number will never be a variable length. It is always 10 characters, excluding dashes and parentheses.

If you don't want to issue the `USE` statement first before creating a table, you can explicitly identify the database name so that you are assured that the table is created where you expect it to be. To explicitly state where you want the table created, type the database name, followed by `.dbo.`, followed by your table name. For example, the following statement creates the table `Contact` in the `Customer` database:

```
CREATE TABLE Customer.dbo.Contact
(ContactID integer,
LastName varchar (30),
FirstName varchar (30),
Address varchar (30),
City varchar (30),
State char (2),
Zip varchar (10),
Phone char (10))
```

Additionally, you can specify constraints for the table at the same time as you create the table. A `column_constraint` is a limitation placed on a table, such as an index. If you want to indicate that the `ContactID` column in the `Contact` table is a primary key, use this statement:

```
CREATE TABLE Contact
(ContactID integer CONSTRAINT Primary1 PRIMARY KEY,
LastName varchar (30),
FirstName varchar (30),
Address varchar (30),
City varchar (30),
State char (2),
Zip varchar (10),
Phone char (10))
```

The preceding statement adds a constraint clause. This statement actually creates an index with the name `Primary1` and defines it as a primary key for the `Contact` column. For more information about primary keys, see Chapter 3.

Okay, all this is well and good, but what if you want to force a user to type a last name and first name for a contact? How do you indicate this to SQL Server? You need to tell SQL Server that it shouldn't accept blank values (called *null* values). Do this with the `NOT NULL` keywords. Therefore, to create a `Contact` table that forces you to put data into the `LastName` and `FirstName` fields, issue this SQL statement:

```
CREATE TABLE Contact
(ContactID integer,
LastName varchar (30) NOT NULL,
FirstName varchar (30) NOT NULL,
Address varchar (30),
City varchar (30),
State char (2),
Zip varchar (10),
Phone char (10))
```

How do I speed up my queries?

An index is a mechanism for SQL Server to speed up querying the database. Because an index is used to speed up queries, you must first know how your data will be accessed. For example, if your data will always be accessed by a `ContactID`, you probably want to place an index on that column. If, on the other hand, your data will be looked up by `Last Name`, you probably want to place an index on that column. If your data will be accessed by using either column, you probably want to place an index on both columns.

You also need to decide on the type of index used. Your choices are clustered and nonclustered:

- A *clustered* index uses a binary tree search algorithm and indicates that SQL Server will physically order the records based in order of the values in a specific column or columns of data. Because SQL Server has to do more work by physically reordering data, INSERT and UPDATE statements can slow down data accessing, but retrieving data is faster. You can have only one clustered index on a single table. A clustered index is also usually associated with the primary key index.

- A *nonclustered* index also uses a binary tree search algorithm but does not physically order the records. Therefore, querying is usually faster than not using an index at all but not as fast as using a clustered index. A nonclustered index does not generally hurt performance when you use INSERT and UPDATE statements.

To create an index, you use the CREATE INDEX statement. The CREATE INDEX statement uses this general syntax:

```
CREATE [UNIQUE] [CLUSTERED | NONCLUSTERED]
    INDEX index_name ON table (column ASC|DESC[,...n])
[WITH
        [PAD_INDEX]
        [[,] FILLFACTOR = fillfactor]
        [[,] IGNORE_DUP_KEY]
        [[,] DROP_EXISTING]
        [[,] STATISTICS_NORECOMPUTE]
        [[,] SORT_IN_TEMPDB]
]
[ON filegroup]
```

The following keywords are used in the preceding syntax:

UNIQUE indicates that SQL Server 2000 will enforce unique values in the columns represented in the index.

CLUSTERED|NONCLUSTERED specifies that you want to create either a clustered or nonclustered index. These keywords are mutually exclusive, so you cannot specify both. If you specify neither, a nonclustered index will be created.

index_name is the name of the index that you want to create.

table is the name of the table in which to create the index.

column is the name of the column(s) to represent in the created index. If you want to specify more than one column, you specify the column names separated by commas.

ASC|DESC specifies that the column will be sorted in ascending or descending order, with ASC being the default.

PAD_INDEX leaves space open in the intermediate levels of index pages. Specify this keyword only if you use the FILLFACTOR keyword also.

FILLFACTOR specifies how full, by percentage, the leaf index page is before a new index page is created. This percentage can be specified as a number from 1 to 100. Fill factors are not covered in this book.

IGNORE_DUP_KEY is valid only if you also specify the UNIQUE keyword. If specified, the IGNORE_DUP_KEY keyword allows inserts into a table that already contains duplicate values in the columns represented by the index. If this keyword is not specified, the INSERT statement will fail.

DROP_EXISTING specifies that SQL Server 2000 should drop and recreate the index if it already exists.

STATISTICS_NORECOMPUTE specifies that statistics for an out-of-date index are not recomputed. This option can cause problems with performance if it is not used correctly.

SORT_IN_TEMPDB specifies that results will be sorted in the TEMPDB database. This may help in speeding up performance.

ON *filegroup* specifies that the index should be created on a specific filegroup that already exists. If this is not specified, the primary filegroup will be used by default.

If you want to create a clustered index on the Contact table, on the ContactID column you issue this statement:

```
CREATE CLUSTERED INDEX Index1 ON Contact (ContactID)
```

You can substitute the index name, Index1, with any name you choose. This name is used only as an identifier so that you can manipulate the index at a later time. This manipulation includes deleting or dropping the index, as well as altering it.

Clustered and nonclustered index considerations

People generally tend to make the clustered index the primary key, but doing so is not a requirement. A clustered index may be any field in the database. Use the clustered index to group data that will often be retrieved by a GROUP BY clause. When you want to use the clustered index on other than a primary key, you should not use the primary key constraint to create a primary key.

A nonclustered index can be affected by the fill factor used when creating the index. A fill factor leaves blank space in the index to be filled in by future additions to the data. If you do not use a fill factor, then when you do inserts of data, you make the index create extents to hold the data (*extents* are chained storage spaces). Many extents can slow down inserts.

Likewise, you can create a nonclustered index on the same table and column by issuing this statement:

```
CREATE NONCLUSTERED INDEX Index1 ON Contact (ContactID)
```

A multiple key index is one whose specified fields are made up of more than one column in a table. If you want to create a multiple key index, simply specify the columns in the index. To ensure that the ContactID and LastName columns are part of an index, use this statement:

```
CREATE NONCLUSTERED INDEX Index1 ON Contact (ContactID,
           LastName)
```

It is important to know that SQL Server 2000 does not allow you to create a multiple key index when you use the CREATE TABLE statement. You must first create the table and then use the CREATE INDEX statement to specify multiple keys. However, if you aren't trying to create multiple key indexes, you may find it useful to specify the index (constraint) within the CREATE TABLE statement.

Seeing things differently

If you want to hide columns from a table in a database, you can do that with a view. A *view* is a database object that allows you to define which columns and/or rows, in one or more tables, are exposed to the view. Being exposed to a view means that you define the columns that you want to be visible in the view. In other words, a view is a logical table.

To create a view, use the CREATE VIEW statement. The CREATE VIEW statement follows this general syntax:

```
CREATE [owner] VIEW view_name [(column [,....n])]
          [WITH ENCRYPTION]
          AS
          select_statement
          [WITH CHECK OPTION]
```

The following keywords are used in the preceding syntax:

   owner is the name of the owner of the view. If no owner is specified, the owner of the view will be dbo.

   view_name is the name of the view to create.

   column is the name of one or more column(s) that are represented in the view, separated by commas. These are known as column aliases because the names that you choose do not have to be the same name as the columns in the *select_statement*.

WITH ENCRYPTION is a keyword that instructs SQL Server 2000 to encrypt the Transact-SQL statement that defines the view. This is necessary when you don't want anyone to know what underlying tables make up the view. Without this keyword, the Transact-SQL statement that defines the view will be visible in the syscomments table.

select_statement is any valid SQL statement, which can contain joins to multiple tables but cannot contain ORDER BY, COMPUTE, or COMPUTE BY clauses. It also cannot contain the INTO keyword or reference a temporary table.

WITH CHECK OPTION is a keyword that instructs SQL Server 2000 to ensure that if data is modified through the view, that the criteria set forth in the *select_statement* is applied.

As an example, suppose that you have a table named Employee with columns named Employee_ID, Last_Name, First_Name, and Salary. You probably don't want to show the Salary column to just anyone, so you can create a view on the Employee table, like this:

```
CREATE VIEW Dont_Show_Salary
AS
SELECT Employee_ID, Last_Name, First_Name
FROM Employee
```

With the preceding statement, you define a view with the name Dont_Show_Salary. The columns exposed in the view are defined in the SELECT statement after the AS clause. For more information about the SELECT statement, see "Querying data," later in this chapter.

Then, to use the view, you can access it as if it were a table, like this:

```
SELECT *
FROM Dont_Show_Salary
```

Ruling the world

Okay, if not the world, at least your database! A rule defines what values are valid to be placed in a column. As you may have guessed, you use the CREATE RULE statement to suit this purpose. The CREATE RULE statement follows this general syntax:

```
CREATE RULE rule_name
AS condition_expression
```

The following keywords are used in the preceding syntax:

rule_name is the name of the rule that you want to create.

condition_expression is the heart of the rule. This defines the condition of the rule defined in rule_name. This can contain one or more expression(s) that can be found in any valid WHERE clause, with one exception. No database objects can be referenced in this expression.

For example, suppose that you want to create a rule to allow only the numbers 1 through 5. You use the CREATE RULE statement like this:

```
CREATE RULE Between_1_and_5
AS
@val >= 1 and @val <= 5
```

The rule is given a name, Between_1_and_5. Then it is defined using a variable name. I use @val. Then this value is tested to ensure that it is greater than or equal to 1 and less than or equal to 5.

Now that the rule is defined, it can be used, or *bound,* to any of the columns in the database in which the rule was created. To bind the rule to a column, you must use a system-stored procedure, called sp_bindrule. For more information about system stored procedures, see Chapter 7.

The sp_bindrule system stored procedure follows this general syntax:

```
sp_bindrule 'rule_name', 'object_name', 'future_only'
```

The following keywords are used in the preceding syntax:

rule_name is the name of the rule that you have already created. This value must be enclosed in single quotation marks (called ticks).

object_name is the name of the table and column that you want to bind rule_name to. This value must also be enclosed in single quotation marks.

future_only is a flag to be used if the rule is bound to a user-defined type only. It indicates that the rule should be applied only to new values, not values already existing in the table.

Use the sp_bindrule system stored procedure like this:

```
EXEC sp_bindrule 'Between_1_and_5', 'Employee.Employee_ID'
```

The system stored procedure binds the Between_1_and_5 rule to the Employee_ID column in the Employee table.

Whose default is it, anyway?

It's not my fault if you don't specify data for columns in your INSERT statement. However, I know how to fix the situation. You can specify a default value for any column of data that is left null when you insert data. Doing so ensures that there is a value in the column. Defaults are especially important where they concern columns that do not allow null values. To create a default, you use the `CREATE DEFAULT` statement, which follows this general syntax:

```
CREATE DEFAULT default_name
AS condition_expression
```

The following keywords are used in the preceding syntax:

> *default_name* is the name of the default that you want to create.
>
> *condition_expression* is the constant expression that you want the default to use if a value is not specified in a column. No database objects can be referenced in this expression.

Here's an example of how to create a default:

```
CREATE DEFAULT DEF_Level1
AS 'Level 1'
```

The preceding statement creates a default named `DEF_Level1` and assigns a constant value of `Level1`. This can be used for a situation in which you specify a salary level for an employee. If you leave the salary level null, the value `Level1` will automatically be inserted.

However, just as with a rule, a default must be bound to one or more columns. There is one caveat when binding a column. The column must match the datatype of the default. You bind a default by using a system stored procedure named `sp_bindefault`, which follows this general syntax:

```
sp_bindefault 'default_name', 'object_name', 'future_only'
```

The following keywords are used in the preceding syntax:

> *default_name* is the name of the default that you have already created. This value must be enclosed in single quotation marks (called ticks).
>
> *object_name* is the name of the table and column that you want to bind *default_name* to. This value must also be enclosed in single quotation marks.
>
> *future_only* is a flag to be used if the default is bound to a user-defined type only. It indicates that the default should be applied only to new values, not values already existing in the table.

Here's how you use the `sp_bindefault` system procedure:

```
sp_bindefault DEF_Level1, 'Employee.Salary_Level'
```

This binds the `DEF_Level1` default to the `Salary_Level` column of the `Employee` table.

Horsing around with triggers

Triggers are an important way to enforce referential integrity. *Referential integrity* is a concept that mandates that data in one column of a table be related to the same data value in a field of another table. A trigger can help to enforce this integrity because a trigger runs based on certain events that you define. You can write SQL to enforce your referential integrity rules when these events run (or in other words, fire). The possible events are as follows:

- INSERT
- UPDATE
- DELETE

You create a trigger with the CREATE TRIGGER statement. In this statement, you define what will happen when data is inserted, updated, and/or deleted. The CREATE TRIGGER statement follows this general syntax:

```
CREATE TRIGGER trigger_name ON table|view
      [WITH ENCRYPTION]
      {
            FOR|AFTER|INSTEAD OF trigger_type
            [WITH APPEND]
            [NOT FOR REPLICATION]
            AS
            {     IF UPDATE (column)
                  [{AND | OR} UPDATE (column)]
                        [...n]
                  | IF (COLUMNS_UPDATED()
{bitwise_operator} updated_bitmask)
                        { comparison_operator}
column_bitmask [...n]              }
trigger_code [...n]
      }
```

The following keywords are used in the preceding syntax:

trigger_name is the name of the trigger you are going to create. A trigger is a database object, so it must have a unique name within the database.

table is the name of the table on which you will create the trigger, or you can specify a trigger on the specified view.

WITH ENCRYPTION encrypts the text so that it can not be read from the syscomments table.

trigger_type is the type of trigger you want to create. The type can be INSERT, UPDATE, or DELETE, depending on the type of trigger you are creating.

You can also specify that you want the trigger to fire INSTEAD OF the SQL statement that fired the trigger, or AFTER the statement that fired the trigger. Without specifying these keywords, the trigger will fire after the SQL statement that fired the trigger. See Chapter 5 for more information about these types of triggers.

WITH APPEND is an optional statement that indicates to SQL Server 2000 that if a trigger of the same type already exists, this trigger should also be added.

NOT FOR REPLICATION indicates that any replication operations that affect data in the table should not fire the trigger.

column is used if you want to test for a specific column to have data inserted or updated into it. Multiple columns can be specified.

bitwise_operator, *updated_bitmask*, *comparison_operator*, and *column_bitmask* are all affected by the COLUMNS_UPDATED clause, which is used to test a bit-field representing one or more columns that are updated. These keywords are not covered in this book.

trigger_code is the Transact-SQL code that you will use to implement your business rules, using the inserted and deleted special trigger tables. These special tables exist in memory only and are removed when the trigger code completes.

The best way to learn how to write a trigger is to see one in action. Suppose that you want to create a trigger that inserts a record in the Salary table when a record is inserted into the Employee table. The trigger goes on the Employee table. You do that like this:

```
CREATE TRIGGER TRG_Insert_Salary
ON Employee
FOR INSERT
AS
INSERT Salary (Employee_ID)
SELECT Employee_ID
FROM inserted
```

The trigger that I created is called TRG_Insert_Salary. It is created on the Employee table and fires when a record is inserted into the table. When a row is inserted into a table that contains a trigger, the value(s) that are inserted are duplicated into the inserted table. This way, you can query the table to find out what was inserted.

Likewise, when a row is deleted from a table that contains a trigger, the value(s) that are deleted are stored in the deleted table.

With the preceding SQL Statement, every time a record is inserted into the Employee table, the value that is inserted for Employee_ID is also inserted into the Salary table.

Triggers can also be used for other purposes. An example of such a purpose is executing a stored procedure to e-mail the purchase agent to order more stock if the inventory of a certain product falls below a specified level.

Using Data Manipulation Language (DML) Statements

A *Data Manipulation Language,* or DML, is a SQL statement that is designed to specifically manipulate data that lies within database tables. You'll be spending most of your time with statements in this section. For more information about tables, see Chapter 4. Okay, get going so that you can be on your way trying out this stuff.

DML consists of four keywords. These keywords are also known as *clauses.* They are as follows:

- ✔ INSERT: Adds new rows of data into one or more tables
- ✔ UPDATE: Updates existing rows of data into one or more tables
- ✔ DELETE: Deletes existing rows of data from one or more tables
- ✔ SELECT: Queries existing data from one or more tables

In each of the DML statements, you can manipulate data using literal values (values that you explicitly type into your Transact-SQL) or values that are retrieved from a table. In the case in which values are retrieved from a table, typically a WHERE clause is specified so that the number of records that are affected by the query is limited in some way. Throughout the rest of this chapter, I show you how the WHERE clause is used, but I show you how it is used with one value being equal to another, using the equal sign (=). However, you should know that you can use additional keywords and operators when comparing values in a WHERE clause. These additional keywords and operators, as shown in Table 8-1, apply both to literal values and values retrieved from a table.

Table 8-1	Operators and Keywords for Use in a Transact-SQL WHERE Clause	
Keyword/ Operator	*Description*	*Example*
=	Successful if both values are equal.	WHERE A = B
>	Successful if the left value is greater than the right value.	WHERE A > B

(continued)

Table 8-1 *(continued)*

Keyword/Operator	Description	Example
<	Successful if the left value is less than the right value.	`WHERE A < B`
>=	Successful if the left value is greater than or equal to the right value.	`WHERE A >= B`
<=	Successful if the left value is less than or equal to the right value.	`WHERE A<= B`
<>	Successful if the left value is not equal to the right value. This test can also be specified with ! =	`WHERE A <> B`
LIKE	Pattern matches for a search condition. Placeholder wildcards must be specified with a % symbol and enclosed in quotation marks. There are additional patterns that can be specified but are not covered here.	`WHERE A LIKE 'B%'`
NOT LIKE	The same conditions apply to NOT LIKE as those with LIKE, except that the pattern is tested for a search condition that does not match. Again, placeholder wildcards must be specified with a % symbol and enclosed in quotation marks.	`WHERE A NOT LIKE 'B%'`
BETWEEN	Successful if a search condition is between a range of values.	`WHERE A BETWEEN 1 AND 10`
NOT BETWEEN	Successful if a search condition is outside a range of values.	`WHERE A NOT BETWEEN 1 AND 10`
IS NULL	Successful if the search condition contains a null value (the absence of a value).	`WHERE A IS NULL`
IS NOT NULL	Successful if the search condition does not contain a null value.	`WHERE A IS NOT NULL`
IN	Successful if the search condition is contained within a list of values.	`WHERE A IN (1, 5, 10)`

Keyword/ Operator	Description	Example
NOT IN	Successful if the search condition is not contained within a list of values.	`WHERE A NOT IN (2, 6, 9)`
Subquery	Tests for a condition in another table.	`WHERE A IN (SELECT X FROM #Tmp)`
EXISTS	Tests for the existence of rows in a subquery.	`WHERE EXISTS (SELECT X FROM #Tmp)`
CONTAINS	Similar to the LIKE keyword, but for full-text queries.	See example under the heading "Full-Text Queries," later in this chapter.
FREETEXT	Searches the meaning of one or more words in a full-text query.	See example under the heading, "Full-Text Queries," later in this chapter.

Getting data in

Getting data into a table is a snap. To put data into a table, use the INSERT statement. You have two ways to insert data: by either supplying "hard-coded" data or getting the data from another table. The INSERT statement follows this general syntax:

```
INSERT [INTO]
          {
             table_name [WITH (table_hint [...n])]
             | view_name
             | rowset_function
          }

   {    [(column_list)]
                { VALUES ( {DEFAULT
         |    NULL                              |    expression
                                    }[,...n]
                )
             | derived_table
             | execute_statement
          }
       }
       | DEFAULT VALUES
```

The following keywords are used in the preceding syntax:

table_name is the name of the table to insert data into.

table_hint is a set of properties used to define how SQL Server should handle inserting the data. Table hints are sometimes referred to as *locking hints*. A *table_hint* contains these arguments:

```
{ FASTFIRSTROW
        | HOLDLOCK
        | PAGLOCK
        | READCOMMITTED
        | REPEATABLEREAD
        | ROWLOCK
        | SERIALIZABLE
        | TABLOCK
        | TABLOCKX
        | UPDLOCK
}
```

I do not cover these keywords in this book, as they are advanced topics.

view_name is the name of the view to insert data into.

rowset_function is the OPENROWSET or OPENQUERY function, if used. For more information on these functions, refer to Chapter 13.

column_list is the list of columns to insert data into.

expression is any valid SQL Server expression.

derived_table is the result of any valid SELECT statement that returns rows of data.

execute_statement is any valid EXECUTE statement that returns SELECT data. The columns that are returned from the SELECT statement must have datatypes that are compatible with each column in the INSERT statement.

Supplying "hard-coded" data

"Hard-coded" data indicates to SQL Server that you will specify values and insert one row of data at a time. You can insert a row of data (record) into the Contact table like this:

```
INSERT INTO Contact (ContactID, LastName, FirstName, Address,
        City, State, Zip, Phone)
VALUES (1012, 'Mann', 'Anthony', '123 Main Street, Suite 10',
        'Boston', 'MA', '01111', '6171112222')
```

The values indicated are not significant. I only want to show that when you supply "hard-coded" values, you need to use the VALUES clause to indicate to SQL Server that you will supply the actual values. In addition, I want to show that you need to respect the data types in all columns. This means that a character and date field needs to be surrounded by quotation marks. Numeric and money fields don't have quotation marks.

Getting data from another table

You can insert data into one table based on data in another table. For example, suppose that you have a table named Temp_Contact. It has the same structure as the Contact table. You need to insert the data from Contact into Temp_Contact. This scenario allows you to query data without affecting performance of the Contact table (are you getting all this?). You insert all records from the Contact table into Temp_Contact like this:

```
INSERT Temp_Contact (ContactID, LastName, FirstName, Address,
            City, State, Zip, Phone)
SELECT ContactID, LastName, FirstName, Address, City, State,
            Zip, Phone
FROM Contact
```

This statement inserts all data in each column from the Contact table and inserts it into Temp_Contact in the same columns because the statement specifies the column order. Getting the column order correct is important because, as long as the datatypes are compatible, the SQL statement will succeed. Therefore, it's your responsibility to make sure that the columns specified are in the correct order.

If you want to limit the number of rows, specify a WHERE clause. If you want to limit the insertion shown in the preceding code to all contacts in New Hampshire, you can create this statement:

```
INSERT Temp_Contact (ContactID, LastName, FirstName, Address,
            City, State, Zip, Phone)
SELECT ContactID, LastName, FirstName, Address, City, State,
            Zip, Phone
FROM Contact
WHERE State = 'NH'
```

It's your prerogative to change your data

What if you already have data in a table and you want to change it? This, too, is a piece of cake. Do so with the UPDATE statement.

You use the UPDATE statement to substitute the current value of one or more columns of data with a different value. Using the UPDATE statement works only with existing data; it does not insert new data. To insert new data, you must use the INSERT statement, as shown earlier in this chapter. The UPDATE statement follows this general syntax:

```
UPDATE
                      {
                       table_name WITH (<table_hint> [...n])
                       | view_name
                       | rowset_function
                      }
                      SET
                      {column_name = {expression | DEFAULT |
        NULL}
                       | @variable = expression
                       | @variable = column = expression }
        [,...n]

               {{[FROM {<table_source>} [,...n] ]

               [WHERE
                    <search_condition>] }
               |
               [WHERE CURRENT OF
               { { [GLOBAL] cursor_name } |
        cursor_variable}
               ] }
               [OPTION (<query_hint> [,...n] )]
```

The following keywords are used in the preceding syntax:

table_name is the name of the table that will have data updated.

table_hint is a set of properties used to define how SQL Server should handle updating the data (which I don't cover in this book). A *table_hint* contains these arguments:

```
{ FASTFIRSTROW
        | HOLDLOCK
        | PAGLOCK
        | READCOMMITTED
        | REPEATABLEREAD
        | ROWLOCK
        | SERIALIZABLE
        | TABLOCK
        | TABLOCKX
        | UPDLOCK
}
```

view_name is the name of the view to insert data into.

rowset_function is the OPENROWSET or OPENQUERY function, if used. For more information on these functions, refer to Chapter 13.

column_name is the name of the column to update in the table or view.

expression is any valid SQL Server expression.

@variable = expression sets the value of the declared variable to be that of the column value, but before the update occurs.

@variable= column = expression sets the value of the declared variable @variable to the same value as the column.

table_source is the name of the table(s), view(s), rowset function, or derived table. Rowset functions are covered in Chapter 13.

search_condition is one or more conditions that determine which rows are updated with the statement. The search_condition can also be used to specify join information if it is not specified in the FROM clause.

cursor_name or cursor_variable is the name of a declared cursor or cursor variable. Cursors are covered in Chapter 9.

query_hint instructs the SQL Server optimizer to use specific options when processing the query as a whole. A *query_hint* follows this syntax, but isn't covered any further in this book:

```
{        { HASH | ORDER } GROUP
             { CONCAT | HASH | MERGE       } UNION
             {LOOP | MERGE | HASH} JOIN
             FAST number_rows
             FORCE ORDER
             MAXDOP
             ROBUST PLAN
             KEEP PLAN
    }
```

Suppose that a customer moves and you want to update his/her address. For this example, assume that there is a Customer table with the following columns:

Cust_ID – number (integer)

Cust_Name – varchar (30)

Address_1 – varchar (30)

Address_2 – varchar (30)

City – varchar (30)

State – char (2)

Zip – varchar (10)

Phone – char (10)

Fax – char (10)

Email – varchar (30)

I take you through a couple of different scenarios to understand the UPDATE statement. The first scenario is that the customer's ZIP Code changed. The key to being able to update this record is that you know the Cust_ID and that every customer has a different Cust_ID. Knowing this, you know exactly which record to update. In this scenario, you can update the ZIP Code for the customer from whatever it currently is to 00112. The SQL statement to perform the update looks like this:

```
UPDATE Customer
SET Zip = '00112'
WHERE Cust_ID = '2345'
```

If it were possible to have more than one Cust_ID with the value of 2345, all rows containing this value would be updated. That's why you have to be very careful when using the UPDATE statement.

You can join statements in the WHERE clause to further qualify the update. For example, suppose that you want to additionally qualify the update to specify that the record(s) will be updated also only when the Zip column contains a value of 01101. This statement looks like this:

```
UPDATE Customer
SET Zip = '00112'
WHERE Cust_ID = '2345'
AND Zip = '01101'
```

For the second scenario, suppose that you want to update more than one field. This is how you would update a customer's entire address record:

```
UPDATE Customer
SET Address_1 = '123 Main Street',
Address_2 = 'Suite 44',
City = 'BOSTON',
State = 'MA',
Zip = '00112',
Phone = '6171111111',
Fax = '6172222222',
Email = 'someone@anywhere.com'
WHERE Cust_ID = '2345'
```

Notice that every field that gets updated is separated by a comma. The WHERE clause applies to all fields in the statement only if the Cust_ID is 2345. Bear in mind, if you left out the WHERE clause, every row in the table would be updated.

You can even update data in one table based on the data in another table by using the concepts I show in the "Querying data" section later in this chapter.

Wiping data out

Well, through all these tests, you now have a bunch of bogus data in your database. You can delete this bogus data by using the DELETE statement. The DELETE statement follows this general syntax:

```
DELETE [FROM]                {
                    table_name WITH ( <table_hint> [...n])
                    | view_name
                    | rowset_function
                    }
              [FROM {<table_source>} [,...n] ]

              [WHERE
                    {<search_condition>}
                    |
                    [CURRENT OF
                    { { [GLOBAL] cursor_name } |
         cursor_variable}
                    ] }
                    [OPTION (<query_hint> [,...n] )]
```

The following keywords are used in the preceding syntax:

table_name is the name of the table to delete data from.

table_hint is a set of properties used to define how SQL Server should handle deleting the data (which I don't cover in this book). A *table_hint* contains these arguments:

```
{ FASTFIRSTROW
            | HOLDLOCK
            | PAGLOCK
            | READCOMMITTED
            | REPEATABLEREAD
            | ROWLOCK
            | SERIALIZABLE
            | TABLOCK
            | TABLOCKX
            | UPDLOCK
    }
```

view_name is the name of the view to delete data from.

rowset_function is the OPENROWSET or OPENQUERY function, if used. For more information on these functions, refer to Chapter 13.

table_source is the name of the table(s), view(s), rowset function, or derived table. Rowset functions are covered in Chapter 13.

search_condition is one or more conditions that determine which rows are deleted with the statement. The search_condition can also be used to specify join information if it is not specified in the FROM clause.

cursor_name or *cursor_variable* is the name of a declared cursor or cursor variable.

query_hint instructs the SQL Server optimizer to use specific options when processing the query as a whole. A query_hint follows this syntax but isn't covered any further in this book:

```
{          { HASH | ORDER } GROUP
          | { CONCAT | HASH | MERGE       } UNION
          | {LOOP | MERGE | HASH} JOIN
          | FAST number_rows
          | FORCE ORDER
          | MAXDOP
          | ROBUST PLAN
          | KEEP PLAN
}
```

With the DELETE statement, either all data can be deleted or data can be targeted so that only specific rows of data are deleted. But realize that the DELETE statement deletes all columns of data in an entire row! It does not delete specific columns of data within a row. If you want to delete specific columns of data, use the UPDATE statement (see "It's your prerogative to change your data," earlier in this chapter).

To delete all rows of data in a Customer table, use this statement:

```
DELETE FROM Customer
```

To delete only row(s) in the Customer table for the customer with a Cust_ID of 1001, you construct the statement like this:

```
DELETE FROM Customer
WHERE Cust_ID = 1001
```

You can even delete data in one table based on the data in another table by using the concepts I show in "Querying data," next.

Querying data

What good is your data if you can't query it? *Querying* data means running a report, based on criteria that you specify. Querying data is done by using the SELECT statement. The SELECT statement is the most common of all SQL statements. Because it is so common, there are lots of ways to use it, and I cruise you through the important ones. The SELECT statement follows this general syntax:

```
SELECT select_list
[INTO new_table_name]
FROM table_source
[WHERE search_condition]
[GROUP BY group_by_expression]
[HAVING search_condition]
```

```
[ORDER BY order_expression [ASC|DESC]]
[ FOR XML { RAW | AUTO | EXPLICIT }
     [ , XMLDATA ]
     [ , ELEMENTS ]
     [ , BINARY BASE64 ]]
```

The following keywords are used in the preceding syntax:

select_list is either a comma separated list of columns or the * wildcard character. Also, an expression or calculation can be in the select list, such as ItemQty * 5. Additionally, a string literal or constant expression can be in the select list.

new_table_name is the name of the new table to create with the results of the SELECT statement.

table_source is the name of the table from which you're requesting data.

search_condition is the way you specify the actual rows in the table that are to be retrieved. If you omit the WHERE clause, every row in the table will be retrieved. So specifying a WHERE clause in your queries is generally a good idea.

Group_by_expression is an expression or set of columns that are used with aggregate data.

Order_expression specifies one or more columns used to sort data.

FOR XML clause returns a recordset in XML format. You have a choice of one of the following XML modes:

RAW: Each row of data is returned with an XML <row/> identifier

AUTO: Returns data in a simple nested XML tree

EXPLICIT: Allows you to explicitly define the format of the XML tree that will be used to return data

In addition to the XML formats, you can specify any or all of the following keywords:

XMLDATA: Returns the XML schema, appended to the XML document, but without the root element.

ELEMENTS: Indicates that each column will be returned as an element, instead of being an attribute (which is the default). This option is available only for AUTO mode.

BINARY BASE64: Default for AUTO mode, specifies that XML documents are returned in the base64-encoded format.

If you are unsure of what rows an UPDATE statement will affect, transform the UPDATE statement into a SELECT statement using the same WHERE clause. This procedure shows you the rows that will be updated if you issue the UPDATE statement instead.

Simple selects

A *simple select* is a query that looks up data in only one table. You can think of the main parts of the SELECT statement like this:

```
SELECT what
FROM location
WHERE limitations
```

The SELECT, FROM, and WHERE keywords are all considered to be *clauses*.

If you want to query the database to find all customers who live in New Hampshire, you can issue this statement:

```
SELECT Cust_ID, Cust_Name
FROM Customer
WHERE State = 'NH'
```

This statement returns only the Cust_ID and Cust_Name for all customers who live in New Hampshire. If you want to retrieve all columns of data for every customer in New Hampshire, you can specify every column in the Customer table by name, separated by a comma, or you can use the * wild-card. The * wildcard indicates that you want all possible columns. You use the * wildcard like this:

```
SELECT *
FROM Customer
WHERE State = 'NH'
```

This statement also returns all columns for customers who live in New Hampshire, but returns the data in a RAW XML format:

```
SELECT *
FROM Customer
WHERE State = 'NH'
FOR XML RAW
```

I do not cover XML in this book. If you want to learn about XML, refer to *XML For Dummies,* 2nd Edition, by Ed Tittel.

Compound selects

A *compound select* is a query that looks up data in more than one table. To look up data in more than one table, you must perform what is called a join in the WHERE clause of the SQL statement. A *join* is just like the name suggests. It specifies the columns that are to be joined between tables. In addition, you must specify all the tables used in the query in the FROM clause. If you specify only the criteria you desire in the SELECT statement without specifying join information, you won't achieve the desired results — or the statement will result in error. For example, consider this statement:

```
SELECT Cust_Name
FROM Customer,Orders
WHERE State = 'NH'
AND Order_Date = '01/01/2000'
```

The `Cust_Name` and `State` fields exist in the `Customer` table. The `Order_Date` exists in the `Orders` table. However, nothing is in the statement to indicate how to join the two tables together.

With these two tables, the "glue" to link the tables is the `Cust_ID` field. It exists in both tables and allows you to look up fields in one table based on the values in another. The following statement is the correct statement to link the two tables together:

```
SELECT Cust_Name
FROM Customer,Orders
WHERE State = 'NH'
AND Order_Date = '01/01/2000'
AND Customer.Cust_ID = Orders.Cust_ID
```

LINGO

The reason for the syntax in the last line of the statement that specifies the table name is that SQL Server needs to know the specific table if one or more tables contain the same column name. If the table names are not specified, this is known as an *ambiguous join*.

The data will be returned in no specific order, unless you add an `ORDER BY` clause to the end of the statement. If you want all customer's names to be ordered alphabetically, add this clause:

```
ORDER BY Cust_Name
```

I hope I don't confuse you on this one, but I think I should show you another way to construct joins. Microsoft recommends creating joins in the `FROM` clause. A join is performed in the `FROM` clause with the `JOIN` and `ON` keywords. Look at this statement:

```
SELECT Customer.Cust_Name
FROM Customer JOIN Orders ON Customer.Cust_ID =
           Orders.Cust_ID
WHERE Customer.State = 'NH'
AND Orders.Order_Date = '01/01/2000'
```

The `JOIN` keyword indicates that the `Orders` table is joined with the `Customer` table. The `ON` keyword indicates the columns in the respective tables to be joined. Therefore, the `Cust_ID` column of the `Orders` table (noted on the right side of the equal sign) is joined with the `Cust_ID` column of the `Customer`.

Using an alias

Want to see something really cool? Suppose that you don't want to repeat your table names, such as Customer or Orders, all the time. You can use a reference to a table name with fewer characters than the full table name, known as an *alias*. An alias is specified with the AS keyword in the FROM clause. Consider this SQL statement used for a compound select statement:

```
SELECT C.Cust_Name
FROM Customer AS C JOIN Orders AS O ON C.Cust_ID = O.Cust_ID
WHERE C.State = 'NH'
AND O.Order_Date = '01/01/2000'
```

Any series of characters directly after the AS keyword is the alias used in the entire SQL statement. Customer is aliased as C and Orders is aliased as O. Rather than specify the entire table names, you can use the defined aliases.

Inner joins

In the preceding section, I show you how to perform a join. This join that I discuss is called an *inner join*. Using an inner join may not return the results you expect, as you can see in the next section, "Outer joins."

An inner join matches values on columns between tables. If there is no match, then no record is returned from either table. However, you may want to know that there is a missing (or null) value in one of the tables. Suppose that you have two tables (with the column names listed in parentheses):

- ✔ Customer (Cust_ID, Cust_Name)
- ✔ Orders (Cust_ID, Order_Date)

Because a customer does not have to place an order, there can be a record in the Customer table but not the Orders table. Therefore, if you perform a query joining the Cust_ID columns between the two tables, the only customers that will be shown are those with orders. This will not list *all* of the customers or their order dates.

To illustrate my point, refer to Table 8-2 for the Customer table and Table 8-3 for the Orders table.

Table 8-2	Sample Customer Table
Cust_ID	*Cust_Name*
1001	John Smith
1002	Fred Jones
1003	Mary Smith

Table 8-3	Sample Orders Table
Cust_ID	*Order_Date*
1001	10/24/1996
1001	01/01/1997
1003	05/04/1995

If you want to retrieve all `Order_Dates` for all customers and order them by `Cust_Name`, you may think that you should issue this Transact-SQL statement:

```
SELECT Cust_Name, Order_Date
FROM Customer JOIN Orders ON Customer.Cust_ID =
         Orders.Cust_ID
ORDER BY Cust_Name
```

. . . or this statement:

```
SELECT Cust_Name, Order_Date
FROM Orders, Customer
WHERE Orders.Cust_ID = Customer.Cust_ID
ORDER BY Cust_Name
```

You'd be right, except you may not get back the data you expect. (Don't you just hate when that happens?) The data returned is shown in Table 8-4.

Table 8-4	Sample Results of Inner Join
Cust_ID	*Order_Date*
John Smith	10/24/1996
John Smith	01/01/1997
Mary Smith	05/04/1995

Notice that Fred Jones does not appear in the result at all because the join used in the WHERE clause in the preceding statement is an inner join. To view all the records, even if it doesn't find a match in the join table, you need to construct an outer join. I talk about outer joins in the next section. Take a deep breath; we're going deep!

Outer joins

An *outer join* is a join that returns all records from one of two tables, even if there are no corresponding records in any of the join tables. If you want to return all customers and their corresponding orders (if they have any), using the data shown in Tables 8-1 and 8-2, you must issue a SELECT statement with an outer join, like this:

```
SELECT Cust_Name, Order_Date
FROM Customer LEFT OUTER JOIN Orders ON Customer.Cust_ID =
        Orders.Cust_ID
ORDER BY Cust_Name
```

The preceding statement returns the following results, shown in Table 8-5.

Table 8-5	Sample Results of Outer Join
Cust_Name	*Order_Date*
Fred Jones	NULL
John Smith	10/24/1996
John Smith	01/01/1997
Mary Smith	05/04/1995

There are three types of outer joins. One is a *left outer join,* or sometimes referred to as a left join. The second type is a *right outer join,* or sometimes referred to as a right join. The last type is a *full outer join,* or sometimes referred to as a full join. Determining which type of join to use depends on how you construct the SQL statement.

A left join specifies that all rows in the table on the left part of the SQL statement will return every row of data, even if there is no data that matches in the table on the right part of the SQL statement. A right join is exactly the opposite of a left join. The table on the right part of the SQL statement will return every row of data, regardless of a match in the table on the left part of the SQL statement. A full join is actually a combination of the two joins. All data from both tables are returned, regardless of matching values in the opposite table.

Here's how it works. The SQL statement that I show you at the beginning of this section is equivalent to this statement:

```
SELECT Cust_Name, Order_Date
FROM Orders RIGHT OUTER JOIN Customer ON Orders.Cust_ID =
          Customer.Cust_ID
ORDER BY Cust_Name
```

In either type of outer join statement, the join is not performed in the WHERE clause. It is actually performed in the FROM clause. The FROM clause specifies not only the tables to be joined but also the columns to be joined. You specify columns directly after the ON keyword, and you specify the tables directly after the FROM keyword.

If you want all records to be returned in both tables, use this statement:

```
SELECT Cust_Name, Order_Date
FROM Orders FULL OUTER JOIN Customer ON Orders.Cust_ID =
          Customer.Cust_ID
ORDER BY Cust_Name
```

I know you're probably new at all this — but this is important stuff. So I'm going to help you. If you don't know which type of join to construct, or in what order, you can follow these rules:

- ✓ If the table that can contain missing data is specified directly after the FROM keyword, use the RIGHT OUTER JOIN keywords, followed by the table that cannot contain missing data.

- ✓ If the table that can't contain missing data is specified directly after the FROM keyword, use the LEFT OUTER JOIN keywords, followed by the table that can contain missing data.

- ✓ If you need to return each and every row of data regardless of matching values in the tables, use the FULL OUTER JOIN keywords.

Using transactions with your queries

A *transaction* is one or more SQL statements that manipulate data in a database that are treated as a complete unit. If any error occurs, the entire set of statements isn't executed. If errors do not occur, the entire set of statements is executed, thereby affecting the database. For more information about transactions, see Chapter 3 and Chapter 13.

DCL consists of three sets of statements. They are as follows:

- ✓ BEGIN TRANSACTION: Starts a transaction
- ✓ COMMIT TRANSACTION: Accepts all changes made to the database since the last BEGIN TRANSACTION statement

✔ ROLLBACK TRANSACTION: Discards all changes made to the database since the last BEGIN TRANSACTION statement

These statements are very easy to use because they require no parameters or optional arguments. What you see is what you get!

To see how transactions are used, refer to these statements:

```
BEGIN TRANSACTION
INSERT Orders (Order_ID,Cust_ID,Order_Date,Order_Total)
VALUES (1234,3225, '05/22/98',344.68)
INSERT Orders (Order_ID,Cust_ID,Order_Date,Order_Total)
VALUES (5678,3225, '04/1/97',500.00)
IF @@error = 0
          COMMIT TRANSACTION
ELSE
          ROLLBACK TRANSACTION
```

In this example, I insert two rows of data into the Orders table within a transaction. If any error occurs, the transaction is rolled back. If no errors occur, the transaction is committed. The transaction ensures that either both or no rows of data are inserted.

That's all there is to transactions. Aren't they as easy as I said they were? Transactions really do give you a great way to control your SQL statements in case of failure.

Using Data Control Language (DCL) Statements

A *Data Control Language,* or DCL, is a SQL statement that allows you to control permissions on objects DCL consists of a set of three Transact-SQL statements. They are as follows:

✔ GRANT: Explicitly grants permission on an object

✔ DENY: Explicitly denies permission on an object

✔ REVOKE: Removes a previous explicitly granted or denied permission on an object. The result of using the REVOKE Transact-SQL statement is that no permissions are explicitly assigned on an object

Each of the three statements can be used in two different ways. The first way to use DCL is to assign statement permissions, while the second is to assign object permissions.

Statement permissions

A statement permission allows you to grant, deny, or revoke permissions on Transact-SQL statements. This means that you can determine, through permissions, which users or roles will have the ability to issue certain types of Transact-SQL statements. The Transact-SQL statements that apply to statement permissions are the following:

- CREATE DATABASE
- CREATE DEFAULT
- CREATE FUNCTION
- CREATE PROCEDURE
- CREATE RULE
- CREATE TABLE
- CREATE VIEW
- BACKUP DATABASE
- BACKUP LOG

To assign statement permissions, follow this general syntax:

```
DCL_keyword { ALL | TSQL_statement [ ,...n ] }
TO security_account [ ,...n ]
```

The following keywords are used in the preceding syntax:

DCL_keyword is either GRANT, DENY, or REVOKE.

ALL indicates that the permission indicated with DCL_keyword will be applied to all possible Transact-SQL statements. This keyword cannot be used with the TSQL_statement.

TSQL_statement is the specific Transact-SQL statement that you want to assign permissions for.

security_account is the user name or role to which you want to assign permissions.

Here's an example of how to use DCL to grant the ability to use the CREATE RULE Transact-SQL statement to the public role:

```
GRANT CREATE RULE TO public
```

Object permissions

An object permission allows you to grant, deny, or revoke permissions on specific objects, such as tables and stored procedures. You can, for example, grant the ability to run, or execute, a stored procedure to the public role. The object permissions that you can assign to objects are as follows:

- EXECUTE: Allows the execution of a stored procedure
- SELECT: Allows the retrieval of data within the designated table or view
- INSERT: Allows the insertion of data within the designated table or view
- UPDATE: Allows the updating of data within the designated table or view
- DELETE: Allows the deletion of data within the designated table or view

Many options are available when you assign object permissions, but in the real-world, you won't use most of them. Don't be too scared. I want to show you all these options for completeness. To assign object permissions, follow this general syntax:

```
DCL_keyword [ GRANT_OPTION_FOR ]
    { ALL | permission [ ,...n ] }
    {
        ON { table | view } [ ( column [ ,...n ] ) ]
        | ON { object }
    }
{ TO | FROM }
    security_account [ ,...n ]
[ CASCADE ]
[ WITH GRANT OPTION ]
[ AS { group | role } ]
```

The following keywords are used in the preceding syntax:

DCL_keyword is either GRANT, DENY, or REVOKE.

GRANT_OPTION_FOR is available only if the *DCL_keyword* is REVOKE. This set of keywords that indicates that the permissions are being revoked where they were previously assigned using the WITH_GRANT_OPTION.

ALL indicates that the permission indicated with *DCL_keyword* will be applied to all possible permissions. This keyword cannot be used with *PRIVILEGES*.

permission is one or more specific privilege(s) that you want to assign, such as INSERT and UPDATE.

table or *view* is the name of a specific table or view on which you want to apply permissions. If you supply this name, you can also optionally indicate which column(s) within the table or view will be assigned specific permissions. If you supply a table or view, you cannot also use the object argument.

column is the name of a specific column in the table or view on which you want to apply permissions.

object is the name of a stored procedure, extended procedure, or user-defined function. If you supply an object name, you cannot also use table, view, or column arguments.

TO or FROM indicates that the list of security accounts is to follow. The FROM keyword is available only if you specify the REVOKE keyword.

security_account is the user name or role to which you want to assign permissions.

CASCADE is available only for DENY and REVOKE. This keyword indicates that permissions that were granted by the security_account will also have the new permissions assigned.

WITH GRANT OPTION is available only for GRANT. This keyword indicates that permissions that are being granted to security_account will also have permission to grant this permission to other security_accounts.

AS group or role is available only for GRANT or REVOKE. This keyword indicates that the specific Windows NT group or SQL Server role will be used rather than the currently logged on account because that account has the ability to use the GRANT or REVOKE statement.

Here's a typical, real-world example of how to use DCL to grant the ability to execute the usp_RunQuery stored procedure to the public role:

```
GRANT EXEC ON usp_RunQuery TO public
```

Full-Text Queries

Since SQL Server, version 7.0, you could issue queries against fields that were declared with the text datatype. This is known as a full-text query. A *full-text* query allows you to build an external catalog of significant words, called nonnoise words, from which SQL Server will search. Because full-text queries function from this external catalog, a new set of Transact-SQL statements was generated to allow you to access that catalog.

Six Transact-SQL statements are available in SQL Server 2000, with which you can write queries against full-text catalogs. They are shown in Table 8-6.

Table 8-6	Transact-SQL Commands for Full-Text Searching
Command	**Description**
CONTAINS	WHERE clause used for general searching of full-text catalogs based on conditions that you specify. The CONTAINS keyword is to full-text queries as the LIKE keyword is to other queries.
FREETEXT	WHERE clause used to search for words that are similar to or mean the same thing as the specified text.
CONTAINSTABLE	Very similar to the CONTAINS keyword, except that it returns a table that can be referenced in the FROM clause instead of the WHERE clause.
FREETEXTTABLE	Very similar to the FREETEXT keyword, except that it returns a table that can be referenced in the FROM clause instead of the WHERE clause.

The CONTAINS keyword (which is used in a WHERE clause) follows this general syntax:

```
CONTAINS ( {column_name | *}, 'search_condition' )
```

The following keywords are used in the preceding syntax:

column_name is the name of the column defined in the full-text catalog that you want to search, or specify * for all columns.

search_condition is the condition you want to search for. There are many more ways to search a column in the full-text catalog using CONTAINS that are not presented in the example below. Refer to Books Online for more information.

Here's an example of how you would use the CONTAINS keyword to conduct a full-text search of a catalog that has the Resume column registered in the Employee table:

```
SELECT LastName, FirstName
FROM Employee
WHERE CONTAINS (Resume, 'Visual Basic')
```

The preceding example will return data only if the words Visual Basic are found in an employee's résumé.

The FREETEXT keyword (which is also used in a WHERE clause) follows this general syntax:

```
FREETEXT ( {column_name | *}, 'search_condition' )
```

The following keywords are used in the preceding syntax:

> *column_name* is the name of the column defined in the full-text catalog that you want to search, or specify * for all columns.

> *search_condition* is the condition you want to search for. Again, there are many more ways to search a column in the full-text catalog using FREETEXT that are not presented in the example. Refer to Books Online for more information.

Here's an example of how you would use the FREETEXT keyword to conduct a full-text search of a catalog that has the Resume column registered in the Employee table:

```
SELECT LastName, FirstName
FROM Employee
WHERE FREETEXT (Resume, 'work')
```

The preceding example does not differ much from the CONTAINS example, but it does differ in functionality. This example returns the LastName and FirstName for an employee that has words similar to work in his/her résumé. Such words could be worked, working, works, or others. As you can see, FREETEXT is a very powerful search tool.

As described in Table 8-6, the CONTAINSTABLE keyword functions basically the same as the CONTAINS keyword, but it can be used in a FROM clause because it returns a table of values. The CONTAINSTABLE keyword is typically used to join one table with another. This table returned by the CONTAINSTA-BLE keyword contains only two columns:

- ✔ KEY: Contains the primary key or unique key values that must be joined to the original table to retrieve rows. A table cannot be enabled for full-text searching without a primary or unique key.

- ✔ RANK: a value from 0 to 1000 that indicates the quality of the match in the full-text search.

The CONTAINSTABLE keyword follows this general syntax:

```
CONTAINSTABLE ( table_name, {column_name | *},
        'search_condition' [, top_n] )
```

The following keywords are used in the preceding syntax:

> *table_name* is the name of the table that contains the column defined in the full-text catalog that you want to search.

> *column_name* is the name of the column defined in the full-text catalog that you want to search, or specify * for all columns.

search_condition is the condition you want to search for. There are many more ways to search a column in the full-text catalog using CONTAINSTABLE that are not presented in the example. Refer to Books Online for more information.

top_n is a number that you specify to return only a certain number of rows that best match the criteria in descending order.

Sticking with the same example, here's how you would use the CONTAINSTA-BLE keyword to conduct a full-text search of a catalog that has the Resume column registered in the Employee table:

```
SELECT FT_TBL.LastName, FT_TBL.FirstName, KEY_TBL.RANK
FROM Employee AS FT_TBL
    JOIN CONTAINSTABLE(Employee, Resume, 'Visual Basic', 10)
            AS KEY_TBL
    ON (FT_TBL.EmployeeID = KEY_TBL.[KEY])
ORDER BY KEY_TBL.RANK DESC
```

The preceding example probably looks confusing to you, so I'll break it down. I start in the middle of the query, where the CONTAINSTABLE keyword is. Remember that this keyword returns a table that contains only a KEY and a RANK column. The KEY column contains the value of the primary key. Assuming that EmployeeID is the primary key in the Employee table, the join is constructed based on the EmployeeID column in the Employee table (which is aliased as FT_TBL) being equal to the KEY column in the table that is returned by CONTAINSTABLE (which is aliased as KEY_TBL). The join allows for only the 10 highest ranking matches to be returned from the query. WHEW!

The final keyword that I want to cover in this section on full-text queries is the FREETEXTTABLE keyword. If you understand the FREETEXT keyword and you followed my example for CONTAINSTABLE, this will be a piece of cake. The FREETEXTTABLE keyword functions basically the same as the FREETEXT keyword, but it can be used in a FROM clause because it returns a table of values, just as CONTAINSTABLE did. It also consists of two columns; KEY and RANK.

The FREETEXTTABLE keyword follows this general syntax:

```
FREETEXTTABLE ( table_name, {column_name | *},
        'search_condition' [, top_n] )
```

The following keywords are used in the preceding syntax:

table_name is the name of the table that contains the column defined in the full-text catalog that you want to search.

column_name is the name of the column defined in the full-text catalog that you want to search, or specify * for all columns.

search_condition is the condition you want to search for. There are many more ways to search a column in the full-text catalog using FREETEXTTABLE that are not presented in the example. Refer to Books Online for more information.

top_n is a number that you specify to return only a certain number of rows that best match the criteria in descending order.

Again, sticking with the same example, here's how you would use the FREETEXTTABLE keyword to conduct a full-text search of a catalog that has the Resume column registered in the Employee table:

```
SELECT FT_TBL.LastName, FT_TBL.FirstName, KEY_TBL.RANK
FROM Employee AS FT_TBL
    JOIN FREETEXTTABLE(Employee, Resume, 'work', 10) AS
        KEY_TBL
    ON (FT_TBL.EmployeeID = KEY_TBL.[KEY])
ORDER BY KEY_TBL.RANK DESC
```

The explanation of the preceding code is exactly the same as that of the CONTAINSTABLE keyword, except that all words similar to work will be returned, just as with the FREETEXT keyword.

Chapter 9

Now That I Have a Structure, How Do I Use It?

In This Chapter

▶ Delving into details about SQL Server Query Analyzer

▶ Connecting to SQL Server 2000

▶ Navigating with cursors

▶ Accessing SQL Server 2000 data from a Web page

*I*n chapters 1 through 8, I walk you through the process of creating your database structure and objects in Microsoft SQL Server 2000. In this chapter, I provide a step-by-step trek to another exciting destination — the actual use of your structure! If you need a quick refresher on Transact-SQL before you take the next leap, check out Chapter 8 — you can be up-to-speed in no time.

This chapter gets a little complex, but it contains information that you need to know, so read it slowly and carefully. If it doesn't make sense to you, perhaps you need to reread Chapters 1–8.

Using SQL Server Query Analyzer

The SQL Server Query Analyzer is a wonderful, user-friendly tool from Microsoft that enables you to issue Transact-SQL statements and view the results of Transact-SQL queries. In addition, I want to let you know that as you get more proficient with SQL Server 2000, you can use the Query Analyzer to view the query plan chosen by the SQL Server. A *query plan* is how SQL Server 2000 decides to optimize your query by choosing the correct indexing scheme. Because this is an advanced topic, I don't discuss analyzing query plans in the book.

Executing queries

To use the SQL Server Query Analyzer, follow these steps:

1. **To start the SQL Server Query, choose Start⮕Programs⮕Microsoft SQL Server⮕Query Analyzer.**

2. **Log in to the SQL Server by filling in the following fields in the Connect to SQL Server dialog box (see Figure 9-1); then click OK.**

Figure 9-1:
The Connect
to SQL
Server
dialog box.

- **SQL Server:** You can select the desired SQL Server from the drop-down list of registered SQL Servers. By default, the registered SQL Server on the current computer is presented. My SQL Server is called HAWKEYE.

- **Windows NT Authentication:** This option uses Windows NT authentication. This means that you are authorized to use the SQL Server Query Analyzer to connect to the selected SQL Server if Windows NT validates the login you gave when you logged into Windows NT. The login name and password are those you used when you logged into the network.

- **SQL Server Authentication:** This option uses SQL Server to validate your login when you attempt to connect to the selected SQL Server. When this option is chosen, the Login Name and Password text boxes become enabled. You must supply the Login Name and Password in the text boxes.

After you log in to a SQL Server, you see the SQL Server Query Analyzer, as shown in Figure 9-2.

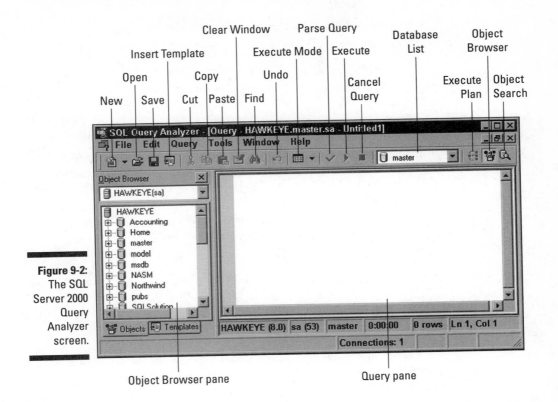

Clear Window   Parse Query

Insert Template   Execute Mode | Execute   Database List   Object Browser

Open   Copy   Undo   Cancel Query   Execute Plan | Object Search

New | Save   Cut | Paste | Find

Figure 9-2:
The SQL Server 2000 Query Analyzer screen.

Object Browser pane   Query pane

3. **In the SQL Server Query Analyzer, choose your database from the Database drop-down list, which contains all the databases on the server that you logged in to.**

   Alternatively, you can use Transact-SQL to change the database — just type the USE keyword, followed by the name of the database, and then execute your query. For example, this statement changes the active database to the pubs database:

   ```
   USE pubs
   ```

4. **Type in your Transact-SQL.**

   You can type in any valid Transact-SQL. What's a valid Transact-SQL statement, you ask? These are valid types of Transact-SQL Statements:

   • Programmatic functions and constructs (see Chapter 6)

   • Stored procedures (see Chapter 7)

   • Extended procedures (see Chapter 7)

- Dynamic Data Language, or DDL (see Chapter 8)
- Data Manipulation Language, or DML (see Chapter 8)
- Data Control Language, or DCL (see Chapter 8)

Here's an example of a valid Transact-SQL statement:

```
SELECT *
FROM authors
ORDER BY au_lname
```

You can even place Transact-SQL commands in a batch. A *batch* is a process that contains multiple Transact-SQL commands or statements that are executed as a single unit. Batches are separated by the GO keyword between them.

For example, these statements represent two batches because there is a GO keyword separating the Transact-SQL statements:

```
USE pubs
GO
SELECT *
FROM authors
ORDER BY au_lname
GO
```

5. **Click the Query menu and then click an execute option.**

   There are three execute options, which control where the results of your queries go. These options are *mutually exclusive,* which means that only one option can be selected at any one time.

   - **Results in Text:** Executes your query and displays the results in a text box at the bottom of the screen (see Figure 9-3).

   - **Results in Grid:** Executes your query and displays the results in the Grids tab at the bottom of the screen. This grid looks very similar to an Excel workbook (see Figure 9-4).

   - **Results in File:** Executes your query and writes the results to a file for later analysis. When you execute the query, you are prompted for the filename (see Figure 9-5).

6. **Execute your query.**

   Execute your query by clicking Query⇨Execute. Doing so displays the results using the option you chose in the prior step.

Because you will execute many queries using the Query Analyzer, you should become familiar with some of the shortcut keys available. These shortcut keys appear to the right of each menu option where they are available. For example, the shortcut key to execute your query is F5.

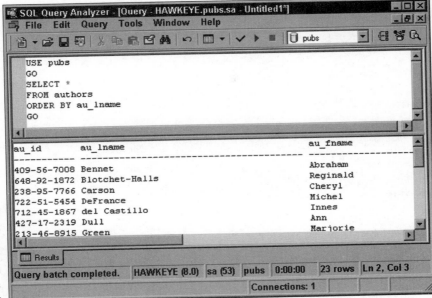

Figure 9-3:
Viewing
query
results in
text form.

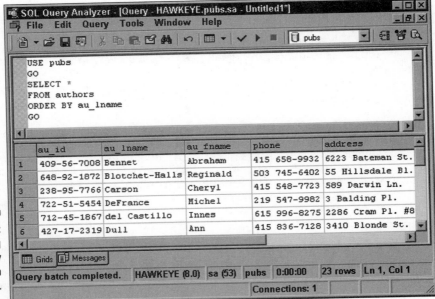

Figure 9-4:
Viewing
query
results in
grid form.

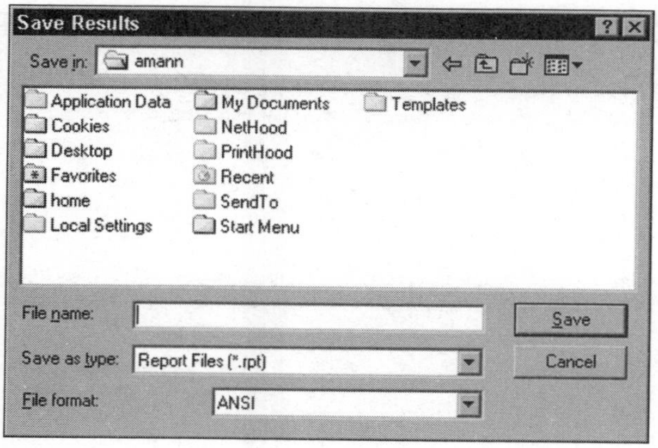

Figure 9-5:
Viewing
query
results in
file form.

Browsing objects

If you are familiar with Microsoft Visual Studio, you know all about the object browser. The Visual Studio object browser allows you to view all the objects that are available to your project, either in a library or the functions that you wrote. Within each of these objects, you can view members, such as properties, methods, and events.

Well, the SQL Server 2000 Query Analyzer now comes with an object browser. This is a very helpful feature because there are so many database objects, functions, routines, and datatypes to remember, you will not remember them all. In prior versions of SQL Server, you found yourself constantly switching between the Query Analyzer, Enterprise Manager, and Books Online. That's all over now.

The first time you run the Query Analyzer in SQL Server 2000, the Object Browser comes up also. However, if you don't see it, simply click Tools⇨ Object Browser or press the F8 shortcut key. You can drill down on all of the objects using the hierarchical treeview in the Object Browser. After you drill down to the desired object or function, you can drag and drop it onto the query pane to help build your query.

Using templates

Templates are a new feature in SQL Server 2000. A template is a basic Transact-SQL shell that gives you the structure of Transact-SQL code but requires you to fill-in the specifics for your situation. For example, there is a template for creating a basic table, called `Create Table Basic Template.tql`. This is the Transact-SQL code that makes up the template:

```
-- ================================================
-- Create table basic template
-- ================================================
IF EXISTS (SELECT name FROM sysobjects WHERE name =
           '<table_name, sysname, test_table>' AND type =
           'U')
    DROP TABLE <table_name, sysname, test_table>
GO

CREATE TABLE <table_name, sysname, test_table>
(<column_1, sysname, c1> <datatype_for_column_1, , int> NULL,
 <column_2, sysname, c2> <datatype_for_column_2, , int> NOT
           NULL)
GO
```

Doesn't this help a lot? You simply substitute your information for the parameter placeholders in the template. Microsoft has made this very easy also. Read on and you'll see how.

To open a Transact-SQL template, simply click Edit⇔Insert Template. You are prompted to select from the available template files (with a .TQL extension). There are a bunch of templates that come with SQL Server 2000, but you can also write your own, because they are simply comprised of Transact-SQL. These templates are located in the \Tools\Templates\SQL Query Analyzer folder of wherever you installed SQL Server 2000.

When you open your template file into the Query Analyzer window, you must go through it and substitute your parameters for the ones that are represented as placeholders. You can either overwrite the placeholders manually or use the neat little tool that Microsoft gives you. This tool takes the form of a dialog box called Replace Template Parameters. It is located on the Edit menu (see Figure 9-6).

Simply enter your desired replacement value for each field in the `Value` column. When you are ready to replace the values, click the Replace All button. Then, you simply execute your query as shown previously, in the "Executing queries" section, and you've created a table (or performed whatever action was designed by the template).

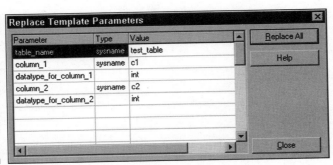

Figure 9-6:
Replace
Template
Parameters
dialog box.

Technologies to Connect to SQL Server 2000

You can connect to a database via several different methods, each of which refers to a separate technology that boasts its own benefits and involves individual costs. Because Microsoft comes out with new technologies all the time and usually continues to support the old ones, these connection issues can cause confusion. Rather than suggest that this potential puzzle is a bad thing, I just call it the nature of the beast. In Table 9-1, I outline various technologies used to connect to SQL Server 2000 and the technical terms that relate to those connections.

Table 9-1	SQL Server 2000 Connectivity Technical Talk	
Term	*Stands For*	*Definition*
COM	Common Object Model	The Microsoft architecture for components talking to each other on the Desktop.
DCOM	Distributed Common Object Model	The Microsoft architecture for components talking to each other from multiple (distributed) computers.
ODBC	Open Database Connectivity	An underlying database communication technology. Microsoft recommends using ODBC for application development outside the COM environment. However, ODBC remains the most common, but not the fastest, way to connect to a database, even within the COM environment.
DAO	Data Access Objects	Set of programmable objects, originally used within Microsoft Visual Basic for the connection and manipulation of Microsoft Access objects. DAO is now supported by multiple environments, such as Visual Basic, Visual C++, and Microsoft Access. Using DAO to request data from a client application to SQL Server can be slow. This is an older technology and should be used only when necessary.

Term	Stands For	Definition
RDO	Remote Data Objects	Set of programmable objects, used to request data from a client application to SQL Server. This connection is quite fast. RDO is now supported by multiple environments, such as Visual Basic and Visual C++. This is an older technology and should be used only when necessary.
ADO	ActiveX Data Objects	Set of programmable objects, also used to request data from a client application to SQL Server. This connection is very fast. Microsoft recommends using ADO for developing your business applications in a COM-based environment. Later in this chapter, I show you how to use ADO from Visual Basic 6.
SQL-DMO	Structured Query Language-Distributed Management Objects	SQL-DMO is a set of objects that enables you to administer and manage SQL Server 2000 through standard SQL queries.
OLE DB	Object Linking and Embedding for Databases	An underlying communication technology. Microsoft recommends using OLE DB when you develop low-level applications within the COM environment. This is typically how different SQL Server components talk to each other. You can also use the OLE DB technology through ODBC. This is done through a concept called a provider. This provider defines the communication between two objects. Therefore, you can use the OLE DB provider for ODBC. ADO is based on the OLE DB technology.
MDAC	Microsoft Data Access Components	This is a set of technologies and components that can access data from ADO, OLE DB, and ODBC data sources.
RDS	Remote Data Service	Allows for customization of the way ADO handles accessing OLE DB or ODBC applications.

(continued)

Term	Stands For	Definition
Table 9-1 *(continued)*		
UDL	Universal Data Link	UDL is a file that is stored on your hard drive that provides connection information for an OLE DB data source. This is very similar to the way you can store ODBC information about ODBC data sources in the Windows Control Panel.
Net-Library		The network protocol that's used between the client application and the server. The network protocol can be either Named Pipes, TCP/IP (using Windows sockets), NetBEUI, Novell SPX/IPX, Banyan Vines, Shared Memory, Multiprotocol, or AppleTalk. SQL Server 2000 enhances the Net-Library so that clients don't need to perform any configuration. It now also supports secure database connections.
DB-Library		The library (DLL) that's used for the client request to talk to a specific database. The client application makes a request through the DB-Library and transmits that request to the server through the Net-Library.

If you want any more information about technologies used to access data with Microsoft SQL Server 2000, visit the Web site at:

```
http://www.microsoft.com/data/
```

Navigating with Cursors

A cursor is more than a blinking blip on your monitor. In database terms, the cursor is a way to manipulate your result sets. A *result set* is a set of data that matches your query request. It can contain any number of rows of data. A *cursor* is a user-definable subset of the entire result set. A cursor can be one row or a set of rows.

One advantage of using a cursor is the efficiency of working with a small set of data rather than the large record set. However, it does take some overhead to create the cursor. _Overhead_ is a term that describes the extra time or resources (memory or disk space) that a process requires.

When would you use a cursor? That's a tough one. It's hard to describe the circumstances that may require a cursor. Let me tell you a situation where I have needed to use a cursor and maybe that will give you a better idea. I have run into situations in which I wanted to return a list of every table in a database, as well as the number of rows in each of those tables. This cannot be done in a single Transact-SQL statement. First, I needed to query to get a list of each table in the database. Within each of those tables, I needed to issue a Transact-SQL statement to get a count for each table. Therefore, I used a cursor to do this.

In order for SQL Server to know how and when to create the cursor, the cursor must first be declared in one of two ways:

✔ By using Database API cursor-specific functions

✔ By using Transact-SQL statements

Transact-SQL statements are the most common way to access cursors, which you can discover in the upcoming sections. For more information about database API cursor functions, refer to the specific documentation for the API you're using. Cursor-specific functions are available in the following database APIs:

✔ ODBC

✔ OLE DB

✔ DB-Library

There are four different types of cursors, each of which is outlined in Table 9-2 along with its pros and cons.

Table 9-2	Cursor Types	
Cursor Type	_Pros_	_Cons_
Static	Requires few resources Cursor can be scrolled	Does not detect if data changes are made Cursor is read-only
Dynamic	Detects if data changes are made Cursor can be scrolled Cursor is read-write	Requires more resources

(continued)

Table 9-2 *(continued)*

Cursor Type	Pros	Cons
Forward-only	Detects if data is changed in rows that have not been fetched	Does not detect if data changes are made in rows that have been fetched Cursor can't be scrolled backwards
Keyset-driven	Data changes to keyset columns are available through a SQL Server variable	Does not detect if data changes are made to nonkey set columns

Cursor Transact-SQL statements are executed just like any other Transact-SQL — through a client program or through the SQL Server Query Analyzer. The following list shows the types of functionality each cursor statement performs:

- Declaring the cursor
- Opening the cursor
- Using the cursor
- Closing the cursor
- Removing the cursor

Declaring the cursor

Where does it all start, you may wonder. The answer: with the DECLARE CURSOR statement. If you don't declare the cursor, no other operations can be performed on it. The DECLARE CURSOR statement follows this general syntax:

```
DECLARE cursor_name [INSENSITIVE] [SCROLL] CURSOR
    FOR select_statement
    FOR {READ ONLY | UPDATE [OF column_list]}]
```

The preceding statement is made up of these parts:

cursor_name is the name of your cursor.

INSENSITIVE is an optional keyword. If it is supplied, cursor data is temporarily copied to a table in the tempdb database.

SCROLL is an optional keyword. If it is supplied, the cursor can be scrolled in all directions (FIRST, PREVIOUS, NEXT, and LAST).

select_statement is the SELECT statement that generates the record set.

FOR READ ONLY is an optional set of keywords. If it is supplied, the cursor will not be updatable. This can't be used with the FOR UPDATE keywords.

FOR UPDATE is an optional set of keywords. If it is supplied, the cursor will be updatable. This can't be used with the FOR READ ONLY keywords.

OF *column_list* is an optional list of columns that can be updated, if the FOR UPDATE keywords are specified.

Here is an example of the DECLARE CURSOR statement:

```
DECLARE CUR_Temp SCROLL CURSOR
FOR SELECT au_lname FROM Authors
FOR UPDATE
```

This example declares an updatable, scrollable cursor, called CUR_Temp. The cursor is comprised of all records and columns in the Authors tables.

Opening the cursor

Opening the cursor is how the cursor generates a record set. When the cursor is opened, the record set (as defined in the DECLARE statement) is populated. The keyword for opening a cursor is OPEN (imagine that?) and it follows this general syntax:

```
OPEN { { [GLOBAL] cursor_name } | cursor_variable_name}
```

The preceding statement is made up of these parts:

GLOBAL is an optional keyword. If supplied, this indicates that the global cursor is to be opened. A global cursor is available to any procedure that has access to the open connection. This is useful only when there is a global and local cursor with the same name.

cursor_name is the name of the already declared cursor. This can't be used with a *cursor_variable_name*.

cursor_variable_name is the name of the already declared cursor variable. This can't be used with a *cursor_name*.

An example of an OPEN statement is as follows:

```
OPEN CUR_Temp
```

Using the cursor

You can use the cursor after it's declared and opened. Remember, a cursor is simply a result set (or a subset of a result set). Either way, it contains specific rows of data. Using the cursor means accessing those rows of data to manipulate them. To use the cursor, the FETCH keyword is used. It follows this general syntax:

```
FETCH
    [ [NEXT | PRIOR | FIRST | LAST
    | ABSOLUTE {n | @nvar} | RELATIVE {n | @nvar}]
    FROM ] { { [GLOBAL] cursor_name } | cursor_variable_name}
    [INTO @variable_name[,...n] ]
```

The preceding statement is made up of these parts:

NEXT is an optional keyword. If it's supplied, the very next row in the cursor is retrieved. This can't be used with the PRIOR, FIRST, LAST, ABSOLUTE, or RELATIVE keywords.

PRIOR is an optional keyword. If it's supplied, the row just prior to the current row in the cursor is retrieved. This can't be used with the NEXT, FIRST, LAST, ABSOLUTE, or RELATIVE keywords.

FIRST is an optional keyword. If it's supplied, the very first row in the cursor is retrieved. This can't be used with the NEXT, PRIOR, LAST, ABSOLUTE, or RELATIVE keywords.

LAST is an optional keyword. If it's supplied, the very last row in the cursor is retrieved. This can't be used with the NEXT, PRIOR, FIRST, ABSOLUTE, or RELATIVE keywords.

ABSOLUTE is an optional keyword. If it's supplied, the keyword moves the current row in the cursor n number of rows from the beginning of the cursor (if n is positive) or n number of rows from the end of the cursor (if n is negative). Rather than a value for n in the SQL statement being specified, a variable, @nvar can be used. This can't be used with the NEXT, PRIOR, FIRST, LAST, or RELATIVE keywords.

RELATIVE is an optional keyword. If it's supplied, the keyword moves the current row in the cursor n number of rows from the current position. If n is positive, the cursor rows are advanced. If n is negative, the cursor rows are reversed. Rather than a value for n in the SQL statement being specified, a variable, @nvar can be used. This can't be used with the NEXT, PRIOR, FIRST, LAST, or ABSOLUTE keywords.

GLOBAL is an optional keyword. If supplied, this indicates that the FETCH is to apply to the global cursor. This is useful only when there is a global and local cursor with the same name. As a review a local cursor (or variable) is available only within the procedure in which the variable was declared. Likewise, a global cursor (or variable) is available outside the procedure in which the variable was declared to any procedure that has access to the existing SQL Server connection.

cursor_name is the name of your cursor.

INTO is an optional keyword. If supplied, @variable_name is the name of the variable that is to contain the result set of the FETCH. If you use the INTO keyword, you must specify enough variables (separated by commas) to contain every column returned by the fetch. I have found that the INTO keyword is used most of the time.

An example of the FETCH statement is as follows:

```
FETCH
FIRST
FROM CUR_Temp INTO @LastName
```

This statement simply fetches the first record from the cursor and displays it. Suppose that you declare a cursor to select all records from the Authors table in the pubs database. Figure 9-7 shows the results of the first fetch in the SQL Server Query Analyzer.

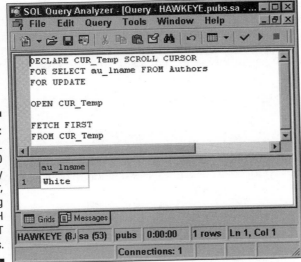

Figure 9-7: The SQL Server 2000 Query Analyzer, showing FETCH FIRST results.

Use the NEXT keyword to move to the next record. Here's how:

```
FETCH
NEXT
FROM CUR_Temp INTO @LastName
```

SQL Server 2000 has a system function that stores the FETCH status; it's called @@FETCH_STATUS. You can use this function in your procedures to perform specific actions when the function returns certain values. These are the possible values returned by @@FETCH_STATUS:

- ✔ 0: Fetch is successful.
- ✔ -1: Fetch failed or the row was beyond the result set.
- ✔ -2: Row fetched is missing.

The `@@FETCH_STATUS` function is commonly used to loop through rows in a cursor until there are no more rows. You can issue a statement similar to this:

```
WHILE @@FETCH_STATUS = 0
BEGIN
    FETCH NEXT
    FROM CUR_Temp INTO @LastName
END
```

This code enters a loop (with the `WHILE` statement) and loops as long as `@@FETCH_STATUS` returns zero. If it doesn't return zero, there are no more rows in the cursor.

Closing the cursor

Closing the cursor releases the record set from memory and frees any locks that the cursor is holding. Note that closing the cursor does not delete it. The keyword for closing a cursor is the `CLOSE` keyword. It follows this general syntax:

```
CLOSE { { [GLOBAL] cursor_name } | cursor_variable_name}
```

The preceding statement is made up of these parts:

> `GLOBAL` is an optional keyword. If supplied, this indicates that the global cursor is to be closed. This is only useful when there is a global and local cursor with the same name.

> `cursor_name` is the name of the already declared cursor. This can't be used with a `cursor_variable_name`.

> `cursor_variable_name` is the name of the already declared cursor variable. This can't be used with a `cursor_name`.

An example of the `CLOSE` statement is as follows:

```
CLOSE CUR_Temp
```

Removing the cursor

Removing the cursor is known as *deallocating* the cursor, primarily because any variable assigned with the `DECLARE` keyword needs to be removed from memory. Therefore, as you may expect, the keyword for removing a variable from memory is `DEALLOCATE`. It follows this general syntax:

```
DEALLOCATE { { [GLOBAL] cursor_name } | cursor_variable_name}
```

The preceding statement is made up of these parts:

GLOBAL is an optional keyword. If supplied, the keyword indicates that the global cursor is to be deallocated. This is only useful when there is a global and local cursor with the same name.

cursor_name is the name of the already declared cursor. This can't be used with a cursor_variable_name.

cursor_variable_name is the name of the already declared cursor variable. This can't be used with a cursor_name.

An example of the DEALLOCATE statement is as follows:

```
DEALLOCATE CUR_Temp
```

Putting it all together

Earlier in this chapter, I mention how I've used cursors in the past. Although I would consider the code I'm about to show to be an advanced Transact-SQL batch, I'm going to show you anyway. I think it's important to see how Transact-SQL is used in the real world. Note that this is not the only way to retrieve these table counts. It is just a good way to illustrate how cursors can be used.

```
--declare a variable to hold the table name
DECLARE @TableName varchar(50)

--declare a variable to hold the command string to execute
DECLARE @sCmd varchar(100)

--declare the cursor to get all user-defined tables from the
            sysobjects system table
DECLARE curTable CURSOR

FOR
SELECT      [name]
FROM        sysobjects
WHERE       type = 'U'
ORDER BY [name]


--open the cursor
OPEN curTable

--Fetch the first record
FETCH NEXT
FROM curTable
INTO @TableName

--check cursor status and loop
```

```
WHILE @@FETCH_STATUS = 0
        BEGIN
            --now that we have a table name, we can get a
    count
            SET @sCmd = ''
            SET @sCmd = @sCmd + 'SELECT ''' + @TableName
    + ''', count(*)'
            SET @sCmd = @sCmd + 'FROM pubs.dbo.' +
    @TableName

            --execute the statement to get the count,
    based on this iteration
            EXECUTE (@sCmd)

            --Fetch the next record
            FETCH NEXT
            FROM curTable
            INTO @TableName
        END

--close the cursor
CLOSE curTable

--deallocate the cursor
DEALLOCATE curTable
```

Examining SQL Server from an ASP Web Page

Okay, now you have a SQL Server database. What if you want to write a program that accesses your SQL Server database? Lots of companies want you to write an application that uses the data in SQL Server. One of the most common computer languages is Microsoft Visual Basic, which can be used to write such an application.

Another extremely popular way to access your data is from a Web page using Active Server Pages (ASP) using VB Script or Java Script on Microsoft's Internet Information Server, version 4 or 5 (which comes with Windows 2000). Also, you can write ASP pages and host them with Microsoft's Personal Web Server (PWS) on a Windows 95 or 98 computer.

Although this book is not about Visual Basic or VB Script, I want to show you how to communicate with SQL Server from a Web page using VB Script and ASP. This section isn't designed to equip you with a full understanding of VB Script or ASP. Rather, I offer just enough information to help you build a basic understanding of how you can access SQL Server data from a Web page using ADO and VB Script. If you want to pick up the details of Visual Basic 6, you can refer to *Visual Basic 6 For Dummies,* by Wallace Wang (from IDG Books Worldwide, Inc.). You can also refer to another book I wrote (from SAMS),

Visual Basic 5 Developer's Guide. Likewise, IDG publishes books on VBScript, Active Server Pages, and Internet Information Server (IIS).

The great thing about writing Web pages is that they are just text. They can be edited using any editor, such as Microsoft Visual InterDev, Microsoft Word, or even Notepad. After you save your file in a directory that your Web administrator gives you, the page will be available through your Web browser.

In an ASP page, you are actually combining a scripting language with static HTML code. The script is processed on the server and rendered into HTML dynamically as the Web server renders the Web page. This HTML is combined with the static HTML and sent to the browser. To denote the difference between script code and static HTML code to the Web server, you must include any script code between tags, like this:

```
<%
script code here...
%>
```

Your ASP page can (and probably will) contain many of these tags. With these tags, the Web server knows what it has to process by the script engine.

You'll also notice that in my code, I use the Response object. A Response.Write call will actually write text to the Web browser within a piece of script.

To create an ASP page that retrieves all data from the Authors table in the pubs database, simply follow these steps:

1. **Open the editor of your choice.**

2. **Type in the following code:**

    I have commented the code so that you can understand what each line is doing. You'll have to change the name of the server, from HAWKEYE (which is my database server) to the name of your server. Also, you may have to provide a different user name and password.

```
<%@ Language=VBScript %>
<HTML>
<BODY>
<%
        dim sConn
        dim oConn
        dim sCmd
        dim rs
        dim oField

        'create ADO connection object
        set oConn =
        Server.CreateObject("ADODB.Connection")

        'define connection string
```

```
sConn  =
"Provider=SQLOLEDB.1;SERVER=HAWKEYE;UID=sa;
PWD=;DATABASE=PUBS"

'open the connection
oConn.Open sConn

'construct Transact-SQL statement
sCmd = "SELECT * FROM Authors"

'Execute Transact-SQL statement and assign
to rs object
set rs = oConn.Execute(sCmd)

'construct HTML table of data
Response.Write "<TABLE Border=1>"
if not rs.eof then
     'write out column headings
     Response.Write("<tr>")
     for each oField in rs.fields
          Response.Write("<th>" & oField.name
& "</th>")
     next
     Response.Write("</tr>")

     'write out each record
     while not rs.eof
          Response.Write("<tr>")
          'write out each field within each
record
          for each oField in rs.fields
               Response.Write("<td>" &
oField.value & "</td>")
          next
          Response.Write("</tr>")

          'move to the next record
          rs.movenext

     wend
end if
Response.Write "</TABLE>"

'clean-up objects by closing and deallocating
rs.close
set rs = nothing
oConn.Close
set oconn = nothing

%>
</BODY>
</HTML>
```

Obviously, it is not secure to store the user names and passwords inside your ASP pages. I show it this way for example purposes only. Typically, you would use a UDL file (briefly mentioned earlier) or some other similar mechanism, such as an ODBC data source name.

3. **Save the file on your Web server, giving it whatever name you want.**

   When you save your file, make sure to save it in an appropriate folder on your Web server. Typically, the Web server hierarchy begins at `\inetpub\wwwroot` on whatever drive IIS was installed on. Make sure to save the file with an .ASP extension or you'll never be able to access it.

4. **Test the file in a Web browser (see Figure 9-8).**

   Launch your Web browser and open the file by clicking File⇨Open. This allows you to test your ASP/VB Script code.

http://hawkeye/testasp.asp - Microsoft Internet Explorer
File Edit View Favorites Tools Help
Back Search Favorites History
Address http://hawkeye/testasp.asp Go
Links Homelink Internosis Mail Yahoo All SQL SQLServer7 Hotmail TCT Web Campus
au_id au_lname au_fname phone address city state zip contract
172-32-1176 White Johnson 408 496-7223 10932 Bigge Rd. Menlo Park CA 94025 True
213-46-8915 Green Marjorie 415 986-7020 309 63rd St. #411 Oakland CA 94618 True
238-95-7766 Carson Cheryl 415 548-7723 589 Darwin Ln. Berkeley CA 94705 True
267-41-2394 O'Leary Michael 408 286-2428 22 Cleveland Av. #14 San Jose CA 95128 True
274-80- Straight Dean 415 834- 5420 College Oakland CA 94609 True
Done
Local intranet

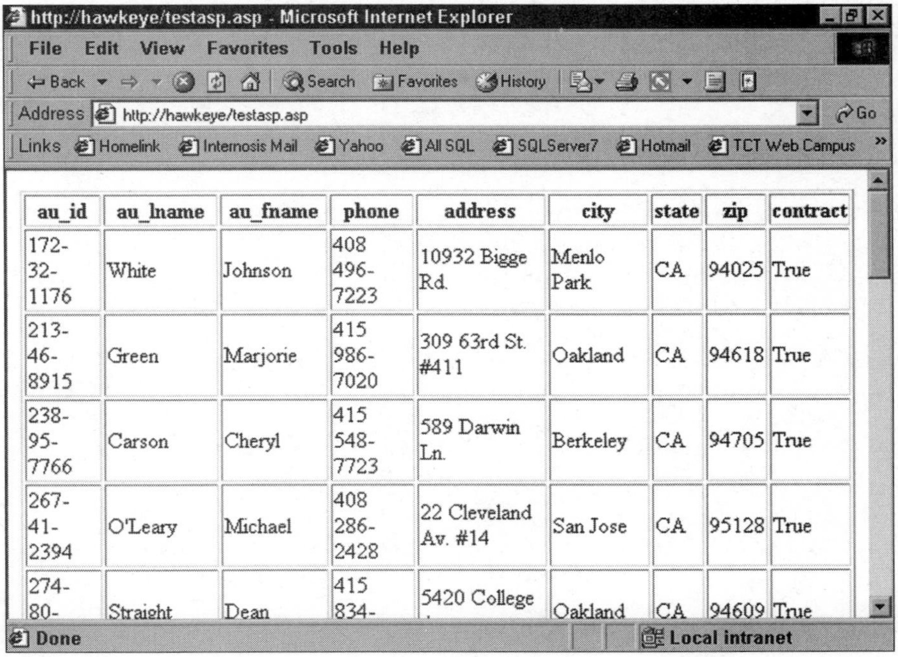

Figure 9-8: Viewing your ASP file in Microsoft Internet Explorer 5.

Chapter 10

Maintaining Flexibility by Importing and Exporting Data

In This Chapter

▶ Bringing data into SQL Server by importing

▶ Sending out your data by exporting

*W*hen it comes to data, you must maintain flexibility. Flexibility refers to the ability to use data in multiple locations. If there were no provision to use data from some other location into SQL Server (Importing) or from SQL Server to some other location (Exporting), many companies would never use SQL Server. The lack of flexibility is too limiting. Companies need to be able to use data from other databases or locations. In this chapter, I show you how to import and export using SQL Server 2000.

I have seen many times that some people confuse the terms *importing* and *exporting*. The confusion seems to come not when thinking of a single system importing or exporting but rather when thinking of one system importing and another exporting to complete some process. It's the same type of confusion that sets in when discussing debits and credits in accounting. Therefore, look at it this way: Suppose that you owe a friend $100. This person is going to import (deposit) the money you give into an account. However, for your friend to import the money, you need to export it (withdrawal). The side of the transaction you are looking at dictates whether you have an import or an export. Keep this in mind as you read this chapter.

Different data-source options need different types of data specified. Therefore, as you choose specific options within the wizards that I show you in this chapter, the screen automatically adjusts itself to allow you to fill in the data necessary for the data source that you choose. For example, if your data source is Microsoft Access, you need to specify the filename (database) that contains the data. If you specify a different data source, you don't have to specify the filename, but you specify other information, as determined by the data source. You can see what I mean as you read the rest of this chapter!

To help you follow the flow of the wizards that I show you in this chapter, see the flowcharts in Appendix A.

What is DTS, Anyway?

DTS stands for Data Transformation Services. This is a set of services built into Microsoft SQL Server, starting with version 7 and expanded in SQL Server 2000. DTS is comprised of a complete set of programmatic objects that allows for very complex transformations of data. A single *data transformation* refers to the process of taking data from one place, moving it to another, but transforming it along the way. As an example, consider Figure 10-1.

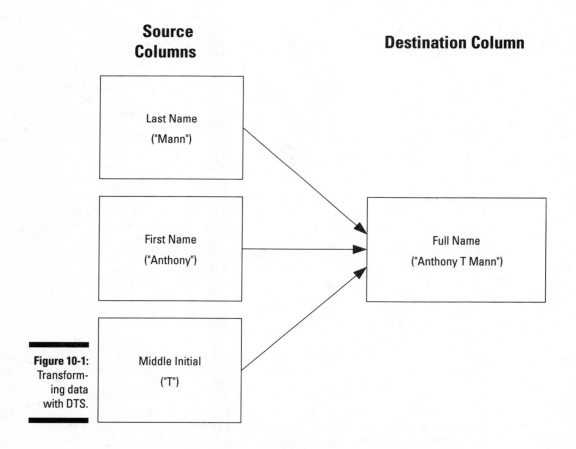

Figure 10-1: Transforming data with DTS.

Notice in the figure that in the source data, there are three columns of data (First Name, Last Name, and Middle Initial) that have to be converted, or transformed, into one column of data at the destination, called Full Name. This is an example of a very simple transformation, but it illustrates the need for transformation of data between the source and destination tables. On the other hand, many times, no transformation needs to take place. The source data is simply copied into the destination table.

SQL Server 2000 gives you an Import/Export Wizard to easily move data to and fro. How do wizards work, you ask? Well, the concept is quite simple. Microsoft wrote a custom program that acts as a wrapper around the object model exposed by DTS services. You can do the same thing but, unfortunately, I cannot show you that in this book. Look for another upcoming book that I will write on programming the DTS object model. But for now, I will limit my DTS instruction to using the Import Wizard and the Export Wizard.

In SQL Server 7, there was a separate Import and Export Wizard. In SQL Server 2000, this wizard is combined into the DTS Import/Export Wizard.

Importing Data to a SQL Server Database

Knowing how to construct your database and insert data is one thing. But what if you need to use *legacy data,* data that's stored in another database system that you no longer use? One way to use that legacy database is to import the data. In this section, I show you how to import data located in another system into Microsoft SQL Server 2000.

The DTS Import/Export Wizard guides you through the process of importing your data. A series of steps prompts you for information.

In this section, I use an example of importing from a Microsoft Access database into Microsoft SQL Server 2000. Therefore, if you are going to follow along with this example, you must have Microsoft Visual Basic installed on your computer, along with the sample databases.

To import your data using the DTS Import/Export Wizard, follow these steps:

1. **Choose Start⇨Programs⇨Microsoft SQL Server⇨Import and Export Data.**

   Alternatively, you can start the DTS Import/Export Wizard by using the Enterprise Manager. Within the Enterprise Manager, choose Tools⇨ Wizards to bring up the Select Wizard dialog box. Under the Data

Transformation Services item, you see options to import and export data. Each of the options brings up the DTS Import/Export Wizard.

2. **After you read the introduction screen, click Next.**

3. **Choose a Data Source relating to the source data (see Figure 10-2); then click Next.**

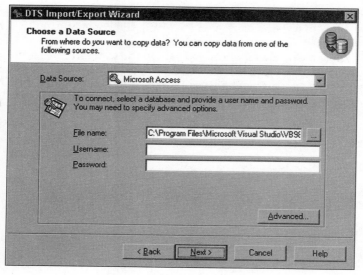

Figure 10-2: Selecting Microsoft Access as the data source in the DTS Import/ Export Wizard.

Source data indicates the location of data used for your import. The fields in this dialog box that you need to provide information for are the following:

- **Source:** The data that you are importing into SQL Server. All other fields on this screen relate to the source data. Therefore, the screen will physically change, depending on the type of source data that you select.

  If you entered the DTS Import/Export Wizard by selecting one of the menu options that indicate "Export" in the menu name, then the database selected will automatically be set to the current database with the current login information already entered.

  If you are following my example, choose Microsoft Access as the source. I'm showing you how to import the data from the Microsoft Access Biblio database into the SQL Server 2000 pubs database.

- **File Name:** Click the ellipsis button (. . .) to choose the filename of the Microsoft Access database you want to import data from. If you have Visual Basic installed on your computer, the Microsoft Access database BIBLIO.MDB is most likely also installed. If you used all the default locations when you installed Microsoft Visual Studio 6, the path to the Biblio database is `C:\Program Files\ Microsoft Visual Studio\VB98`.

- **Username:** If your database uses security, you need to type in a user name (and password). If you are following my example, the `Biblio` database does not use security, so you can leave this field blank.

- **Password:** If your database uses security, you need to type in a password (and user name). If you are following my example, the `Biblio` database does not use security, so just leave this field blank.

Click Next when you are ready to continue.

4. **Choose a Data Source relating to the destination data (see Figure 10-3); then click Next.**

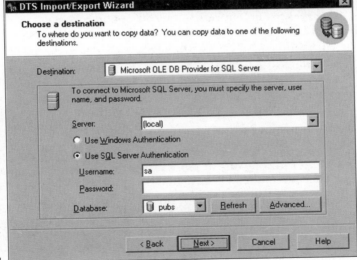

Figure 10-3:
Selecting SQL Server as the destination in the DTS Import/ Export Wizard.

Destination data indicates the location of the recipient of the data used for your import. The fields in this dialog box that you need to provide information for are the following:

- **Destination:** The data location that will receive the imported data. In my example, I am importing Microsoft Access data into Microsoft SQL Server 2000. All other fields on this screen relate to the destination data. Therefore, the screen will physically change, depending on the type of destination data that you select.

If you entered the DTS Import/Export Wizard by selecting one of the menu options that indicate "Import" in the menu name, then the database selected will automatically be set to the current database with the current login information already entered.

If you are following my example, choose Microsoft OLE DB Provider for SQL Server as the source. Remember, you are importing the data from the Microsoft Access Biblio database into the SQL Server 2000 pubs database.

- **Server:** Enter or select the server that contains the database you will import into. By default, (local) is selected, indicating that the computer that is running the DTS Import/Export Wizard will be used.

- **Use Windows NT Authentication:** Use this option if you want the user's login name and password to be used for authentication within a Windows NT or Windows 2000 domain.

- **Use SQL Server NT Authentication:** This option is used if you want to indicate in the Username and Password fields the data for SQL Server to authenticate. After this option is chosen, the Username and Password fields become enabled. Enter the desired name and password. I use sa as my login with no password in my example.

- **Database:** Select from the drop-down list of databases the database that contains the table you will use to import data into. For my example, choose the pubs database. If you don't see your desired database, click the Refresh button.

Click Next to move to the next step.

5. **In the Specify Table Copy or Query dialog box (see Figure 10-4), specify whether to copy one or more tables or the results of a query from the data source; then click Next.**

This dialog box prompts you to specify whether you want to copy all records from the source table or use a query that limits the records to a specific subset of data. Choose the appropriate option. For my example, choose Copy table(s) and View(s) from the Source Database, which is also the default option.

If the source and destination data sources are both SQL Server databases (version 7.0 or 2000), another option, Copy Objects and Data between SQL Server Databases, becomes enabled. This option allows you to move any SQL Server objects, such as tables, indexes, stored procedures, and more.

Click Next to move to the next step.

6. **In the Select Source Tables and Views dialog box (see Figure 10-5), select the source tables to import; then click Next.**

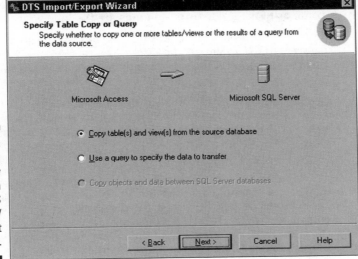

Figure 10-4:
Selecting
the Copy
Table Option
in the DTS
Import/
Export
Wizard.

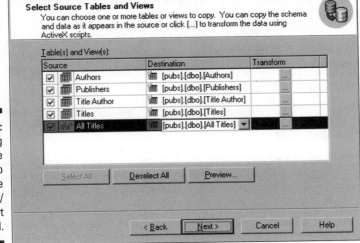

Figure 10-5:
Selecting
the source
tables to
import in the
DTS Import/
Export
Wizard.

This dialog box prompts you to specify the source tables to copy to specific destination tables. A *source table* is the table where data is coming from. A *destination* table is the table where data is going to.

The tables are presented in a grid format, allowing for multiple rows and three columns of data. The three columns are the following:

- **Source Table:** Select the check box(es) next to the source table name(s) to use to import data from. The table names presented in this grid come from the source data that you selected earlier.

- **Destination Table:** If the source table is checked, you can specify a destination table. By default, the destination table name is the same as the source table name, only it's in the destination database. If the destination table already exists, SQL Server automatically appends data to the end of the table. If the destination table doesn't exist, SQL Server creates a new table.

- **Transform:** This option specifies additional information about the import. For example, you can specify the data types for the different columns of data. To access the transform screens, click the ellipsis button (. . .). Because the transform option is an advanced topic, it is outside the scope of this book, and I don't cover it here. Consult Books Online for more information.

If you want to import all tables, simply click the Select All button. Likewise, if you want to clear all your selections, click the Deselect All button. If you want to see the data in the table, click the Preview button. You will see only the first 100 rows of data.

One final option in this step is labeled Include all Primary & Foreign Keys. This option, if checked, will create the same primary and foreign keys on the destination tables as what exists in the source tables. For more information about primary and foreign keys, refer to Chapter 3.

After you select all desired options, click Next.

7. **In the Save, Schedule, and Replicate Package dialog box (see Figure 10-6), select the save, schedule, and replicate option that you want; then click Next.**

This dialog box prompts you to specify whether you want to save and/or schedule the DTS package that is automatically created by the DTS Import/Export Wizard. A *DTS package* is the entire set of instructions that you configured either manually or by using the DTS Import/Export Wizard.

Select or enter data for these fields:

- **Run Immediately:** Select this check box if you would like the DTS package to run when you are finished using the wizard. This option is checked automatically.

- **Use Replication to Publish Destination Data:** If this option is checked, data will be transferred to the destination using replication. Refer to Chapter 12 for more information on replication.

- **Schedule DTS Package for Later Execution:** Select this check box if you wish for the DTS package to run later or on a recurring schedule. Clicking the ellipsis button (. . .) allows you to change the default schedule of running every day at midnight.

  Note that you will not be allowed to schedule the DTS package if you do not save it (using the Save DTS Package option).

- **Save DTS Package:** Select this check box if you wish to save the specified import information for use in the future. If you save the package, you can run it again at a later time. If you don't save it, the information you specified is lost after this specific import.

  If you click this option, you will have the further choice of defining where you want the packaged saved. You can choose from SQL Server, SQL Meta Data Services (formerly known as the repository), Structured Storage File, or Visual Basic File.

In my example, I am performing a one-time import, so the DTS package is not being saved. However, if you are going to save the DTS package, you are prompted with an additional screen to name the package and select some properties for it. After you select all desired options, click Next.

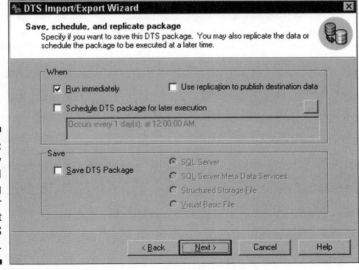

Figure 10-6:
Specify saving and scheduling options for resultant DTS package.

8. **In the Completing the DTS Import/Export Wizard dialog box, review your choices; then click Finish.**

This dialog box prompts you to review your choices. After you review your choices, you can click the Back button to change any information that you typed earlier, or click the Finish button to begin the import. If you have followed my example, data from the Microsoft Access database BIBLIO.MDB is transferred into the Microsoft SQL Server 2000 database, called pubs.

Exporting Data from a SQL Server 2000 Database

Use the DTS Import/Export Wizard when you need to export data from a database in SQL Server 2000 to another data source, such as a database or file. In this section, I show how the DTS Import/Export Wizard guides you through a series of steps to perform the exporting process, prompting you for data at each step.

In this section, I use an example of exporting the Authors table in the Microsoft SQL Server 2000 pubs database into a text file. Therefore, if you are going to follow along with this example, you must have this database installed, but it is installed by default during the setup process. pubs is a sample database that includes book, author, and publisher information for some books. I can't believe that after writing seven books, I'm *still* not in the database!

To export your data using the DTS Import/Export Wizard, follow these steps:

1. **Choose Start➪Programs➪Microsoft SQL Server➪Import and Export Data.**

   Alternatively, you can start the DTS Import/Export Wizard by using the Enterprise Manager. Within the Enterprise Manager, choose Tools➪ Wizards to bring up the Select Wizard dialog box. Under the Data Transformation Services item, you'll see options to import and export data. Each of the options brings up the DTS Import/Export Wizard.

2. **After you read the introduction screen, click Next.**

3. **Choose a Data Source relating to the source data (see Figure 10-7); Then click Next.**

   Source data indicates the location of data used for your export. The fields in this dialog box that you need to provide information for are the following:

   • **Source:** The data that you are exporting from in SQL Server. All other fields on this screen relate to the source data. Therefore, the screen will physically change, depending on the type of source data that you select.

If you entered the DTS Import/Export Wizard by selecting one of the menu options that indicate "Export" in the menu name, then the database selected will automatically be set to the current database with the current login information already entered.

If you are following my example, choose Microsoft OLE DB Provider for SQL Server as the source. I'm showing you how to export the data from the Authors table in the pubs database into a text file.

- **Server:** Enter or select the server that contains the database you will export from. By default, (local) is selected, indicating that the computer that is running the DTS Import/Export Wizard will be used.

- **Use Windows NT Authentication:** Use this option if you want the user's login name and password to be used for authentication within a Windows NT or Windows 2000 domain.

- **Use SQL Server NT Authentication:** This option is used if you want to indicate in the Username and Password fields the data for SQL Server to authenticate. After this option is chosen, the Username and Password fields become enabled. Enter the desired name and password. I use sa as my login with no password in my example.

- **Database:** Select from the drop-down list of databases the database that contains the table you will use to export data from. For my example, choose the pubs database. If you don't see your desired database, click the Refresh button.

Click Next to move to the next step.

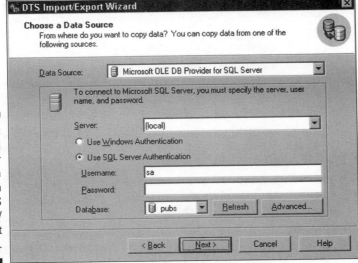

Figure 10-7:
Selecting
SQL Server
as the data
source in
the DTS
Import/
Export
Wizard.

4. Choose a Data Source relating to the destination data (see Figure 10-8); then click Next.

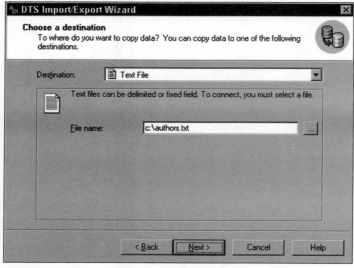

Figure 10-8:
Selecting a
Text File as
the data
destination
in the DTS
Import/
Export
Wizard.

Destination data indicates the location of the recipient of the data used for your import. The fields in this dialog box that you need to provide information for are the following:

- **Destination:** The data location that will receive the imported data. In my example, I am exporting from Microsoft SQL Server 2000 into a text file. All other fields on this screen relate to the destination data. Therefore, the screen will physically change, depending on the type of destination data that you select.

  If you entered the DTS Import/Export Wizard by selecting one of the menu options that indicate "Import" in the menu name, then the database selected will automatically be set to the current database with the current login information already entered.

  If you are following my example, choose Text File as the source. Remember, you are exporting the data from the SQL Server 2000 `pubs` database into a text file.

- **File Name:** Type the name of the text file you want to create, or choose an existing text file by clicking the ellipsis button (. . .). Type **C:\Authors.txt** for this example.

5. In the Specify Table Copy or Query dialog box (refer back to Figure 10-4), specify whether to copy one or more tables or the results of a query from the data source; then click Next.

This dialog box prompts you to specify whether you want to copy all records from the source table, or use a query that limits the records to a specific subset of data. Choose the appropriate option. For my example, choose Copy Table(s) and View(s) from the Source Database, which is also the default option.

If the source and destination data sources are both SQL Server databases, another option, Copy Objects and Data between SQL Server Databases, becomes enabled. This option allows you to move any SQL Server objects, such as tables, indexes, stored procedures, and more.

Click Next to move to the next step.

6. **In the Select Destination File Format dialog box (see Figure 10-9), select the destination file format of the text file you want to export; then click Next.**

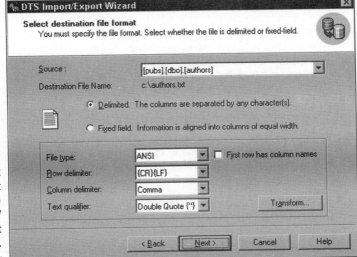

Figure 10-9: Selecting a destination file format for the text file in the DTS Import/ Export Wizard.

This dialog box prompts you to specify the file format of the text file you are using to export data from. The fields you need to provide information for are the following:

- **Source:** Choose the table from the available source tables used for the export. The data from this table is exported in the format you select in this dialog box. Choose the table `[pubs].[dbo].[authors]`.

Notice that the list didn't just show the table name of authors. The format [database].[owner].[table] is a very precise specification for the name of a table. You can normally use the table name alone (without specifying the database and owner), but doing so indicates that the table you've selected is in a specific database and created by a specific owner. If your table is *not* in the current database, then you *must* specify that database and the table name.

- **Delimited:** Click this option when you want every field in your text file to be separated by a character that you specify. Often, a record is made up of variable-length fields, separated (or delimited) by commas. This step enables you to specify the delimiters in your text file. This is the default option. If you are following my example, ensure that this is option is selected.

- **Fixed Field:** Click this option when you want every field in your text file to be the same width (number of characters). This option is used less often than the Delimited option.

- **File Type:** Choose the type of file, ANSI, OEM, or Unicode, that you want your file to be, from the drop-down list. ANSI is a standard by which you can only use the characters chosen in the current character set. Unicode is a standard by which you can use characters defined by a much larger standard that may cross character sets. Using Unicode takes up twice as much storage space as using ANSI, which is the default. OEM specifies that the default code page will be used. A *code page* is the way that SQL Server maps-out characters to be displayed.

- **Row Delimiter:** Choose from the drop-down list of choices how you want to indicate that there are no more fields (columns) in a record. The default is {CR}{LF}, which is a carriage return and a line feed. {CR}{LF} is typically used in a text file export or import.

- **Column Delimiter:** Choose how you want to separate column data from the drop-down list. (This field is enabled only if you choose the Delimited option.) The default is Comma, which is typically used in a delimited text file export or import.

- **Text Qualifier:** Choose how you want to indicate that a field is a text field, rather than a numeric field, from the drop-down list. The default is Double Quote {"}, and is typically used in a text file export or import. You want to qualify text fields because some systems don't accept what appears to be a numeric field in a text file into a character field. For example, 93843 appears to be a numeric field. If a system attempts to import it into a character field, the import may fail. This field should appear as "93843" to import into a character field.

- **First Row Has Column Names:** Check this check box when you want the first row of data to contain the actual names of the fields in the table from which it came, which makes the text file easier to read. This doesn't affect how the computer reads the data. That is, unless you know that the system that handles the import requires the column names in the first row, don't check this box. This option is not selected by default.

- **Transform:** This button allows you to specify additional information about the export. For example, you can specify the data types for the different columns of data. To access the transform screens, click this button. Because the Transform option is an advanced topic, it is outside the scope of this book, and I don't cover it here. Consult Books Online for more information.

7. **In the Save, Schedule, and Replicate Package dialog box (refer back to Figure 10-6), select the save, schedule, and replicate option that you want; then click Next.**

This dialog box prompts you to specify whether you want to save and/or schedule the DTS package that is automatically created by the DTS Import/Export Wizard. A *DTS package* is the entire set of instructions that you configured either manually or by using the DTS Import/Export Wizard.

Select or enter data for these fields:

- **Run Immediately:** Select this check box if you would like the DTS package to run when you are finished using the wizard. This option is checked automatically.

- **Use Replication to Publish Destination Data:** If this option is checked, data will be transferred to the destination using replication. Refer to Chapter 12 for more information on replication.

- **Schedule DTS Package for Later Execution:** Select this check box if you wish for the DTS package to run later or on a recurring schedule. Clicking the ellipsis button (. . .) allows you to change the default schedule of running every day at midnight.

  Note that you will not be allowed to schedule the DTS package if you do not save it (using the Save DTS Package option).

- **Save DTS Package:** Select this check box if you want to save the specified import information for use in the future. If you save the package, you can run it again at a later time. If you don't save it, the information you specified is lost after this specific import.

  If you click this option, you will have the further choice of defining where you want the packaged saved. You can choose from SQL Server, SQL Meta Data Services (formerly known as the repository), Structured Storage File, or Visual Basic File.

In my example, I am performing a one-time export, so the DTS package is not being saved. However, if you are going to save the DTS package, you are prompted with an additional screen to name the package and select some properties for it. After you select all desired options, click Next.

8. **In the Completing the DTS Import/Export Wizard dialog box, review your choices; then click Finish.**

This dialog box prompts you to review your choices. After you review your choices, you can click the Back button to change any information that you typed earlier, or click the Finish button to begin the export. If you have followed my example, data from the `authors` table in the `pubs` database in Microsoft SQL Server 2000 is exported to a comma-delimited text file named `C:\AUTHORS.TXT`.

Part IV
Enterprise Issues

The 5th Wave   By Rich Tennant

©RICHTENNANT

"YOU KNOW KIDS – YOU CAN'T BUY THEM JUST ANY WEB AUTHORING SOFTWARE."

In this part . . .

*E*nterprise issues are the hot topic *du jour*. Because it is unlikely that you will personally use SQL Server in your home, you'll probably encounter it at work. Therefore, you'll want to know all about enterprise issues. The "enterprise" represents your entire company, with all of its data. I show you all about views, users, and other neat topics.

I also show you how to replicate your data and back it up, in case there are problems. The icing on the cake is the last topic. I show you how to write distributed queries to access data from multiple data sources.

Chapter 11

Preventing the Inevitable Disaster (Losing Data)

In This Chapter

▶ Manually backing up data to stay in control

▶ Automatic data backups for trusting souls

▶ Restoring data after "D-Day"

Have you ever lost data? If you have, you probably wish that you had backed up your data. I know I have. Backing up is the process of copying data to another location so that you have a way to recover it if your original data is lost. Fortunately, Microsoft made backing up data in SQL Server 2000 easy. You can back up your data either manually or automatically. I illustrate both ways of backing up data in this chapter.

Why Back Up?

Why back up? The answer is simple. You don't want to lose your data! Most companies have had some type of emergency situation where data was lost for some reason. These reasons include:

- ✔ Failed disk drives
- ✔ Failed hardware
- ✔ Inadvertent deletion of data by developers
- ✔ Application problems that violate business rules
- ✔ Data corruption

The only way to recover from bad data is to restore from a backup. After all, how can you recreate the data if you didn't make a snapshot of it at a specific point in time? That's exactly what a backup does for you.

Failover Clustering

To recover from a real-time hardware failure, you can setup your computers to perform failover clustering. Clustering allows for multiple computers to be configured to operate as a single unit so that if one unit fails, the other one takes over. This is handled by the operating system.

To install failover clustering, you must be using Windows NT 4 Enterprise Edition, Windows 2000 Advanced Server, or Windows 2000 Datacenter Server only. You must install the Microsoft cluster services (MSCS). Also, you *must* be using SCSI hard drives, not IDE or EIDE.

SQL Server 2000 supports clustering. Within the SQL Server 2000 setup program, clustering is set up through what is known as a virtual server. A virtual server is the name that you give to represent a collection of SQL Server nodes. These nodes can be added or removed from the cluster. Clustering aids in what Microsoft calls "High Availability." This means that SQL Server will always be available, regardless of the situation that causes failure or slow performance.

Clustering is outside the scope of this book, but I want to at least mention it to make you aware that it exists and that SQL Server 2000 is an enterprise-ready relational database system.

Setting Up a Backup Device

Before you can back up your data, you need to either set up a backup device (which allows you to preconfigure backup location information), or specify a "one-time" location. A backup device can be either a tape or disk. You notify SQL Server about the backup device when you give the device a name and assign it to either a tape drive or a disk drive. If you're using a tape, you specify which tape drive the device uses (even when you have only one tape drive). If you're using a disk, you specify the disk drive and directory that the device uses.

To set up a backup device, follow these steps:

1. **Choose Start⇨Programs⇨Microsoft SQL Server⇨Enterprise Manager to start the SQL Server Enterprise Manager.**

2. **Expand the tree so that you see the Backup folder under the Management folder (see Figure 11-1).**

   For more information about expanding the tree, see the Introduction of this book.

3. **Choose <u>A</u>ction⇨New Backup Device to bring up the Backup Device Properties dialog box.**

Alternatively, you can right-click the Backup Devices folder in the tree. Any method you choose to create a new backup device brings up the Backup Device Properties dialog box, allowing you to configure the new device (see Figure 11-2).

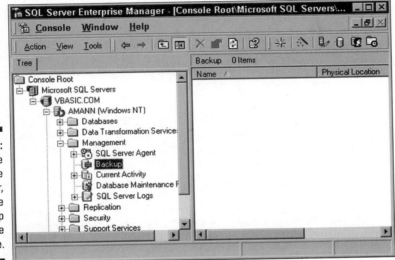

Figure 11-1:
The Enterprise Manager, showing the Backup folder in the tree.

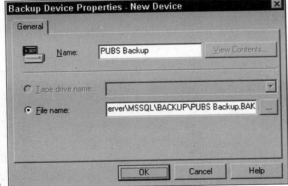

Figure 11-2:
The Backup Device Properties dialog box.

4. **Type information about the new backup device in the following fields:**

   • **Name:** Give your backup device a name. If you intend to use a tape device, you may want to use a name such as `Tape Device`. If you intend to use a disk to back up your data, you may want to use a name such as `Drive C`. In either case, you will be using this name to identify the device later.

- **Tape Drive Name:** If you are using a tape device for your backups, choose from the drop-down list of available devices. If you have more than one tape device, the devices all appear in the drop-down list. If you don't have a tape device, this field will be disabled. This option is chosen by default if you have a tape device on your local computer; otherwise, this option is disabled.

- **File Name:** If you are using a disk drive for your backups, click the ellipsis button (. . .) to choose a drive and directory on your computer. This drive can be a networked drive. The drive and directory you choose is used to place the file containing the SQL Server backup. This option is chosen by default if you do not have a tape device on your computer.

  You need to indicate a filename along with a directory. To help you with this, SQL Server automatically appends the name you entered in the Name field with a `.BAK` extension to the directory you choose. For example, if you give a name of `Drive C`, and you choose a directory `C:\Program Files\Microsoft SQL Server\MSSQL\BACKUP`, SQL Server presents the filename `C:\Program Files\Microsoft SQL Server\MSSQL\BACKUP\ Drive C.BAK`.

The View Contents button is enabled only if you bring up the Backup Device Properties dialog box for an existing backup device. Because you are creating a new device, the button is disabled. If the button is enabled, clicking it will read the medium and allow you to review the data contained within.

5. **Click OK to save your backup device and to close the dialog box.**

   Notice that your newly configured backup device appears on the right pane of the SQL Server Enterprise Manager screen (see Figure 11-3).

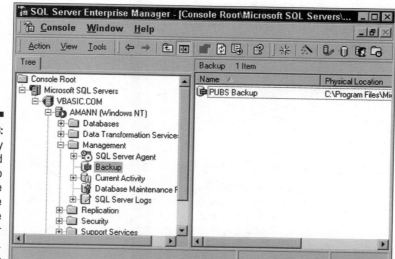

Figure 11-3: The newly configured backup device on the Enterprise Manager screen.

Performing the Backup

Before you back up your data, you need to configure one or more backup devices. Refer to the section "Setting Up a Backup Device," earlier in this chapter, to see how to configure one or more backup devices. To start the backup, follow these steps:

1. **Select Start➪Programs➪Microsoft SQL Server➪Enterprise Manager to start the SQL Server Enterprise Manager.**

2. **Expand the tree so that you see the Databases folder.**

   For more information about expanding the tree, see the Introduction of this book.

3. **Click the database you want to back up.**

4. **Choose Action➪All Tasks➪Backup Database to bring up the SQL Server Backup dialog box.**

   Alternatively, you can right-click the database folder that you want in the tree and choose All Tasks➪Backup Database.

   Each method brings up a dialog box consisting of two tabs (General and Options) to allow you to enter the parameters and data relating to the backup (see Figure 11-4). The General tab appears by default.

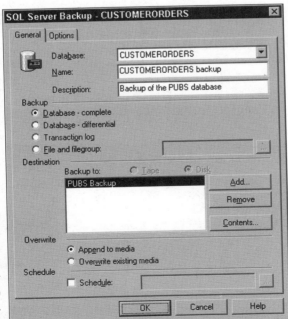

Figure 11-4:
The General tab of the SQL Server Backup dialog box.

You should also know that there is a Backup Wizard that guides you through the backup process. To use this wizard, enter the Enterprise Manager and click Tools⇨Wizards. Doing so brings up the Select Wizard dialog box. The Backup Wizard is located under the Management folder. Also, check out the flowcharts in Appendix A for more information on the Backup Wizard.

In addition, you can use the BACKUP Transact-SQL statement to backup your database. If you use this statement, you can also specify a password for the backup, thereby protecting your data if it sits on a networked file server.

Specifying general data about the backup

Use the General tab to specify general information about the backup — the minimum amount of data necessary — to begin the backup. (See "Specifying optional data about the backup," later in this section, to see the optional data you can specify about the backup.)

To specify general information about the data on the General tab, follow these steps:

1. **Type data in the fields.**

   - **Database:** Choose the database to back up. By default, the database that is selected when you bring up the SQL Server Backup dialog box is shown in the drop-down list. Because I chose the pubs database, pubs is listed in the Database field.

   - **Name:** Give your backup a name. By default, SQL Server enters the name of the database you choose, followed by the word backup. For example, if you choose the pubs database, SQL Server will enter pubs backup.

   - **Description:** This field is optional. You need to enter a description only if the value you typed in the Name field is not descriptive enough.

   - **Backup:** Choose the type of backup you want to perform. The available options are as follows:

     Database - Complete: Backs up all database objects in the current database, such as indexes, tables, and data. You'll want to use this option if you are concerned about being able to do a complete restore of the database in case it becomes corrupted. By default, this option is automatically selected.

     Database - Differential: Backs up only the changes made since the last complete backup.

Transaction Log: Backs up only the SQL Server transaction log. A *transaction log* is a log that SQL Server maintains automatically to know what operations have been performed on the SQL Server. This information allows a user or a process to roll back changes to a prior state, if necessary.

File and Filegroup: Allows you to break up a large database into separate files or groups of files. Click the . . . button to choose the file or filegroup name.

- **Destination:** Choose either the Tape or Disk option button. After you choose an option, click the Add button. Doing so allows you to add any device that has been previously set up or to specify a device (for tapes) or location (for files). By default, the Tape option is chosen if you have a tape drive on your server.

- **Overwrite:** Choose the type of action you want to perform. The available options are as follows:

  Append to Media: Appends data onto the end of the data already existing on the tape or disk. This is the default option selected.

  Overwrite Existing Media: Overwrites the data that already exists on the tape or disk.

2. **Specify a schedule by clicking the Schedule check box.**

   Make sure that the Schedule check box has a check mark in it (by clicking it) if you wish for the backup of your database to be on a specified schedule. After you click this check box, you can click the ellipsis button (. . .) to specify the scheduling options (see Figure 11-5).

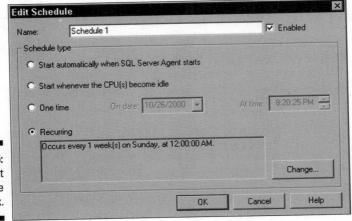

Figure 11-5:
The Edit
Schedule
dialog box.

If you create a schedule, SQL Server creates a job for you. For more information about jobs, see Chapter 14. You can specify from these options:

- **Name:** Give your schedule a name. By default, SQL Server enters Schedule 1.

- **Start Automatically When SQL Server Agent Starts:** Choose this option if you want your backup to begin every time you start the SQL Server Agent service.

- **Start Whenever the CPU(s) Become Idle:** Starts the job whenever the system processor(s) is not busy. If a very calculation-intensive query is running, there is no time for the job to run. This option enables you to perform periodic system processing without sacrificing CPU cycles for a user's query.

- **One Time:** Runs the job once, at a specified date and time. Choosing this option enables the On Date and At Time fields, allowing you to specify the date and time, respectively.

- **Recurring:** Runs the job on a recurring basis, at intervals that you specify. Because this is the most popular option for a job, it is selected by default. Also by default, the schedule runs once a week, on Sunday, at midnight. To change the Recurring option, click the Change button.

3. **Click OK to save data and begin the backup.**

   You can close the dialog box and begin the backup by clicking OK, or you can choose additional options (refer to the next section, "Specifying optional data about the backup").

Specifying optional data about the backup

Use the Options tab to specify additional data about the backup that isn't mandatory to begin the backup (see Figure 11-6).

To specify optional data on the Options tab, type information in the following fields.

Options

Choose the options you want. Check boxes are next to each option — you can choose any or all of these options. The available options are the following:

- **Verify Backup upon Completion:** I always choose this option. This option ensures that the data copied to the tape or disk is an exact copy of the original data, but it takes more time to verify than backing up alone.

- **Eject Tape After Backup:** Ejects the tape when the backup completes. This option is enabled only if you choose Tape Device under the Destination section on the General tab.

- **Remove Inactive Entries from Transaction Log:** Inactive transaction log entries will be removed before the backup takes place. This can happen if you do not set the Truncate Log on Checkpoint database option. If this option is not set, completed transactions will not be removed from the transaction log, but are no longer needed. Therefore, they should be removed before backing up. This option is enabled only if you choose Transaction Log under the Backup section on the General tab.

- **Check Media Set Name and Backup Set Expiration:** This option checks the Media Set Name and the expiration data listed in the After and On fields to determine whether it can be overwritten.

- **Backup Set Will Expire:** Designates when the backup will expire. After that time, it can be overwritten. This option is available only if you choose the Overwrite Existing Media option in the Overwrite section on the General tab. If you choose this option, you must select the number of days or a specific date the backup will expire. To do this, click the appropriate option button and type the data related to the number of days or a specific date you want the backup to expire on.

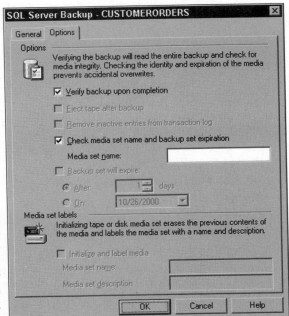

Figure 11-6:
The Options tab of the SQL Server Backup dialog box.

Media set labels

This section allows you to first initialize (delete) the media that you selected for backup. A media set is a way to group all the media used in a backup together. For example, a media set can be made up of five disk drives (in a striped array), or three tape drives. There are two fields that you must fill out if you choose this option. This option is not available unless you choose the Overwrite existing media option in the Overwrite section on the General tab.

- ✔ **Media Set Name:** Type the name of the media set. This will be used to check whether the data can be overwritten. The data typed in this field will be written to the tape or disk drive.

- ✔ **Media Set Description:** Type the description of the tape if the Media Set Name is not descriptive enough. The data typed in this field will be written to the tape or disk drive.

Click OK to save data and begin the backup.

Restoring Your Data

Backing up your data is an important safeguard against losing important data. But what if you need the data you have backed up? Restoring data is the only way to use the backed up data. To restore data from a backup (also referred to as a restore), follow these steps:

1. **Select Start➪Programs➪Microsoft SQL Server➪Enterprise Manager to start the SQL Server Enterprise Manager.**

2. **Expand the tree so that you see the Databases folder.**

   For more information about expanding the tree, see the Introduction of this book.

3. **Click the database you want to restore.**

4. **Choose Action➪All Tasks➪Restore Database to bring up the SQL Server Backup dialog box.**

   Alternatively, you can right-click the database folder that you want in the tree and choose All Tasks➪Restore Database.

   Each method brings up a dialog box consisting of two tabs (General and Options) to allow you to enter the parameters and data relating to restoring your data from backup (see Figure 11-7). The General tab appears by default.

You can use the RESTORE Transact-SQL statement to restore your data from a backup. If you use this statement, you can also specify a password, if one has been used during the backup. This protects your data if it sits on a networked file server.

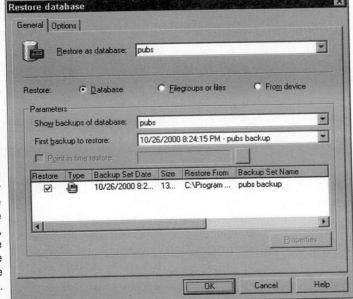

Figure 11-7:
The General
tab of the
SQL Server
Restore
Database
dialog box,
showing the
Database
restore
option.

Specifying general data about the restore

Use the General tab to specify general information about the restore — the minimum amount of data necessary — to begin the backup. (See "Specifying optional data about the restore," later in this section, to see the optional data you can specify about the restore.)

To specify general information about the restore on the General tab, type data or select from these fields:

- ✔ **Restore As Database:** Choose the database to restore into. The database that you choose to restore into does not have to be the same database that you backed up from. However, if you want to restore to a new database, you must type the name of the new database. It will automatically be created.

- ✔ **Restore:** Choose the type of restore that you want. Depending on the type of restore that you choose, the parameters section at the bottom of the screen will change. In all three types of restore operations, SQL Server knows what backups have been performed because it keeps track of the backups that have been made and stores them in the msdb database for later retrieval. You can choose from the following types of restore:

- **Database:** Choose this option if you want your restore to be an exact image of the way your database looked when you performed the backup (refer to Figure 11-7). I recommend this option. It is also the default option.

  If you choose this option, there are options that become enabled in the Parameters section. The first is Show Backups of Database. Choose from the list of databases to restore. Next is First Backup to Restore. Choose from the drop-down list of prior backups that you wish to restore. The third option is Point In Time Restore. Check this option if you want to restore your database as it was at a specific point in time. For example, you can restore a database to look the way it did on January 15, 1998 at 3:00 p.m. (assuming that you performed a backup at that time). After you check this option, the ellipsis button **(. . .)** becomes enabled, allowing you to change the time for the restore. The final option is a grid that shows a list of available backups to restore. Ensure that there is a check mark in the first column for each backup you want to restore.

- **Filegroups or Files:** Choose this option if you want to restore one or more specific filegroups or files (see Figure 11-8).

  If you choose this option, options in the Parameters section become enabled. The first is Show Backups of Database. Choose from the list of databases to restore. The next option is Select a Subset of Backup Sets. Check this option if you want to restore only a *subset* of a prior backup. A *subset* of a backup is any part of the complete backup. If you check this option, the Selection Criteria button becomes enabled, allowing you to select the criteria that defines the subset. The last option is a grid that shows a list of available backups to restore. Ensure that a check mark is in the first column for each backup you wish to restore.

- **From Device:** Choose this option if you wish to restore the data exactly as it is stored on a device that you have already configured (see Figure 11-9). If you choose this option, several options become enabled in the Parameters section.

  The first is the list of previously configured devices. Select the devices to restore by clicking the Select Devices button and choosing the desired backup devices. After they are selected, these devices will appear in the list. The next option is the Backup Number. Enter the number of the backup you wish to restore. The first backup is number 1, the second is number 2, and so on. If you want to be sure that you are selecting the correct backup, click the View Contents button to view the contents of the selected backup.

  Next is Restore Backup Set. You can choose from among Database - Complete, Database - Differential, Transaction Log, or File or Filegroup.

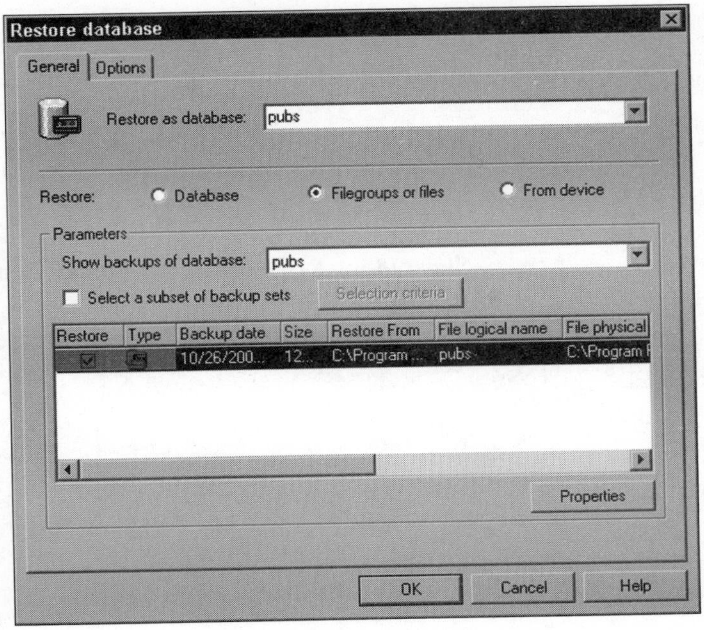

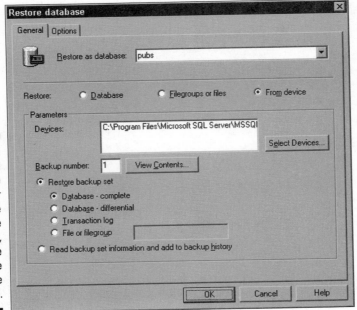

Figure 11-8:
The General
tab of the
SQL Server
Restore
Database
dialog box,
showing the
Filegroups
or Files
restore
option.

Figure 11-9:
The General
tab of the
SQL Server
Restore
Database
dialog box,
showing the
From Device
restore
option.

The last option is Read Backup Set Information and Add to Backup History. If you choose this option, every backup set stored on the backup will be restored. Therefore, you do not need to specify a specific backup set.

Specifying optional data about the restore

Use the Options tab to specify additional data about the restore that isn't mandatory to begin the backup (see Figure 11-10).

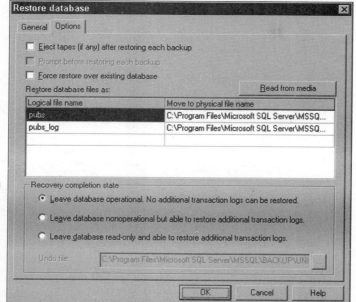

Figure 11-10:
The Options tab of the SQL Server Restore Database dialog box.

To specify optional data on the Options tab, select from the following options:

- ✔ **Eject Tapes (If Any) After Restoring Each Backup:** Check this option if you want your tapes to be ejected after each backup. Your tape drive(s) must have the capability to eject a tape for this option to work.

- ✔ **Prompt Before Restoring Each Backup:** Check this option if you want to be prompted before restoring each backup in a backup set.

✔ **Force Restore Over Existing Database:** Check this option if you want to overwrite an existing database with the data that was backed up.

✔ **Restore Database Files As:** This grid lists all original filenames for databases and transaction logs, as well as the filenames that they will be restored to. You can change the filenames and/or locations that the files are restored to. To do so, simply click the desired file name in the grid and type the desired filename.

✔ **Leave Database Operational. No Additional Transaction Logs Can Be Restored:** This option is chosen by default. While the restore is being completed, the database is left in an operational state. This is very useful when you are taking the server offline in order to bring a standby server online.

✔ **Leave Database Nonoperational, but Able to Restore Additional Transaction Logs:** While the restore is being completed, the database is left in a nonoperational state. This state allows for the transaction logs to be restored, but no other user can access the database.

✔ **Leave Database Read-Only and Able to Restore Additional Transaction Logs:** While the restore is being completed, the database is left in an operational state, but users cannot write any data to the database. It is read-only. This state allows for the transaction logs to be restored and users to have limited access to the database. This option is generally used on a standby server to keep it in sync with the primary server. If you choose this option, you can then choose an undo file, which allows the system to automatically undo (or roll back) the restore of a transaction log, if it needs to be rolled back.

You No Longer Have to Ship Your Logs by UPS!

Okay, bad joke, but SQL Server 2000 has a great new feature called log shipping. SQL Server 2000 now includes the ability to automatically backup the transaction log and send it to another database in real time. What does this do for you, you might ask? Well it lets you have a standby server ready and waiting in case your primary server(s) fail.

I mention log shipping here because it is a form of backup, but it is administered using the Enterprise Manager by using the Database Maintenance Plan Wizard. This wizard is covered in Chapter 15.

Chapter 12

So You Want to Be Published?

In This Chapter

▶ Publishing your data

▶ Using the Microsoft SQL Server 2000 Web Assistant

▶ Accessing your published data

▶ Replicating data to another database

Data publishing may sound like a difficult, drawn-out undertaking. Actually, the process isn't that overwhelming. SQL Server 2000 does all the work. Publishing data takes two forms. The first is to publish your data to an HTML Web page. This is very easy. The second is to publish data to another server. The latter is more complex. I cover each of these in this chapter.

Publishing Web Data

Publishing Web data refers to creating an HTML Web page that contains your data in an HTML table. To view the data, you need a browser that supports HTML tables, such as Microsoft Internet Explorer.

Are you an experienced creator of HTML? If you've been there and done that, great! If you're just starting out, not to worry — the Microsoft SQL Server 2000 Web Assistant does everything for you.

If you want to know even more about HTML, check out the *For Dummies* array of titles on the topic, including *HTML For Dummies,* 3rd Edition, by Ed Tittel and Stephen N. James (IDG Books Worldwide, Inc.).

Harnessing the power of the Microsoft SQL Server 2000 Web Assistant

The Microsoft SQL Server 2000 Web Assistant is a wizard that's designed to help you get published — that is, to publish your Web pages. Your Web pages are generated from HTML, but, with the generous help of the Assistant, you don't need to know anything about HTML. Just follow these steps:

1. **Choose Start⇨Programs⇨Microsoft SQL Server⇨Enterprise Manager to start the Enterprise Manager.**

2. **Expand the tree so that you see the name of your server and click either the name of the server or any tree item below the server name.**

    If you need more information about expanding the tree, see the Introduction of this book.

3. **Bring up the Select Wizard dialog box by choosing Tools⇨Wizards.**

4. **Click the Web Assistant Wizard (under the Management folder) and click OK to start the wizard.**

    The Microsoft SQL Server Web Assistant welcome dialog box presents a synopsis of what the wizard can do for you. Click Next when you're ready to move on. To help you understand the logic flow of this wizard, refer to the flowchart diagram in Appendix A. Because the way a dialog box is presented is based upon the options you choose in prior steps, you may want to refer to this flowchart as you go through the rest of this chapter.

5. **Click the name of the database that you want data published from in the Databases name drop-down list; then click Next.**

6. **Specify job information (see Figure 12-1) and then click Next.**

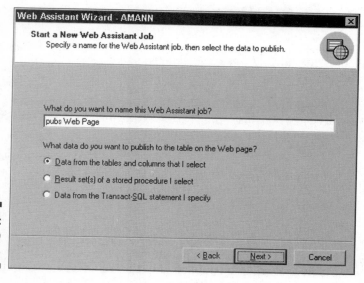

Figure 12-1:
Fill in job
information.

Publishing data is performed by creating a job. For more information about creating jobs, see Chapter 14. This step allows you to configure the job information.

You can enter data and choose from these fields:

- **What Do You Want to Name This Web Assistant Job?:** Type the name of your job. By default, SQL Server enters the name of your database, followed by `Web Page`. In my example, the name `pubs Web Page` is automatically entered.

- **Data from the Tables and Columns That I Select:** Select this option if you want to specify the tables and columns for HTML Web publication. This option is chosen by default.

- **Result Set(s) of a Stored Procedure I Select:** Select this option if you want to indicate a specific stored procedure, the results of which will be contained in the HTML Web publication.

- **Data from the Transact-SQL Statement I Specify:** Select this option if you want to enter a SQL statement directly, the results of which will be contained in the HTML Web publication.

Because so many options are available in the Web Assistant Wizard, I supplement the numbered steps with the letters a, b, and c. The reason that I do this is not to confuse you, but rather to clarify. The letters indicate that different dialog boxes are presented at a specific step number, based on options that you choose. Please take a few minutes to see the diagram in Appendix A to see what I mean. In other words, the option that you choose in this step will dictate the screens that you see using the rest of this wizard.

7a. **In the Select a Table and Columns dialog box, specify a table and columns; then click Next.**

You can publish from one table and multiple columns. This step is available only if you chose the Data from the Tables and Columns That I Select option.

You can enter data and choose from these fields:

- **Available Tables:** Choose the desired table from the drop-down list of available tables. These are all the tables in the database chosen earlier.

- **Table Columns:** Choose the desired columns of data to publish to the Web. You may choose one or more columns by clicking the desired columns and clicking the Add button. You can also click choose all the columns by clicking the Add All button.

- **Selected Columns:** This list shows all the columns in the chosen table that are to be published to the Web. If you want to remove any of the columns, click the desired columns and click the Remove button.

8a. In the Select Rows dialog box, specify how rows are to be limited; then click Next.

You can opt to limit the number of rows to be published to the Web. This step is available only if you chose the Data from the Tables and Columns That I Select option.

You can enter data and choose from these fields:

- **All of the Rows:** Choose this option if you do not want to limit the number of rows that are published to the Web. This option is selected by default.

- **Only Those Rows That Meet the Following Criteria:** Choose this option if you want to limit the number of rows that are published to the Web, based on criteria that you specify. If you choose this option, the fields that allow you to specify that criteria become enabled. For example, you can choose to publish all authors with a last name beginning with letter *M*. (Where do you think I got that example from?)

- **Only Those Rows That Qualify using the following Transact-SQL WHERE Clause:** Choose this option if you want to limit the number of rows that are published to the Web, based on a SQL WHERE clause that you specify. If you choose this option, the text box that allows you to specify that SQL WHERE clause becomes enabled. For more information about SQL or a WHERE clause, see Chapter 8.

7b. In the Select Stored Procedure dialog box, specify a stored procedure and click the Next button when you are finished with this step.

Whatever columns of data have been specified in the stored procedure that you select will be published to the Web. This step is available only if you chose the Result Set(s) of a Stored Procedure I Select option.

To select a stored procedure, simply click the desired stored procedure from the Stored Procedures list box.

8b. Specify Stored Procedure Parameters and then click Next.

After you have chosen a stored procedure, you are prompted in this step to enter values for the parameters of that stored procedure. This step is available only if you chose the Result Set(s) of a Stored Procedure I Select option.

For each parameter defined in the stored procedure, you must specify a value if there is no default value indicated in the stored procedure itself. The parameters and data are shown in a grid. Simply click the cell in the grid for each Value you want to enter. Then type in the Value. Continue doing this for every parameter.

7c. Enter your SQL statement; click Next when you are finished with this step.

Type the SQL necessary to return a result set that you want to publish to the Web. This step is available only if you chose the Data from the Transact-SQL Statement I Specify option. After you enter a SQL statement, the Next button becomes enabled.

9. **In the Schedule the Web Assistant Job dialog box, specify the updating and generating schedule; then click Next.**

   After you have defined the record set that is to be published (in Steps 7a and 8a, 7b and 8b, or 7c), you must schedule the job for the Web Assistant to publish the data.

   You can enter data and choose from these fields:

   - **Only One Time, When I Complete This Wizard:** Choose this option if you want the Web Assistant to create the HTML page when the wizard is finished. This option is chosen by default.

   - **On Demand:** Choose this option if you want to create and update your HTML page only when you manually run the job named in Step 7.

   - **Only One Time At:** Choose this option if you want the Web Assistant to schedule a date and time to create the HTML page. However, this job runs only once. If you click this option, text boxes are enabled that allow you to type the date and time desired to run the job.

   - **When the SQL Server Data Changes:** Choose this option if you want the Web Assistant to regenerate the HTML page every time the data changes. This makes for a dynamic solution.

Just because I say this is a dynamic solution does not mean that you are using Dynamic HTML, or *DHTML*. DHTML is HTML that is dynamically determined at the time the Web page is viewed in a browser. The HTML generated here is static text. The data from the table is actually placed in the HTML file. I mention this as being a dynamic solution because the job can regularly run, thereby recreating the HTML with updated data.

   - **At Regularly Scheduled Intervals:** Choose this option if you want the Web Assistant to regenerate the HTML page at intervals that you specify in a later step. This makes for a dynamic solution. (See my earlier note about dynamic HTML!)

   - **Generate a Web Page When the Wizard Is Completed:** Uncheck this check box if you want only to schedule the job and not to create an initial HTML page. This check box is disabled if you choose the Only One Time, When I Complete this Wizard option.

10a. **In the Monitor a Table and Columns dialog box, specify a table and columns to monitor and then click Next when you are finished with this step.**

   You can indicate to SQL Server which columns in a table should be monitored for changes. When these changes are detected, your HTML page is automatically regenerated. This step is available only if you chose the When the SQL Server Data Changes option.

You can enter data and choose from these fields:

- **Available Tables:** Choose the desired table from the drop-down list of available tables. These are all the tables in the database chosen earlier.

- **Table Columns:** Choose the desired columns of data to publish to the Web. You must choose each column one at a time. To do so, click the desired table and click the Add button. Also, you can click the Add All button to select every column in the chosen table to be monitored.

- **Columns to Monitor:** This list shows all the columns in the chosen table that are to be monitored for changes. If you want to remove any of the columns, click the desired table and click the Remove button.

10b. In the Schedule the Update Interval dialog box, specify the update interval and then click Next to continue.

Specify the conditions of the update interval. This step is available only if you chose the At Regularly Scheduled Intervals option.

You can enter data and choose from these fields:

- **Every:** Type the value in the text box that represents the frequency of your desired update schedule. For example, if you want the schedule to run every other day, enter a **2** in this field. 1 is entered by default.

- **Weeks:** Choose this option if you want the schedule to run every x number of weeks, where x is the value in the Every text box. This option is chosen by default.

- **Days:** Choose this option if you want the schedule to run every x number of days, where x is the value in the Every text box.

- **Hours:** Choose this option if you want the schedule to run every x number of hours, where x is the value in the Every text box.

- **Minutes:** Choose this option if you want the schedule to run every x number of minutes, where x is the value in the Every text box.

- **Days of Week:** Check the desired days of the week that you want the schedule to run. You can check any or all of the check boxes to represent the desired days of the week.

- **Start Date and Time:** Enter into the Date and Time text boxes the desired date and time for the update interval to begin. For example, if you want the schedule to run every day but not start until midnight on January 1, 2001, you enter that date and time here.

11. In the Publish the Web Page dialog box, specify the filename of the HTML page to be generated and click Next.

The HTML page that you specify must be a path that can be written by SQL Server. For example, if the security on SQL Server does not allow access to `C:\HTML`, SQL Server can't write the file there. By default, the filename is a sequential filename, named WebPage*x*.htm in the Tools\ HTML subdirectory of wherever you installed SQL Server 2000, where *x* is the sequential number.

Type the desired HTML file into the File Name text box.

12. **Specify the format of the Web page and click Next.**

    You can have the Web Assistant Wizard help you with the formatting of the Web page, or you can choose from an existing template. The format will be derived from this template. You can choose from these fields:

    - **Yes, Help Me Format the Web Page:** Choose this option if you want the Web Assistant Wizard to guide you through formatting the Web page.

    - **No, Use the Template File From:** Choose this option if you are going to use a template HTML file that already contains formatting. After you choose this option, the text box becomes enabled, allowing you to select or type the HTML template file. To browse for the file, click the . . . button.

    - **Use Character Set:** Choose from the possible character sets installed on the server to generate the Web page. Most likely, Unicode (UTF-8) is shown by default.

13. **In the Specify Titles dialog box, specify title information used in the Web page and click Next to continue.**

    Specify the information used to generate the HTML title. This step is available only if you chose the Yes, Help Me Format the HTML Page option. If you don't choose this option, jump to Step 16 that follows.

    You can enter data and choose from these fields:

    - **What Do You Want to Title the Web Page?:** Enter into the text box provided the title that you want to use for your Web page. You may want to enter something that is germane to the result set returned from the query. You can enter something like **All Authors with the Last Name Beginning with 'M'**. By default, SQL Server enters Microsoft SQL Server Web Assistant. Obviously, this does you no good! I suggest that you rename the title.

    - **What Do You Want to Title the HTML Table That Contains the Data?:** Within the HTML page, SQL Server generates an HTML table for the data itself. Enter into the text box provided the title that you want to use for this table. By default, SQL Server enters Query Results. This is an acceptable table title, although you can change it if you want. The title will be displayed on the title bar of the browser that contains the HTML page.

- **What Size Should the HTML Table Title Font Be?:** Click the plus (+) or minus (–) buttons to increase or decrease the size of the HTML table title font. By default, the HTML table title font size is H3.

- **Apply a Time and Date Stamp to the Web Page:** Choose this check box if you want the time and date of creation to be placed on the Web page. This check box is not selected by default.

14. **In the Format a Table dialog box, specify HTML Table formatting information and then click Next.**

   This step allows you to indicate how you want the HTML table to be formatted. This step is available only if you chose the Yes, Help Me Format the HTML Page option. If you don't choose this option, jump to Step 16 that follows.

   You can enter data and choose from these fields:

   - **Yes, Display Column Names:** Choose this option if you want your HTML table to include the names of the columns you chose. This option is chosen by default.

   - **No, Display Data Only:** Choose this option if you don't want your HTML table to include the names of the columns you chose.

   - **Fixed:** Choose this option if you want the font displayed in the table to be a fixed size. This means that every character is the same width. For example, a *W* is the same width as an *I*. Fixed size can be easier to read for result sets because all the characters line up nicely. This option is chosen by default.

   - **Proportional:** Choose this option if you want the font displayed in the table to be a proportional size. This means that every character is as wide as it needs to be. For example, a *W* is wider than an *I*.

   - **Bold:** Choose this check box if you want all the data in the HTML table to be bold. The data in the HTML table can also be italic at the same time.

   - **Italic:** Choose this check box if you want all the data in the HTML table to be italic. The data in the HTML table can also be bold at the same time.

   - **Draw Border Lines around the HTML Table:** Choose this check box if you want all the data in the HTML table to be encompassed by a border. This formatting sometimes makes the data easier to read because it doesn't "float" in the middle of your Web page. This option is chosen by default.

15. **In the Add Hyperlinks to the Web Page dialog box, specify whether to add hyperlinks to your Web page; click Next when you finish with this step.**

This step allows you to indicate whether you want to show hyperlinks to other Web pages in the newly created Web page. This step is available only if you chose the Yes, Help Me Format the HTML Page option. If you don't choose this option, jump to Step 16 that follows.

You can enter data and choose from these fields:

- **No:** Choose this option if you do not want additional hyperlinks to other Web pages added to your Web page. This option is chosen by default.

- **Yes, Add One Hyperlink:** Choose this option if you want to add only one hyperlink to another Web page. After you choose this option, two text boxes become enabled, allowing for you to type the hyperlink data. These text boxes are Hyperlink URL and Hyperlink Label. *URL* stands for Uniform Resource Locator. It is the standard Web address. Additionally, you can specify a label for the URL, such as Visit Our Web Site.

- **Yes, Add a List of Hyperlink URLs. Select them from a SQL Server Table with the Following SQL Statement:** Choose this option if you want to add more than one hyperlink to another Web page. After you choose this option, the text box to specify your SQL statement becomes enabled.

  This option can also be used for one hyperlink that is retrieved from the database with your SQL statement. You don't have to choose the Yes, Add One Hyperlink option.

16. **In the Limit Rows dialog box, specify how to limit data rows and then click Next.**

    This step allows you to not only limit the number of rows returned by SQL Server but also to limit the number of rows displayed in the HTML table.

    You can enter data and choose from these fields:

    - **No, Return All Rows of Data:** Choose this option if you do not want the number of rows returned by SQL Server to be limited. This option is chosen by default.

    - **Yes:** Choose this option if you do want the number of rows returned by SQL Server to be limited. After you choose this option, a text box becomes enabled, allowing you to specify the maximum number of rows to be returned. For example, you might want to show only the first 100 rows.

    - **No, Put All Data in One Scrolling Page:** Choose this option if you want the size of the HTML page to be as large as necessary to hold all the data in the HTML table.

- **Yes, Link the Successive Pages Together:** Choose this option if you want the size of the HTML page to be limited, based on the number of rows that you specify per page. After you choose this option, a text box becomes enabled, allowing you to specify the number of maximum rows to be included in the HTML table per page. For example, you may want to show only 50 rows in the HTML table per page.

17. **Complete the Microsoft SQL Server Web Assistant Wizard by reviewing your choices in the text box provided; then click Finish.**

    Also, you can save the Transact-SQL statement generated by the wizard to a file. To do so, click the Write Transact-SQL to File button and type the filename under which to save the generated SQL.

    If you want to change any of the criteria that you specified in an earlier step, click the Back button until you reach the desired step to change.

Accessing your published data

After you create your Web page using the Web Assistant Wizard, you can access two things. One is the job that you created while using the wizard; the other is the actual HTML page. I show both in the following sections.

Accessing the Web Assistant job

You can access through the Enterprise Manager all jobs created with the Web Assistant Wizard. These jobs will be created only if you have scheduled the publication in the Web Assistant Wizard. To access the Web Assistant jobs, follow these steps.

1. **Choose the Start⇨Programs⇨Microsoft SQL Server⇨Enterprise Manager to start the SQL Server Enterprise Manager.**

2. **Expand the tree so that you see the name of your server and then the Jobs folder under the Management folder; select it.**

    For more information about expanding the tree, see the Introduction of this book.

    Selecting the Jobs folder populates a list of jobs already created on the right part of the screen. The right part of the screen shows the name of your job, and other bits of data relating to the status of the job.

3. **View the Job Properties by right-clicking the desired job on the right part of the screen and selecting the Properties menu option.**

    For more information about jobs, see Chapter 14.

Accessing the HTML page

Accessing the HTML page is quite simple. You do this with a Web browser that supports tables, such as the Microsoft Internet Explorer. To access the HTML page, follow these steps.

1. **Start the browser.**

   If you would like to use Microsoft Internet Explorer, choose Start⇨ Programs⇨Internet Explorer.

2. **Choose File⇨Open to open the HTML file.**

   This action brings up a dialog box, allowing you to enter or specify your HTML file. You must know the name and location of the HTML file created by the Web Assistant Wizard. The default is the Tools\HTML subdirectory of wherever you installed SQL Server 2000 (see Figure 12-2).

If you want to view the HTML that made up the Web page, click View⇨Source. This action brings up the HTML code in the default editor registered on your system, such as Notepad.

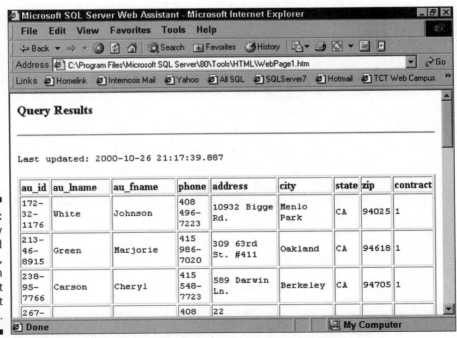

Figure 12-2: The newly created HTML file, as shown in Microsoft Internet Explorer 5.

Microsoft SQL Server Web Assistant - Microsoft Internet Explorer

File   Edit   View   Favorites   Tools   Help

Back ▾ ⇒ ▾ ⊗ ▣ ⌂ | Search Favorites History | ▾ ▾ ▾ ▾

Address ▤ C:\Program Files\Microsoft SQL Server\80\Tools\HTML\WebPage1.htm ▾ | Go

Links ▤Homelink ▤Internosis Mail ▤Yahoo ▤All SQL ▤SQLServer7 ▤Hotmail ▤TCT Web Campus »

Query Results

Last updated: 2000-10-26 21:17:39.887

au_id	au_lname	au_fname	phone	address	city	state	zip	contract
172-32-1176	White	Johnson	408 496-7223	10932 Bigge Rd.	Menlo Park	CA	94025	1
213-46-8915	Green	Marjorie	415 986-7020	309 63rd St. #411	Oakland	CA	94618	1
238-95-7766	Carson	Cheryl	415 548-7723	589 Darwin Ln.	Berkeley	CA	94705	1
267-			408	22				

Done   My Computer

Publishing to Another Computer

Publishing your data to another computer is more complex than publishing data to the Web. It involves some concepts that you must understand first. These concepts can be likened to a subscription that you have to a magazine. All these concepts together describe *replication*. The concepts are centered around the following terms:

Publisher: The computer that stores the written publication. The publisher wants to give the publication to the distributor so that it can be given to a subscriber. The publisher may or may not know about who is going to subscribe to the publication.

Distributor: Receives a publication from a publisher and gives it to authorized subscribers. If you don't subscribe to a magazine, you don't expect to receive it, do you? It may seem as though the distributor is not necessary. This may be true, but it is required in the replication model. However, a computer can be a Publisher/Distributor at the same time.

Subscriber: The computer that intends to receive the publication from the distributor.

Article: The smallest unit of data available in a publication. A publication is made up of one or more articles.

Regardless of which computer is the publisher, distributor, or subscriber, there is other terminology, that you might already be aware of, which indicates who is controlling the flow of data:

Push: Data is pushed by the publisher to the distributor and initiated by the publisher. Data can also be pushed by the distributor to the subscriber and initiated by the distributor. This is a typical paradigm when you receive informative (or not-so-informative) e-mails.

Pull: Data is pulled from the publisher to the distributor and initiated by the distributor. Data can also be pulled by the subscriber from the distributor and initiated by the subscriber. This paradigm basically indicates "give me what I want when I want it, but only when I ask for it."

Also, three different types of publications can be available in SQL Server 2000:

Transactional: Publication is updated in near real-time from the distributor to the subscriber.

Merge: Publication is updated upon a specific schedule, but changes can be made by either the distributor or the subscriber. The merge agent, which controls replication, handles the merging of data.

Snapshot: Publication is updated upon a specific schedule, but changes can be made only by the publisher. A snapshot is taken of the data at this time. The subscriber can pull this data from the distributor whenever he/she wants.

All these terms come together by using a couple of wizards that come with SQL Server 2000. This may seem a little confusing, so take your time.

Configuring publishers, distributors, and subscribers

Publishers, distributors, and subscribers are configured using the Configure Publishing and Distribution Wizard. Follow these steps to use the wizard:

1. **Choose Start⇨Programs⇨Microsoft SQL Server⇨Enterprise Manager to start the Enterprise Manager (refer back to Figure 12-1).**

2. **Expand the tree so that you see the name of your server and click either the name of the server or any tree item below the server name.**

   If you need more information about expanding the tree, see the Introduction of this book.

3. **Bring up the Configure Publishing and Distribution Wizard dialog box by choosing Tools⇨Replication⇨Configure Publishing, Subscribers, and Distribution.**

   The Configure Publishing and Distribution Wizard welcome dialog box presents a synopsis of what the wizard can do for you. Click Next when you're ready to move on.

4. **Select which computer will be the distributor; then click Next.**

   You can choose from these fields:

   - **Make *x* Its Own Distributor; SQL Server Will Create a Distribution Database and Log:** Select this option if you want your computer to be the distributor. *x* will be the name of the server that you are running the wizard on. You will find many times that you want the publisher and distributor to be on the same computer. This option is chosen by default.

   When you installed SQL Server 2000, you selected an account for use by the SQL Server services. If you chose the local system account, replication will not work. You must adjust the login accounts so that replication uses an account that can be accessed throughout, and possibly across, your domain.

- **Use the Following Server, Which Has Already Been Configured as a Distributor:** Select this option if you want to use another computer as a distributor. This other computer must have already been configured as a distributor to use this option.

5. **Customize your configuration and click Next.**

   Indicate whether you want to change some of the automatic defaults or customize the configuration. You can choose from these fields:

   - **Yes, Let Me Set the Distribution Database Properties, Enable Publishers, or Set Publishing Settings:** Select this option if you want to change the default options (see the next description in this list). Many times, you do not need to use this option.

   - **No, Use the Following Default Settings:** Select this option if you want to use all the default settings, chosen by the wizard. Most of the time, this option is the one you need. This option is selected by default. The default settings are as follows:

   - Configure the current server as a publisher and a distributor

   - Configure all registered servers in the Enterprise Manager to allow for subscriptions from the distributor.

   - Stores the distribution database and log file in the data directory of wherever you installed SQL Server 2000 in a database called `Distribution`.

6. **Complete the Configure Publishing and Distribution Wizard by reviewing your choices in the text box provided; then click Finish.**

   If you want to change any of the criteria that you specified in an earlier step, click the Back button until you reach the desired step to change. After you click Finish, you will be all set up for publishing and distribution.

Configuring publications

Now that you have configured publishers and distributors, you need to publish something. Otherwise, what's the point in configuring those things? You configure publications using (what else?) the Create Publication Wizard. Follow these steps to use the wizard:

1. **Choose Start➪Programs➪Microsoft SQL Server➪Enterprise Manager to start the Enterprise Manager (shown in previous figure, Figure 12-1).**

2. **Expand the tree so that you see the name of your server and click either the name of the server or any tree item below the server name.**

If you need more information about expanding the tree, see the Introduction of this book.

3. **Bring up the Create Publication Wizard dialog box by clicking Tools⇨ Replication⇨Create and Manage Publications and clicking the Create Publication button.**

   The Create Publication Wizard welcome dialog box presents a synopsis of what the wizard can do for you. Click Next when you're ready to create your publication.

4. **Choose the publication database; then click Next.**

   Select the database to create the publication from in the listbox provided. You can choose only one database.

5. **Select a publication type; then click Next.**

   For a description of these options, see the definitions at the beginning of this section. You can choose from these fields:

   • **Snapshot Publication:** This option uses the least server resources but is not necessarily up-to-date. This option is selected by default.

   • **Transactional Publication**: This option uses the most server resources because it has to maintain transactional integrity. Updates can be made only by the publisher, not the subscriber. For more information about transactions, see Chapter 3.

   • **Merge Publication:** This option uses a moderate amount of server resources and merges only changes made to data. Data can be changed by either the publisher or subscriber.

6. **Specify the Subscriber Type(s); then click Next.**

   Choose the types of subscribers that will possibly be subscribing to the publication. There are some new options available in SQL Server 2000 that won't be used if you select any option other than SQL Server 2000. You can select one or more options. Choose from these options:

   • **Servers Running SQL Server 2000:** This option is selected by default.

   • **Servers Running SQL Server version 7.0:** Selecting this option ensures that new replication features of SQL Server 2000 are not used for SQL Server 7 databases.

   • **Heterogeneous Data Sources, Such as Oracle or Microsoft Access; or Servers Running Earlier Versions of SQL Server:** Replication was not available prior to SQL Server version 7.0, so earlier versions are lumped into the "other" category.

7. **Specify article(s) to publish (see Figure 12-3); then click Next.**

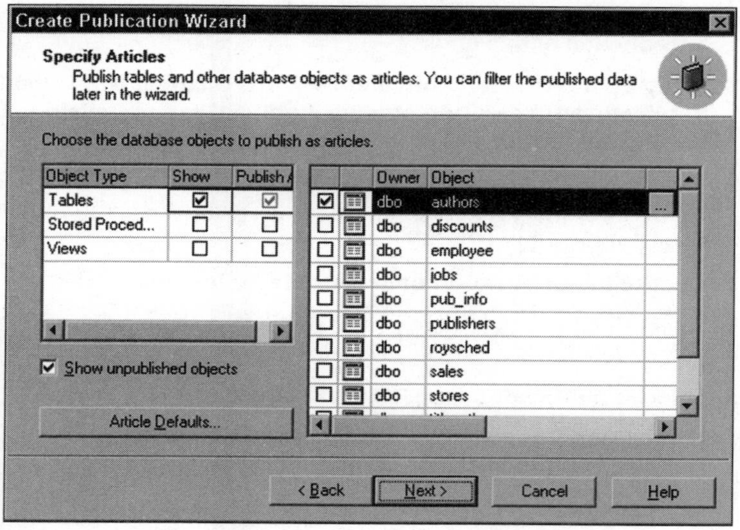

Figure 12-3:
Specifying
which
article(s) to
publish.

Choose the article(s) that you want to publish. Articles are data that is stored or made available in tables, stored procedures, and views. You will filter, or limit, the data that is returned in a later step. This step shows two grids; one on the left and one on the right. Although they are not labeled, the one on the left controls the objects that you can see or those that are selected in the right grid. In this step, you can select from these fields:

- **Show:** Select this check box once for each row in the left grid for the type of object that you want to view in the right grid.

- **Publish All:** Select this check box if you want to publish all articles for the object type shown in the first column of the grid. If you select this option, you will see checks placed in the appropriate cells in the right grid.

- **(blank check box):** In the right grid, check each check box for the adjacent object(s) that you want to publish.

- **Show Unpublished Objects:** Check this box if you want to see all objects that have not already been published in the right grid. This option is checked by default.

- **Article Defaults:** Click this button if you want to change the default configuration and properties individually for tables, stored procedures, or views. Because this is a very advanced option, I do not cover it in this book.

8. **Specify the Publication Name and Description; then click Next.**

Enter the name and description that you would like to use for the articles specified for your publication. Enter or select data from these fields:

- **Publication Name:** Enter the name of your publication. This name will be visible for all enabled subscribers, so name your publication accordingly. By default, the chosen database is the name of your publication.

- **Publication Description:** Enter the description of your publication. Again, this will be visible for all enabled subscribers, so make sure to be explicit enough if the name is not obvious as to the articles contained in the publication.

- **List This Publication in the Active Directory:** Select this check box if you want the publication to be listed in the Active Directory. This option allows for a query to be made across the entire enterprise to determine which publications are available on the network. This option is not checked by default.

9. **Customize your configuration; then click Next.**

   Indicate whether you want to change some of the automatic defaults or customize the configuration. You can choose from these fields:

   - **Yes, I Will Define Data Filters, Enable Anonymous Subscriptions, or Customize Other Properties:** Select this option if you want to change the default options (see the next description in this list). Many times, you do not need to use this option.

   - **No, Create the Publication As Specified:** Select this option if you want to use all the default settings chosen by the wizard. Most of the time, this option is the one you need. This option is selected by default. The default settings are as follows:

   - No filters will be applied. Every row of data in the table or view will be available in the article(s). A stored procedure may already limit the data, based on the nature of a stored procedure.

   - Anonymous subscribers will not be allowed. Each subscriber must be explicitly configured.

10. **Complete the Create Publication Wizard by reviewing your choices in the text box provided and then click Finish.**

    If you want to change any of the criteria that you specified in an earlier step, click the Back button until you reach the desired step to change. After you click Finish, you will be all set up to publish articles. However, be aware that your articles may not be published until a specific time. Read the review box carefully.

Subscribing to articles

Earlier, you configured publishers and distributors. You also published articles. So, how do you get them? You need to subscribe to them. How do you do that? Again, you use a trusty wizard. You subscribe to articles using the Pull Subscription Wizard. Follow these steps to use the wizard:

1. **Choose Start➪Programs➪Microsoft SQL Server➪Enterprise Manager to start the Enterprise Manager.**

2. **Expand the tree so that you see the name of your server and click either the name of the server or any tree item below the server name.**

   If you need more information about expanding the tree, see the Introduction of this book.

3. **Bring up the Pull Subscription Wizard dialog box by choosing Tools➪ Replication➪Pull Subscriptions and clicking the Pull New Subscription button.**

   The Pull Subscription Wizard welcome dialog box presents a synopsis of what the wizard can do for you. Click Next when you're ready to subscribe to your publication.

4. **Look for Available Publications (see Figure 12-4); then click Next.**

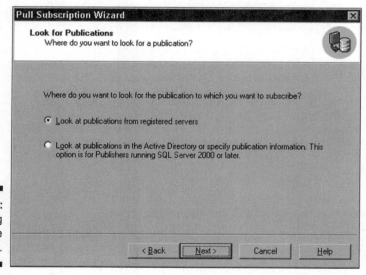

Figure 12-4: Searching for available publications.

Indicate whether you want to change some of the automatic defaults or customize the configuration. You can choose from these fields:

- **Look at Publications from Registered Servers:** Select this option to search for publications from all servers that are registered in the Enterprise Manager. This option is selected by default. For my example, I choose this option.

- **Look at Publications in the Active Directory or Specify Publication Information:** Select this option if you want to read the active directory or specify the publication you want to subscribe to from a SQL Server 2000 database.

5. **Choose a publication; then click Next.**

   Drill-down on the desired registered server to see a list of available publications. Click the desired publication and click Next.

6. **Specify Synchronization Agent Login; then click Next.**

   To subscribe to a publication, you must log into the server. Therefore, you must choose from these options:

   - **Impersonate the SQL Server Agent Account:** Select this option if you want to use the account that was specified on the distribution server for the SQL Server Agent. As long as this account was not specified as the local system account, this option should be fine. This option is also selected by default.

   - **Use SQL Server Authentication:** Select this option if you don't want to use the account specified for the distributor's SQL Server Agent Account. Chances are you won't need to use this option unless the SQL Server Agent account is configured to log in as the local system account.

7. **Choose the destination database and click Next.**

   This destination database is used to store the articles that you subscribe to. You can click the New button to create a new database to store your articles.

8. **Initialize the Subscription and click Next.**

   If you have never subscribed to this publication before, you must initialize the schema and data. This basically means that the structure of the database and table(s) will be created. Then the data will be copied.

9. **Indicate how to deliver the snapshot files and then click Next.**

   If you initialize your publication in the preceding step, you need to indicate where SQL Server will get the files for initialization. By default, the default snapshot folder will be used. Unless you have a lot of experience using replication, don't change this option.

10. **Set Distribution Agent Schedule; then click Next.**

    Indicate when the subscription be updated by clicking one of the following fields:

    - **Continuously:** Select this option if you want to provide close to real-time updates to the publication. This option uses the most server resources.

- **Using the Following Schedule:** Select this option if you want the publication to be updated at a schedule that you specify. This option is selected by default. Also by default, the schedule is to receive updates every five minutes. This option uses a moderate amount of server resources. To change the schedule, click the Change button.

- **On Demand Only:** Select this option if you want to control when the publication is synchronized with the distributor. This option uses the least server resources.

11. **Select the Required Services to Start and then click Next.**

    For a pull subscription to take place, SQL Server and SQL Server Agent services need to be started. If they are not started, this screen allows you to select the services that will be started. This screen is more of a confirmation screen because you have no choice if you want the subscription to succeed. By default, all services are checked. Click Next.

12. **Complete the Pull Subscription Wizard by reviewing your choices in the text box provided; then click Finish.**

    If you want to change any of the criteria that you specified in an earlier step, click the Back button until you reach the desired step to change. After you click Finish, data will be replicated from the distributor to the subscriber. However, be aware that your articles may not be available until a specific time, depending on how you scheduled the subscription. Read the review box carefully.

Chapter 13

Distributed Queries

· ·

In This Chapter

▶ Using linked data sources

▶ Accessing distributed data

▶ Understanding distributed transactions

· ·

Simply put, a distributed query is a query that accesses data from multiple data sources, located on multiple computers. In this chapter, I show you how to set up the server to allow for distributed queries and transactions. I also show you how to write queries that access data from multiple servers. I think you'll really enjoy this chapter.

Actually, a query that runs on the same computer but crosses databases is also considered to be a distributed query.

How Do Distributed Queries Work?

I break up the category of distributed queries into two separate subcategories that I term *distributed nontransactional* and *distributed transactional* queries. Distributed queries are easier to understand this way. Each type is described in the next two sections. For a review of the theory of transactions, refer to Chapter 3.

For distributed queries, you need to either set up a linked server or issue the type of query that allows you to specify server connection information at run time. The latter is called an *ad-hoc* server connection. You'll see later in this chapter how to do all of this.

Distributed nontransactional queries

A nontransactional distributed query is a query that needs to access data from one or more remote data sources but does not take part in a transaction.

An example of a nontransactional distributed query is simply a Transact-SQL SELECT statement that grabs data from multiple servers. The concept is quite simple. You'll see later in this chapter how this is done.

Distributed transactional queries

A distributed transactional query is just like any other type of distributed query except that it has to support transactions. Again, if you need a refresher on transactions, see Chapter 3. A distributed transaction is much more complicated than a nontransactional distributed query.

An example of a distributed transactional query is this scenario. You make an online purchase. When you make the purchase, the inventory database on Server A has to remove the item from inventory, and the record of the transaction must be recorded in the accounting database on Server B. Therefore, this transaction is distributed because it involves more than one server. It is transactional because you cannot afford to have the Accounting database to indicate that a purchase was made but fail to remove the inventory item from the inventory database.

For a distributed transactional query to function, you must have the Distributed Transaction Coordinator, or DTC, service running. To ensure that the DTC is running, open the Service Manager by choosing Start⇨Programs⇨ Microsoft SQL Server⇨Service Manager. Ensure that the service is running, as shown in Figure 13-1.

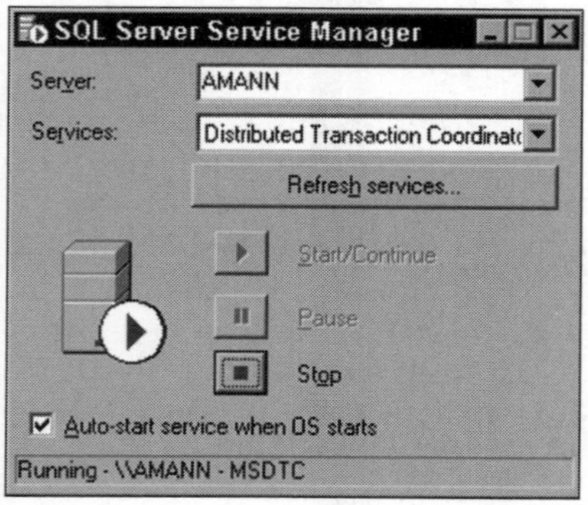

Figure 13-1: The SQL Server 2000 Service Manager, showing the running DTC service.

The DTC service is what communicates with remote data sources to handle the distributed query. The distributed queries function because of a concept called the two-phase commit.

Before the query is executed, the DTC sends a message to the remote computer(s) to let them know that a query is going to be sent. This allows the remote computer to do whatever is necessary to prepare to commit the request. This is called the *prepare phase*. In this phase, locks are acquired and all processing is performed, except that the transaction is not actually committed. The second phase of the two-phase commit is (not surprisingly) called the *commit phase*. This is when the DTC coordinates (through something called a resource manager) the actual committing of the data on each server.

The DTC Service does not need to be running to execute a distributed non-transactional query.

Transaction isolation levels

In Chapter 3, I cover the four different isolation levels available for SQL Server 2000 transactions. These isolation levels apply not only to standard transactions but also to distributed transactions. The DTC and the resource managers handle everything on the server's end to ensure that the isolation level chosen is carried out. That makes it very easy to change in your Transact-SQL queries.

To change the default isolation level of READ COMMITED, use the SET TRANSACTION ISOLATION LEVEL Transact-SQL statement. This statement takes one argument, which is one of the four possible isolation levels, READ COMMITTED, READ UNCOMMITTED, REPEATABLE READ, or SERIALIZABLE.

Here's an example of how you would set the isolation level to SERIALIZABLE (which would guarantee that there is no possibility of data loss):

```
SET TRANSACTION ISOLATION LEVEL SERIALIZABLE
```

Isn't that simple? That's all there is to it. After you set the isolation level, it remains set for the duration of the user's session (also known as the connection).

You should also know that the isolation level can be specified temporarily for a single query by using a hint. I briefly mention locking hints in Chapter 8. I do, however, cover Transact-SQL queries in depth in Chapter 8.

Linking Your Servers Together

Before you can issue a distributed query, you must tell the server that issues the query how to find the remote server(s). You do this by linking a server. A linked server stores connection information about the server(s) that you want to have participate in a distributed query. A linked server has an additional benefit in that it allows you to execute a stored procedure on the remote server. To link a server, follow these few steps:

1. **Choose Start⇨Programs⇨Microsoft SQL Server⇨Enterprise Manager to start the SQL Server Enterprise Manager.**

2. **Expand the tree so that you see the Linked Servers folder under the Security folder; then click the Linked Servers folder.**

   For more information about expanding the tree, see the Introduction of this book.

3. **Choose Action⇨New Linked Server.**

   Alternatively, you can right-click the Linked Servers folder or click anywhere in the right pane; then click New Linked Server.

   Any of these methods brings up a dialog box consisting of three tabs (General, Security, and Server Options) to enable you to type and select the parameters and data relating to the new linked server (see Figure 13-2). The General tab appears by default.

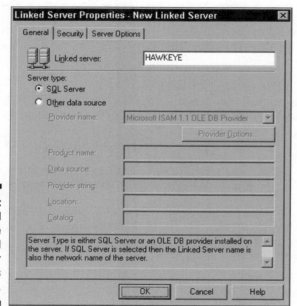

Figure 13-2:
The General tab of the Linked Server Properties dialog box.

SQL Server 2000 supports another kind of linked server, called a remote server. This type of server is supported for backward compatibility only, so I do not cover remote servers in this chapter or book. Microsoft recommends using linked servers instead.

Entering general data for the linked server

In the General tab, you enter data that describes the linked server as a whole. General data includes information such as the linked server name and the type of server that it is. Fill in the following fields to enter data in the General tab:

- **Linked Server:** Type in the name of the linked server. This name will be used in your queries. If you are linking a SQL Server, type in the name of the server instance as it would appear if you browsed the network. For example, you can type **Accounting** if that is the name of the SQL Server to link.

- **SQL Server:** Choose this option if the linked server is another SQL Server. For my example, I click this option. I use SQL Server almost exclusively.

- **Other Data Source:** Choose this option if the linked server is a data source other than SQL Server. Choose the OLE DB provider from the drop-down list of providers available. Then configure the rest of the fields, as they relate the provider. I don't cover these options because this book is about SQL Server.

Securing your data

In the Security tab (see Figure 13-3), you specify how SQL Server is to connect to the remote linked server. This tab is broken up into two separate sections. The top section is a grid that allows you to map logins to the remote data source. The bottom section defines what happens to security if a login is encountered that is not explicitly listed in the top section grid.

Fill in the following grid fields to enter data into the top section of the Security tab:

- **Local Login:** This column in the grid is used for you to specify the logins stored in the local server that are to be mapped to a login in the linked (remote) server. When you click in this column, you see a drop-down list of local logins.

- **Impersonate:** This column in the grid is a check box that is used to specify that the login entered in the Local Login field should be passed to the same login on the remote server.

- **Remote User:** This grid column is a text box that is available only if you uncheck the Impersonate column. This indicates that the login listed in the Local Login field maps to the login listed in this field. This goes hand-in-hand with the Remote Password field.

- **Remote Password:** This grid column is a text box that is available only if you uncheck the Impersonate column. This indicates that the login listed in the Local Login field maps to the login listed in the Remote User field and uses this field as the login password.

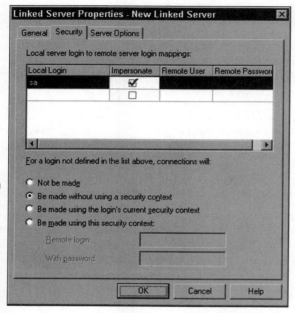

Figure 13-3:
The Server
tab of the
Linked
Server
Properties
dialog box.

Fill in the following fields to enter data into the bottom section of the Security tab to indicate how logins that are not specified in the grid will be handled:

- ✔ **Not Be Made:** Choose this option if only local logins specified in the grid are to be allowed to make a connection to the linked server.

- ✔ **Be Made Without Using a Security Context:** Choose this option if logins not specified in the grid will attempt to access resources on the linked server without any specific security credentials. It is up to the linked server to determine whether doing so is okay. This is the default option.

- ✔ **Be Made Using the Login's Current Security Context:** Choose this option if logins not specified in the grid will attempt to access resources on the linked server by using the current login ID and password.

- ✔ **Be Made Using This Security Context:** Choose this option if logins not specified in the grid will attempt to access resources on the linked server by using the ID and password that you specify in the Remote Login and With Password text boxes.

Choosing options

In the Server Options tab (see Figure 13-4), you specify options for the linked server connection. Some of the fields on this tab require a value to be entered, and some only need a check box selected.

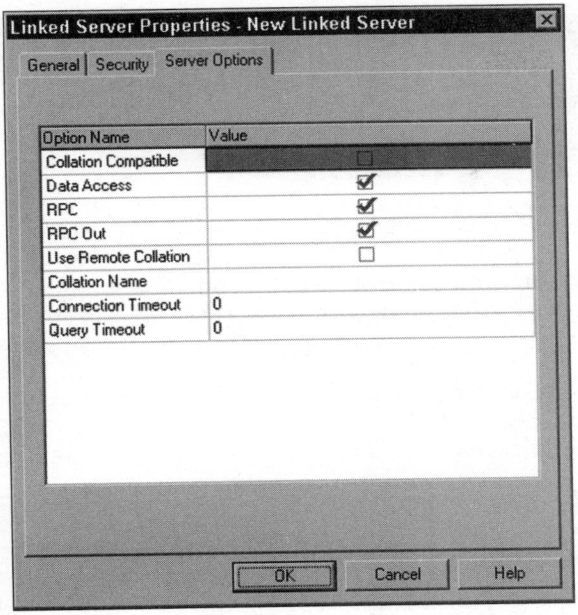

Figure 13-4:
The Server
Options tab
of the
Linked
Server
Properties
dialog box.

Fill in the following fields to enter data into the top section of the Server Options tab:

- ✔ **Collation Compatible:** Check this option if the linked server supports collation. Collation is available only in SQL Server 2000.

- ✔ **Data Access:** Check this option if you want to have data access to the linked server. Obviously, this is why you are creating the linked server, so ensure that this option is checked.

- ✔ **RPC:** Check this option if the linked server supports incoming remote procedure calls. SQL Servers support incoming RPCs.

- ✔ **RPC Out:** Check this option if the linked server supports outgoing remote procedure calls. SQL Servers support outgoing RPCs.

- ✔ **Use Remote Collation:** Check this option if you want collation to be controlled by the linked server. If this option is not checked, collation is controlled by the local server.

- ✔ **Collation Name:** Choose from the drop-down list of available collations. If nothing is selected, the default collation is used.

- ✔ **Connection Timeout:** Enter the number of seconds that are allowed to elapse before the connection is automatically terminated if a connection cannot be made to the linked server. A Connection Timeout value of 0 indicates that the global server configuration timeout value is to be used.

> ✔ **Query Timeout:** Enter the number of seconds that are allowed to elapse before a response from a query must be received from the linked server. A `Query Timeout` value of `0` indicates that the query will wait for an indefinite period of time.

Accessing Remote Data

To access remote data, you use Transact-SQL statements. It may help to go through Chapter 8 before continuing with this section. As I separated distributed queries into two types earlier, I'm doing the same thing here.

Writing distributed queries are really just like those that are used for nondistributed queries, except that you must use four-part names to qualify where SQL Server is to find the remote data. A four-part name follows this syntax:

```
Server.Database.[Owner].Object
```

where you substitute these values:

> *Server:* The name of your server with which a distributed query will take place. If this is not the current server, you need to add the server name as a linked server. I showed you how to do this earlier in this chapter.
>
> *Database:* The name of the database in the linked server that contains the table that will take part in a distributed query.
>
> *Owner:* The owner of the table that you will use. Use the name of the database in the linked server that contains the table that will take part in a distributed query. This is an optional parameter, but only if the owner of the table is `dbo`.
>
> *Object:* The name of the table or view that contains the data that will take part in the distributed query.

Here is an example of a fully-qualified, four-part name:

```
HAWKEYE.Accounting.dbo.Employees
```

In this example, the `Employees` database, owned by `dbo`, is specified in the `Accounting` database on the `HAWKEYE` server (which is the name of one of my servers).

So, this syntax might make for very long queries, right? Well, that's true, but you can alias the fully-qualified, four-part name like this:

```
HAWKEYE.Accounting.dbo.Employees as Emp
```

Now everywhere your table needs to be specified in your query, you can just use Emp to represent your table name, because you have already qualified the name by using all four parts. You can see what I mean in the next couple of sections.

Distributed nontransactional queries

A distributed nontransactional query is my term for a query that accesses data from multiple data sources but does not need to take part in a transaction. This access can take place by using either a linked server or an ad-hoc server connection.

Using a linked server

To write a nontransactional distributed query with a linked server, you simply write the query as you would if you were to join two tables on the same server in the same database, except that you specify the distributed table or view as a four-part, fully-qualified name. I discuss this earlier in this chapter.

An example of selecting data from the local Department table and the remote Employees table, you can write a query like this:

```
SELECT Emp.LastName, Emp.FirstName, Dept.DepartmentName
FROM Department as Dept
    JOIN HAWKEYE.Accounting.dbo.Employees as Emp
    ON (Dept.DepartmentID = Emp.DepartmentID)
```

If you understand how to join tables in your queries, you should be able to follow the above query with no problem. The Department table is joined with the Employees table on the DepartmentID column. The Employees table is located on the HAWKEYE server in the Accounting database and owned by dbo.

Another way to use a linked server is to use the OPENQUERY Transact-SQL statement. The OPENQUERY statement is used with a linked server to return a recordset that can be used as if it were a table. The advantage of using OPEN-QUERY is that it allows for minimal amount of data to be returned by the remote server. The OPENQUERY Transact-SQL statement follows this general syntax:

```
OPENQUERY ( linked_server_name, 'query')
```

linked_server_name is the name of the configured linked server that I show you earlier in this chapter. query is any valid Transact-SQL query that can be issued against the linked remote server.

One nice thing about OPENQUERY is that the local server does not do any parsing of the query whatsoever. The query is passed directly to the linked server. This is called a *passthrough* query.

Here, I show an example of using the OPENQUERY Transact-SQL statement using the same concept that I show in the previous example:

```
SELECT Emp.LastName, Emp.FirstName, Dept.DepartmentName
FROM Department as Dept
    JOIN OPENQUERY(HAWKEYE, 'SELECT * FROM
            Accounting.dbo.Employees') as Emp
    ON (Dept.DepartmentID = Emp.DepartmentID)
```

Using an ad-hoc server connection

If you have not linked a server, you must use an ad-hoc server connection to write a distributed nontransactional query. You can do this using the OPEN-ROWSET Transact-SQL statement. In the OPENROWSET statement, you specify how to connect to the remote server, instead of preconfiguring it as a linked server. The advantage in using the OPENROWSET statement over configuring a linked server is that the OPENROWSET statement is typically used in a one-time situation in which you don't expect to need data from the remote server in multiple queries. A disadvantage in using OPENROWSET over configuring a linked server is that OPENROWSET doesn't allow you to execute a stored procedure on the remote server.

The OPENROWSET Transact-SQL function follows this general syntax:

```
OPENROWSET ( 'provider' ,
    { 'datasource' ; 'login_id' ; 'password'
        | 'provider_string' } ,
    { [ database. ] [ owner. ] object
        | 'query' }
    )
```

where you can substitute the following variables:

provider: Specify the name of the OLE DB provider, as it is listed in the Windows Registry. A SQL Server OLE DB provider is called SQLOLEDB.

datasource: Specify the name of the server. If you specify server, you do not specify provider_string.

login_id: Specify the login account ID that has sufficient access permissions to query the database and table or view that you specify for the ad-hoc server connection. If you specify login_id, you do not specify provider_string.

password: Specify the login account password for the login_id that has sufficient access permissions to query the database and table or view that you specify for the ad-hoc server connection. If you specify password, you do not specify provider_string.

provider_string: Specify the connection string information for the OLE DB provider. This field is not used if you specify provider, datasource, login_id, and password.

database: Specify the name of the database that contains the object that you will access in the distributed query.

owner: Specify the name of the object owner for the object that you will access in the distributed query.

object: Specify the table or view name that you will access in the distributed query. If you specify *object,* you do not specify *query.*

query: Specify a query that is to be processed by the remote data source. If you specify *query,* you do not specify *object.*

The best way for me to show you an example is to use the same example that I show you earlier, in the "Using a linked server" section, except that this example assumes that you have not added HAWKEYE as a linked server:

```
SELECT Emp.LastName, Emp.FirstName, Dept.DepartmentName
FROM Department as Dept
    JOIN OPENROWSET('SQLOLEDB', 'HAWKEYE'; 'sa'; '',
            Accounting.dbo.Employees) as Emp
    ON (Dept.DepartmentID = Emp.DepartmentID)
```

As you can see, the format is exactly the same except where you indicate where the Employees table is located and how to retrieve it.

Distributed transactional queries

A distributed transactional query is my term for a query that accesses data from multiple data sources and also takes part in a transaction. Just as with distributed nontransactional queries, this type of query works by using either a linked server or an ad-hoc server connection.

Using a linked server

To write a transactional distributed query with a linked server, you write the query as the way I show you for nontransactional distributed queries, except that you encapsulate your Transact-SQL statements within a transaction.

To indicate that your Transact-SQL statements are wrapped within a transaction, you use the following special Transact-SQL statement:

```
BEGIN DISTRIBUTED TRANSACTION
```

This statement is just like the BEGIN TRANSACTION Transact-SQL statement except that it alerts the DTC that the transaction needs to be coordinated across remote data sources. This statement requires more resources than a regular transaction, so use it only if necessary.

To commit a distributed transaction, you simply use the same Transact-SQL statement that you use for regular transactions:

```
COMMIT TRANSACTION
```

Likewise, to roll back a distributed transaction, you also use the same Transact-SQL statement as you would for a regular transaction:

```
ROLLBACK TRANSACTION
```

Here's an example of how you might use a distributed transaction with a linked server:

```
--start the transaction
BEGIN DISTRIBUTED TRANSACTION

--first update inventory table in local database
UPDATE Inventory
SET Quantity = Quantity - 1
FROM Inventory
    JOIN HAWKEYE.Accounting.dbo.Invoice as Invoice
    ON (Inventory.ProductID = Invoice.ProductID)
WHERE Invoice.InvoiceID = 123

IF (@@error = 0)
    --no errors - update Invoice
    BEGIN
            --then update products table in remote
        database
            UPDATE HAWKEYE.Accounting.dbo.Invoice
            SET Status = 'COMPLETE'
            WHERE InvoiceID = 123
            IF (@@error = 0)
                --no errors - commit
                COMMIT TRANSACTION
            ELSE
                --errors occurred - rollback
                ROLLBACK TRANSACTION
    END
ELSE
    --errors occurred - rollback
    ROLLBACK TRANSACTION
```

The preceding code is a little complex, so I break it down for you. The basic concept is that first you update the Inventory table, which is in the local database. You know which products to decrement the inventory for based on the items ordered for an invoice, but that invoice is stored in the Invoice table on a remote server called HAWKEYE in the Accounting database.

After the inventory has been decremented, you flag the order as being complete by setting the Status field to COMPLETE for a specific invoice. If all goes well, the transaction is committed. If any errors occur after any Transact-SQL statement is executed, the transaction is rolled back.

Using an ad-hoc server connection

If you have not linked a server, you must use an ad-hoc server connection to write a distributed transactional query. You do this using the OPENROWSET Transact-SQL statement, just as I show you for the distributed nontransactional queries. Use the OPENROWSET syntax.

To continue with my examples, here's how you would use the query from the preceding example with the OPENROWSET Transact-SQL statement to make an ad-hoc server connection to write a distributed transactional query:

```
--start the transaction
BEGIN DISTRIBUTED TRANSACTION

--first update inventory table in local database
UPDATE Inventory
SET Quantity = Quantity - 1
FROM Inventory
    JOIN OPENROWSET('SQLOLEDB', 'HAWKEYE'; 'sa'; '',
        Accounting.dbo.Invoice) as Invoice
    ON (Inventory.ProductID = Invoice.ProductID)
WHERE Invoice.InvoiceID = 123

IF (@@error = 0)
    --no errors - update Invoice
    BEGIN
            --then update products table in remote
        database
            UPDATE OPENROWSET('SQLOLEDB', 'HAWKEYE'; 'sa';
    '', Accounting.dbo.Invoice)
            SET Status = 'COMPLETE'
            WHERE InvoiceID = 123
            IF (@@error = 0)
                --no errors - commit
                COMMIT TRANSACTION
            ELSE
                --errors occurred - rollback
                ROLLBACK TRANSACTION
    END
ELSE
    --errors occurred - rollback
    ROLLBACK TRANSACTION
```

Part V
Administrative
Issues

The 5th Wave   By Rich Tennant

"Look, I've already launched a search for 'reanimated babe cadavers' three times and nothing came up!"

In this part . . .

There are many things during the course of using SQL Server 2000 that come under the heading of administrative issues. These issues are related to automating backups, creating jobs to perform administrative functions, and setting up English Query to allow users to access data. I cover all of these great topics in this part.

Chapter 14

Using Jobs and Alerts to Make SQL Server Work for You

In This Chapter

▶ Creating Jobs

▶ Using Operators

▶ Alerting yourself

*H*ave you ever wondered how to get your job done without actually having to do it? Well, with SQL Server jobs, that's exactly what you can do. A job is a task that can be done automatically.

Think of a *job* as a series of steps that are executed in a sequence at specified times that you determine. A job is treated as a whole — that is, it either completes entirely or not at all — and can notify you or someone else about its status. Knowing the *status* of the job is knowing whether the job has completed successfully.

Think of an *alert* as a response to an error condition. An error condition is when SQL Server encounters a problem and generates an error. An error can be caused by lots of things, such as poor SQL statement syntax. You can specify which error conditions your alert is to respond to. If you were not able to specify the error conditions for an alert, the alert would respond more often than you would like or expect. For example, if you want to know when a backup failed, you need to specify only this error condition in an alert.

An alert works by notifying an operator when the error condition that you specify occurs. An *operator* is a person who is in charge of jobs. In this chapter, I show how to create jobs, operators, and alerts. Also, I show how all these concepts relate together to make SQL Server work for you!

Creating a Job

To create a job, follow these steps:

1. **Choose Start⇨Programs⇨Microsoft SQL Server⇨Enterprise Manager to start the SQL Server Enterprise Manager.**

2. **Expand the tree so that you see the SQL Server Agent folder under the Management folder and click it.**

   Refer to the Introduction of this book to check out how to expand the tree.

3. **Bring up the New Job Properties dialog box by choosing Action⇨ New⇨Job.**

   Alternatively, you can use the mouse to right-click the Jobs icon and select the New Job menu. Another way to create a new job is to click the New Job icon on the toolbar.

   Whichever method you choose to create a new job, each brings up a dialog box consisting of four tabs (General, Steps, Schedules, and Notifications) to allow you to bring up the parameters and data relating to the new job (see Figure 14-1). The General tab appears by default.

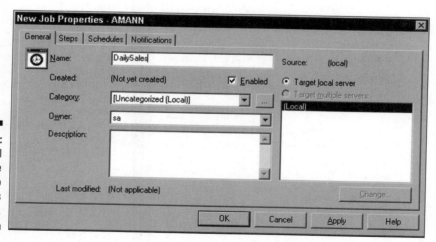

Figure 14-1:
The General
tab of the
New Job
Properties
dialog box.

Entering general data

Enter general data that describes the job as a whole in the General tab. Describing the job involves giving it a name and description and assigning the owners of the job. An *owner* is one who creates the job or is responsible for maintaining the job. To enter general data, make sure that the General tab is selected. A selected folder appears in the foreground and looks like a folder in a filing cabinet.

Fill in the following fields to enter general data in the General tab:

- ✔ **Name:** Give your job a name, such as `Daily Sales`, so that you can identify the job later.

- ✔ **Category:** Choose from the drop-down list of categories. A category is used to list jobs according to their type of function. A job doesn't need to be categorized. By default, `[Uncategorized (Local)]` is shown. This is fine unless you want to change it. An example of when you may want to change the category is if you are creating many jobs relating to backing up. In this case, you should choose the category that closely matches the job function you are trying to achieve, such as `Database Maintenance`. To see what categories are available, click the arrow to expose the drop-down list of categories. Actually, you can add your own categories by clicking the Jobs folder and choosing <u>A</u>ction⇨All Tasks⇨ Manage Job Categories. This brings up a dialog box to allow you to manage existing categories and create new ones.

- ✔ **Owner:** Select the owner from the drop-down list of owners. An owner is one who is responsible for maintaining the job. By default, the currently logged-in user is shown. If you want to select a different owner, you can do so now.

- ✔ **Description:** Give your job some type of description so that you know what it does, in case you forget it! Type in something like `Job that processes daily sales.`

Creating the sequence of steps

The Steps tab is used to review, edit, add, and delete steps in the sequence of steps that make up the job. From here, you can create a new step.

1. **To create a brand new step, click the New button.**

   Clicking the New button enters a new step field within the Steps tab. It then immediately brings up a new dialog box called the New Job Step dialog box, shown in Figure 14-2. This dialog box contains two more tabs, the General tab and the Advanced tab, which allow you to specify attributes of the new step. Many Microsoft programs work this way. It may seem awkward to have tabs within tabs, but it really does make sense to organize the dialog box this way!

   If your machine is slow, this note is for you. After you click the New button, the new step entry within the Steps tab shows up immediately but the dialog box may not show up right away.

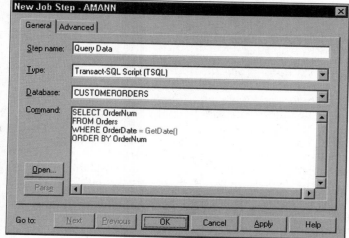

Figure 14-2:
The General
tab of
the New
Job Step
dialog box.

2. **Type general information about the new job step in the General tab of the New Job Step dialog box.**

   • **Step Name:** Give your new job step a name (such as `Query Data`) so that you can identify the job step later.

   • **Type:** Choose the type of step you want to designate from the drop-down list of types. The step type indicates the specific function of the job step. TSQL is chosen by default because most of the time you create jobs that issue TSQL statements. *TSQL,* or Transact-SQL, is one or more SQL statements that is executed to produce some result.

   • **Database:** Choose the database you want to use from the list of databases registered on the server. By default, `master` is shown. I chose `CUSTOMERORDERS`, which is the database used in my query. You choose a database that contains the tables used in your query. If you choose the wrong database, your query can't run.

   • **Command:** Type in the command that you want to use to process the new step that you just defined. The type you select dictates what command is valid for you to use. For example, if you select TSQL, you must type a valid SQL statement in the Command text box. If you select ActiveScripting, you must type in a valid script.

   Because my TSQL command is based on an `Orders` table within my `CUSTOMERORDERS` database, my command looks like this:

```
SELECT OrderNum
FROM Orders
WHERE OrderDate = GetDate()
ORDER BY OrderNum
```

My Orders table contains the columns OrderNum (an automatically generated reference number) and OrderDate (the date the order was placed). For more information about SQL, see Chapter 8. It provides a great overview on the use of SQL.

If you have a command already stored in a file, you can insert the contents of that file by clicking the Open button and selecting the file.

If you want to verify the format of the Command, simply click the Parse button. Doing so results in a message box appearing, letting you know whether there are any problems with your command or whether the parse succeeded. If the parse succeeded, there are no errors.

3. **Click the Advanced tab at the top of the New Job Step dialog box and type advanced information about the new job step (see Figure 14-3).**

   Use the Advanced tab on the New Job Step dialog box to define additional or more advanced information about the new step, such as additional options and what to do upon success or failure of the command entered in Step 2.

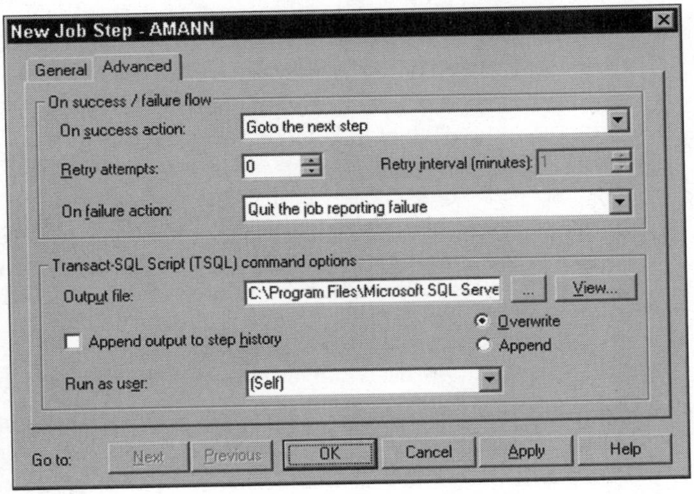

Figure 14-3:
The Advanced tab of the New Job Step dialog box.

- **On Success Action:** Choose On Success Action from the drop-down list of possible actions. By default, Goto the Next Step is shown. The possible actions are as follows:

   Quit the Job Reporting Success: Stops processing the current job that reports a step completed successfully.

   Quit the Job Reporting Failure: Stops processing the current job that reports a step failed.

   Goto the Next Step: Continues to the next step in the current job.

- **Retry Attempts:** Type the number of attempts a failed action should retry. By default, 0 is shown. You may want to enter a number of retry attempts if you believe your Command entered in Step 2 relies on the timing of another process. If this is the case, a number of retries may prove successful. However, in most cases, if a command fails, retrying the command only results in a delay in the job completion (with a failure status).

- **Retry Interval (Minutes):** If you enter a number other than zero in the Retry attempts field, the Retry interval field becomes enabled, allowing you to specify the number of minutes of elapsed time before attempting a retry of executing the command entered in the preceding Step 2.

- **On Failure Action:** Choose On Failure Action from the drop-down list of possible actions. By default, Quit the Job Reporting Failure is shown. The possible actions are as follows:

    Quit the Job Reporting Success: Stops processing the current job that reports a step completed successfully.

    Quit the Job Reporting Failure: Stops processing the current job that reports a step failed.

    Goto the Next Step: Continues to the next step in the current job.

- **Output File:** Type in a filename that stores the results of the Command entered in Step 2. I use a file called `DailySales.out` in the `C:\Program Files\Microsoft SQL Server\MSSQL\Log` directory.

- **Run As User:** Choose Run As User from the drop-down list of database users. Because different users have different permission levels, SQL Server needs to know the user under which the TSQL statement(s) will run. By default, `(Self)` is shown. Self indicates that the job is run as the user you are logged in as at the time the job is created. In other words, whoever you are logged in as right now!

It's important to know that the top part of the Advanced tab dialog box, labeled Transact-SQL Script (TSQL) Command Options, presents different options if you choose anything other than Transact-SQL Script (TSQL) as a type in the preceding Step 2. Table 14-1 shows the fields you need to fill out if you choose any of the other Type options.

Table 14-1	Advanced Tab Options Available for the General Tab Types
Type	*Options Available*
Active Script	None
Operating System Command (CmdExec)	Output file

Type	Options Available
Replication Distributor	None
Replication Transaction-Log Reader	None
Replication Merge	None
Queue Reader	Server and Database
Replication Snapshot	None
Transact-SQL Script (TSQL)	Output file and Run as user

4. Click OK.

The OK button applies all changes and closes the dialog box. You are returned to the Steps tab within the New Job Properties dialog box. Additionally, you see the new job step that you just created listed within this tab.

After you click OK for the job, the last step in the list of steps has the success action changed from the Goto the Next Step option to the Quit the Job Reporting Success option.

Scheduling the frequency of the job

You use the Schedules tab to review, edit, add, and delete the scheduled frequencies at which the job runs. Any of these frequencies encompasses the entire job, not separate steps. Because I use an example about reporting on daily sales, the frequency of the job is to run only once daily.

Click the Schedules tab located at the top of the New Job Properties dialog box to bring up the Schedules tab.

It's a good idea to schedule a query to run in the middle of the night so that it does not affect server performance during the day. This way, network traffic stays at a minimum level when more people need to be accessing the network.

1. To create a brand new schedule, click the New Schedule button.

Clicking the New Schedule button enters a new schedule field within the Schedules tab and then immediately brings up the New Job Schedule dialog box, allowing you to specify attributes of the new schedule. (See Figure 14-4.)

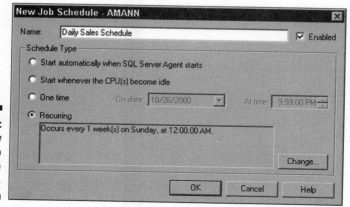

Figure 14-4:
The New
Job
Schedule
dialog box.

2. **Type in information about the new job schedule.**

- **Name:** Give your schedule a name, such as `Daily Sales Schedule`, so that you can identify the schedule later.

- **Enabled:** Choose whether the schedule is enabled, or active. By default, you see a check mark in the box indicating that the schedule is active. You may want to have some schedules that are run only once in a while or that you use for testing. If you are following my example, ensure that the box is checked.

- **Schedule Type:** Select the type of schedule you want to create. You can choose from one of four options:

   Start Automatically When SQL Server Agent Starts: Starts the job when the SQL Server Agent starts (either automatically or manually). This allows you to specify a boot-up schedule.

   Start Whenever the CPU(s) Become Idle: Starts the job whenever the system processor(s) is not busy. If a very calculation-intensive query is running, there is no time for the job to run. This option enables you to perform periodic system processing without sacrificing CPU cycles for a user's query.

   One Time: Runs the job once at a specified date and time. Choosing this option enables the `On Date` and `At Time` fields, allowing you to specify the date and time, respectively.

   Recurring: Runs the job on a recurring basis at intervals that you specify. Because this is the most popular option for a job, it is selected by default. Also by default, the schedule runs once a week on the current day at midnight. To change the Recurring option, continue with the next step.

3. **Click the Change button.**

   Clicking the Change button allows you to change, or edit, the recurring schedule shown within the Recurring option field. Doing so brings up the Edit Recurring Job Schedule dialog box.

4. **Click the Daily option.**

   This option is located within the Occurs section. Other choices are Weekly and Monthly.

5. **Click the Occurs Once At option.**

   This option is located within the Daily Frequency section. You need to check this option because the schedule needs to run only once a day. The other option is the Occurs Every option. It is used to specify a period of time within the time option chosen in the Occurs section to schedule the job.

6. **Type in the time of day you want the job to run.**

   A time in the middle of the night is best for computing intensive daily queries. Type **02:00 AM**.

7. **Type in a Duration.**

   In the Duration section, a Start Date of today is entered by default, and the No End Date option is checked by default. If you want to specify an end date, click the End Date option and type an end date in the box provided.

8. **Click the OK button on the Edit Recurring Job Schedule dialog box.**

   The OK button saves all changes to the Edit Recurring Job Schedule dialog box and closes it. The New Job Schedule dialog box reappears.

9. **Click the OK button on the New Job Schedule dialog box.**

   The OK button applies all changes to the New Job Schedule dialog box and closes it. You are returned to the Schedules tab within the New Job Properties dialog box. Additionally, you see the new schedule that you just created listed within this tab.

10. **Click the OK button on the New Job Properties dialog box.**

    The OK button applies all changes to the New Job Properties dialog box and closes it.

What do I do when the job completes?

The Notifications tab is used to indicate what actions need to be performed when the job completes. A job can complete with one of two statuses: successful or unsuccessful (failure). You use either of these statuses to specify actions to take when the job completes. You actually need not do anything when the job completes — that is, if you don't care about the status of the job completion. However, if you do care about the status of the job completion and want someone or something to be notified, read on!

To bring up the Notifications tab, click the Notifications tab located at the top of the New Job Properties dialog box (see Figure 14-5).

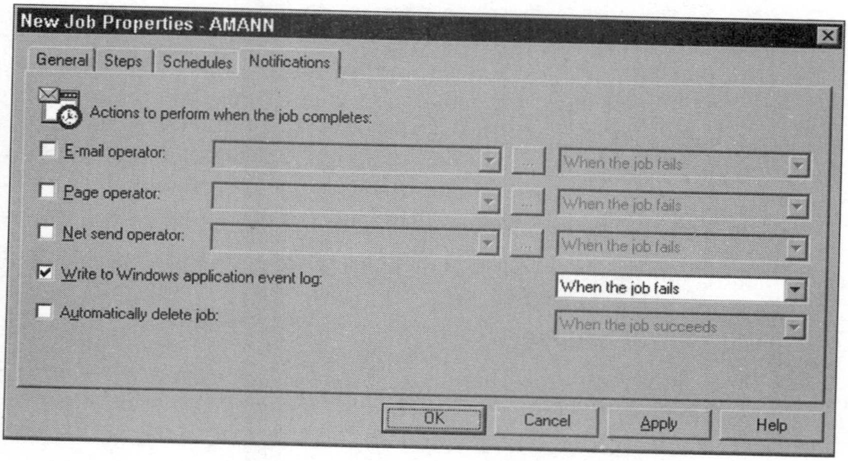

Figure 14-5:
Indicate actions to be performed upon job completion in the Notifications tab.

Either an individual or SQL Server can be notified about the status of a job. The individual is defined as the operator. This means that if you want to have a user notified about a job status, the user must first be set up as an operator. Notifying SQL Server can be specified without setting up an operator.

1. **Specify action(s).**

   You can specify one or more actions to take by clicking the check box next to the action listed on the dialog box in the Notifications tab (refer to Figure 14-5):

   • **E-Mail Operator:** Notifies an operator by e-mail.

   • **Page Operator:** Notifies an operator by paging.

   • **Net Send Operator:** Notifies an operator by sending a pop-up message over the network. This is available only on Windows NT 4.0 and later, not Windows 95 or later.

   • **Write to Windows NT Application Event Log:** Writes the status of the job to the application event log under Windows NT.

   • **Automatically Delete Job:** Deletes the job when complete. This is useful for a one-time-only job.

2. Specify the operator(s).

If you choose E-Mail Operator, Page Operator, or Net Send Operator, you need to specify the name of the operator. To do so, select from the drop-down list for each type of operator that you checked for notification. By default, the name of the operator assigned to the currently logged-in user is shown.

I choose `E-Mail Operator` so that I am notified when a job fails.

To specify a new operator, refer to the section, "Hello . . . Operator?," later in this chapter.

3. Specify condition(s).

If you choose E-Mail Operator, Page Operator, or Net Send Operator, you need to specify the condition under which the operator will be notified. By default, the When the Job Fails option is shown. You can choose a different option if desired. The following are the options available:

- **When the Job Succeeds:** Operator will be notified only if the job completes successfully.

- **When the Job Fails:** Operator will be notified only if the job completes unsuccessfully (failure).

- **Whenever the Job Completes:** Operator will be notified regardless of the status of the job completion.

4. Click the OK button on the New Job Properties dialog box.

The OK button applies all changes to the New Job Properties dialog box and closes it.

Hello . . . Operator?

An *operator* is an individual who is notified of the status of a job. The operator receives a specific type of notification within the time period as defined by the job. If you wish to be set up for notification upon the completion of a job, you must be added as an operator. SQL Server 2000 provides the ability to add new operators. To set up a new operator, follow these steps:

1. Expand the tree so that you see the SQL Server Agent folder and click it.

Refer to the Introduction of this book to check out how to expand the tree.

2. **Bring up the New Operator Properties dialog box by choosing** <u>A</u>ction⇨
   New⇨Operator.

   Alternatively, you can use the mouse to right-click the Operators icon
   and select the New Operator menu.

   Any method you choose to create a new operator brings up a dialog box
   consisting of two tabs, the General tab and the Notifications tab, to allow
   you to type the parameters and data relating to the new operator. The
   General tab comes up first by default.

Entering general data . . . one more time

You type general data about the operator in the General tab, such as name,
contact information (e-mail address, pager name, net send address), and duty
schedule. A *duty schedule* consists of the hours that the specified operator is
available to be notified.

- ✔ **Name:** Give your operator a name. I enter my name as Anthony T.
  Mann. Entering the full name allows for quick reference to an operator.

- ✔ **E-Mail Name:** Type the name of the person to e-mail, as it appears in
  your address book. I enter my e-mail as tmann. If you wish to choose
  from the address book on your system, click the . . . button. After you
  enter an e-mail name, you can test the e-mail by clicking the Test button.

- ✔ **Pager E-Mail Name:** Type the name of the person to page, as it appears
  in your address book. I enter my name as tmann. If you wish to choose
  from the address book on your system, click the . . . button. After you
  enter a pager e-mail name, you can test the pager by clicking the Test
  button.

- ✔ **Net Send Address:** Type the address of the machine to notify using the
  network. After you enter a net send address, you can test the net send
  address by clicking the Test button. Clicking the Test button sends a
  pop-up message to the user that is logged into the network with the
  address (Login ID) you have entered in this field.

- ✔ **Pager on Duty Schedule:** Check the days and type the times the operator is available to be notified. An operator is considered to be available
  24 hours if this person is available Monday through Thursday. For
  Friday, Saturday, or Sunday, you must type the times that the operator is
  available to be notified. By default, these times are between 8:00 a.m.
  and 6:00 p.m.

Click the OK button to apply all changes and close the dialog box.

Viewing an operator's notifications

The Notifications tab shows an operator's capability to receive notifications. You're unable to enter information in this dialog box — notifications are specified when you create a job (see the section, "Creating a Job," earlier in this chapter). This dialog box exists to enable you to view in one place all the notifications assigned to the currently selected (or added) operator.

The dialog box shows the following fields:

- ✔ **Notifications Sent to This Operator By:** Two radio buttons can be selected, Alerts or Jobs.

- ✔ **Grid of check boxes**: If you have selected the Alerts radio button, this grid shows the Alert Name, E-Mail, Pager, and Net Send for each possible category of alert.

  If you have selected the Jobs radio button, this grid shows the Job Name, E-mail, Pager, and Net Send for each possible category of alert. Only the jobs that have already been configured to have this particular operator selected for E-Mail, Pager, or Net Send notification will be listed in the grid.

- ✔ **Operator is Available to Receive Notifications:** This check box can be used to indicate that an operator will not receive any notifications. To specify this, simply uncheck this box. By default, the box is checked, indicating that the operator will receive the notifications listed at the top of the dialog box.

- ✔ **Most Recent Notification Attempts:** Shows the most recent notifications by e-mail, pager, or net send. For a new operator, all fields indicate that notification has never been made.

Click the OK button to apply all changes and close the dialog box.

Using Alerts

An *alert* is an event that responds to criteria you specify. For example, an alert can notify you when a specific error occurs.

Although SQL Server 2000 runs on Windows 95 and Windows 98, alerts are available only on Windows NT 4.0 and Windows 2000. If you are running Windows 95 or Windows 98, the icon for Alerts will not even show up. For an alert to work, you must have the SQL Server Agent service (called SQLAgent$SQL2000) running. To do this in Windows NT 4.0, bring up the Control Panel by choosing

Start⇨Settings⇨Control Panel. Then double-click the Services icon to bring up the dialog box shown in Figure 14-6. In Windows 2000, you can bring up the dialog box by choosing Start⇨Settings⇨Control Panel⇨Administrative Tools⇨Services. Ensure that the `SQLServerAgent` service is started.

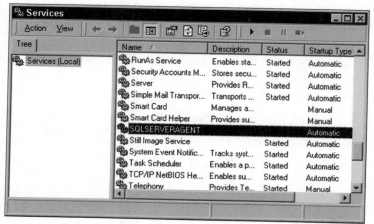

Figure 14-6:
The Services dialog box.

The SQL Server Agent is notified of the job status when the criteria you specify is satisfied, thereby generating the alert, also known as *raising an alert.*

To create a new alert, follow these steps:

1. **Start the SQL Server Enterprise Manager.**

   Select Start⇨Programs⇨Microsoft SQL Server⇨Enterprise Manager.

2. **Expand the tree so that you see the SQL Server Agent folder and click it.**

   Refer to the Introduction of this book to check out how to expand the tree.

3. **Bring up the New Alert Properties dialog box by choosing Action⇨ New⇨Alert.**

   Alternatively, you can use the mouse to right-click the Alerts icon and select the New Alert menu.

   Any method you choose to create a new alert brings up a dialog box consisting of two tabs, the General tab and the Response tab, to allow you to type the definition and response to the new alert. The General tab appears first by default.

Defining alert conditions

You can use the General tab to define alert conditions. This tab is where you specify the criteria for which an alert is raised. First, you determine whether you want the alert to be raised if a specific error occurs, a certain severity of error occurs, or even if the text of the error contains specific characters.

To define alert conditions, type the following information in the General tab:

- **Name:** Give your alert a name (such as `Connect Alert`) so that you can identify the alert later.

- **Type:** At this time, there are only two types of alerts:

    SQL Server Event Alert: Defines specific errors or severity levels for the alert.

    SQL Server Performance Condition Alert: Defines specific performance conditions for the alert. This is a great way to be alerted if performance falls below certain specified levels.

- **Enabled:** Indicates that this alert will be enabled if the check box is checked. If unchecked, this alert will not be enabled. This field is checked by default.

Depending on the Type of alert (specified above), either the Event Alert Definition or Performance Condition Alert Definition section will appear. These fields are available for the Event Alert Definition section:

- **Error Number:** Click this option button if you want to raise the alert when a specific error number occurs. After it's clicked, the text box becomes enabled, allowing you to type the specific error number. Alternatively, you can click the . . . button, which shows you a dialog box containing the possible error numbers to choose from.

- **Severity:** Click this option button if you want to raise the alert when a specific severity of error occurs. The *severity* indicates how critical the error is. An error can simply be informational, or it can be critical to the point that processing can't continue. After this option is clicked, the drop-down list of possible errors becomes enabled. This option is selected by default, and the drop-down list shows `010-Information`. This indicates that the alert will be generated only for errors that are informational, not critical.

- **Database Name:** Select the database name used by SQL Server to determine when to raise the alert. You can choose from any registered database, or all databases. All Databases is chosen by default.

✔ **Error Message Contains This Text:** If you wish to further qualify the conditions of the alert, in addition to the other criteria shown in the General tab, you can type the text that the alert must contain to match the criteria. For example, if you want the alert to respond when there is a connection error, you might type **Connect** in this box.

These fields are available for the Performance Condition Alert Definition section:

✔ **Object:** A number of SQL Server 2000 objects are available for monitoring. Each of these objects has specific counters available (see next bullet).

✔ **Counter:** A specific measurable item for the object selected that allows you to test for specific conditions.

✔ **Instance:** For specific counters, this field becomes enabled. Instance refers to a very specific parameter for a counter, such as a database. In other words, Instance further qualifies the counter.

✔ **Alert If Counter:** A drop-down list of conditions with which to test for the counter. Possible choices are `Falls Below`, `Becomes Equal To`, and `Rises Above`. Make the appropriate choice for the desired test.

✔ **Value:** The number you want to be considered in the test for the specific counter.

Although this is becoming slightly beyond the scope of this book, I want to give you an example. If you wanted be alerted when a lock takes more than two seconds to obtain, you could construct the alert with the parameters shown in Figure 14-7. Note that the value of `2000` is in milliseconds, which equals two seconds.

Click the OK button to apply all changes and close the dialog box. Alternatively, you can click the Apply button to apply changes and leave the dialog box open. Doing so allows you to move to the next section.

Defining alert responses

Enter information in the Response tab to define which operator(s) receive responses to the alert criteria specified in the General tab. For more information about operators, refer to the section, "Hello . . . Operator?" earlier in this chapter. Click the Response tab located at the top of the New Alert Properties dialog box. (See Figure 14-8.)

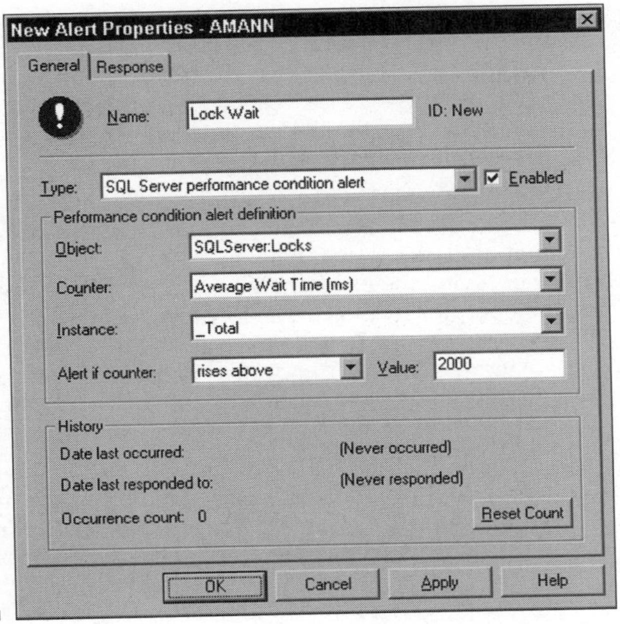

Figure 14-7:
The Response tab of the New Alert Properties dialog box (showing Performance Condition Alert Definition).

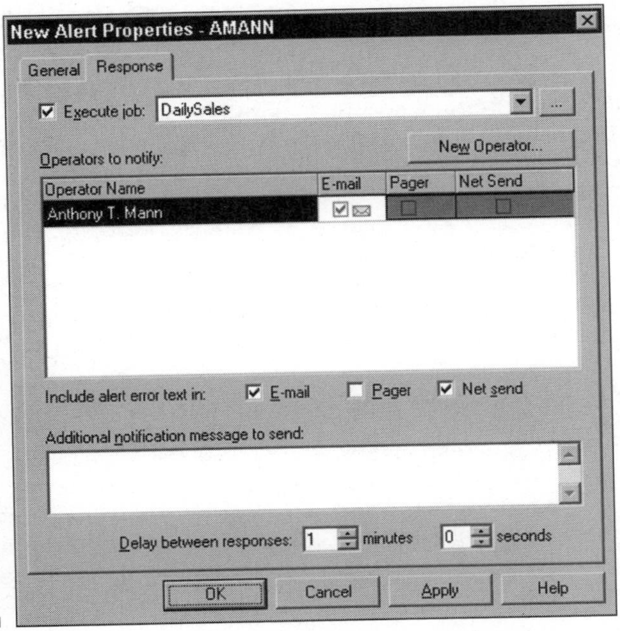

Figure 14-8:
The Response tab of the New Alert Properties dialog box (showing SQL Server event alert definition).

To define which operator(s) receive a response to the alert criteria, enter the following information:

- **Execute Job:** If you want one of the responses to the alert to be to execute a job, check this field. If the field is checked, you can select the name of the job from the drop-down list of jobs.

- **Operators to Notify:** In addition to executing a job, you can have specific operators notified about the alert being raised. This field is a grid containing four columns. The first is the name of the operator. The second is a check box for notifying the operator by e-mail. The third is a check box for notifying the operator by pager. The fourth is a check box for notifying the operator by net send. To use this grid, simply check the types of notification (e-mail, pager, or net send) next to the adjacent operator's name. Doing so notifies any operator with a check mark in the appropriate column when the alert is raised. If you want to specify a new operator, click the New Operator button.

- **Include Alert Error Text In:** This field is a series of three check boxes. You can choose to include the actual text message of the error by clicking any or all of the choices. The choices are `E-Mail`, `Pager`, and `Net Send`.

- **Additional Notification Message to Send to Operator:** If you want additional text (other than the error text) to be sent to the operator, type that text in here. For example, you could type the name of the alert, such as `Connect Alert`.

- **Delay Between Responses for a Recurring Alert:** This field allows you to specify, in minutes and seconds, how much of a delay you want between recurring alerts of the same type. This delay makes it possible not to be notified many times about the same alert. Often an error can appear many times within a short time span. If the error occurs 10 times a minute, you don't want to receive 10 e-mails! Therefore, you may want to leave this value at the default of `1 minute` and `0 seconds`.

Click the OK button to apply all changes and close the dialog box. Alternatively, you can click the Apply button to apply changes and leave the dialog box open.

Chapter 15

Maintenance Plans

· ·

In This Chapter

▶ Maintaining database health

▶ Maintaining index health

▶ Automating your backups

· ·

In most of this book, I have shown you how to create database objects and explained the concepts surrounding those objects. If you have read this book from the very beginning, you should now be able to do many things in SQL Server 2000. However, there are some administrative tasks that you really should do periodically to maintain the health of your system.

This chapter discusses many concepts that may be new to you. Depending on the options that you choose, the wizard that I show you in this chapter may become very tedious to use, but it is necessary, so let's get to it!

For you to create, edit, or delete maintenance plans, you must be a member of the sysadmin fixed server role.

What in the World . . . ?

What is a maintenance plan? Simple! A maintenance plan is a special type of administrative tool that automates the creation of one or more SQL Server jobs. I cover jobs in Chapter 14. Maintenance plans are special types of jobs because the steps involved in the job are preconfigured, depending on the options that you choose. You can choose to perform the following tasks by using a maintenance plan:

✔ Check the integrity of your database(s).

✔ Rebuild your indexes and/or statistics for those indexes.

✔ Back up your databases.

✔ Ship the transaction logs to another server.

Creating a Maintenance Plan

To create a maintenance plan, you use the Database Maintenance Plan Wizard. The first step is to launch the wizard, which you can do in a couple of ways. The next step is to use the wizard. I outline both of these steps next.

Launching the Maintenance Plan Wizard

Launching the wizard can be done in one of two ways. The first way to launch the Maintenance Plan Wizard is to follow these steps:

1. **Choose Start⇨Programs⇨Microsoft SQL Server⇨Enterprise Manager to start the SQL Server Enterprise Manager.**

2. **Expand the tree so that you see the name of your server.**

   For more information about expanding the tree, see the Introduction of this book.

3. **Bring up the Select Wizard dialog box by choosing Tools⇨Wizards.**

   The Select Wizard dialog box appears.

4. **Select the Database Maintenance Plan Wizard item (under the Management category) with the left mouse button and click OK.**

   When the wizard is launched, you are ready to begin. Jump to the "Using the wizard" section of this chapter.

The second way to launch the Maintenance Plan Wizard is to follow these steps:

1. **Start the SQL Server Enterprise Manager by choosing Start⇨Programs⇨ Microsoft SQL Server⇨Enterprise Manager.**

2. **Expand the tree so that you see the Management folder; then select the Database Maintenance Plans folder by clicking it.**

   For more information about expanding the tree, see the Introduction of this book.

3. **Choose <u>A</u>ction⇨New Maintenance Plan.**

   Alternatively, you can right-click the Database Maintenance Plans folder or anywhere in the right pane and then click New Maintenance Plan.

   All these methods bring up the Database Maintenance Plan Wizard. To use the wizard, see the "Using the wizard" section.

Using the wizard

After you launch the wizard, you are ready to begin.

To use the wizard, simply follow these steps:

1. **After you launch the wizard, read the welcome screen and click Next when you are ready.**

2. **Select the desired databases for which you will create maintenance plans.**

   You can choose from these options:

   - **All Databases:** Clicking this option automatically selects all system and user-defined databases.

   - **All System Databases:** Automatically selects only system databases, but not user-defined databases.

   - **All User Databases:** Automatically selects all user databases, but not system databases.

   - **These Databases:** Clicking this option allows you to choose which databases will have the maintenance plan created from the grid of all databases. To select a database, ensure that there is a check mark in the Database column for each row in the table. This option is selected by default.

   - **Ship the Transaction Logs to Other SQL Servers:** Selecting this check box copies the transaction logs of the selected databases to other servers in near real-time. This option is new for SQL Server 2000. Log shipping works by copying the transaction log to a share that you create on another server and specifying additional information. A *share* is a term given to a folder that resides on a computer that has been given a name that can be used by remote computers to access the folder. Log shipping information is specified in later steps. Note that this option is available only if you choose a single database.

3. **Select Data Optimization Information (see Figure 15-1) and click Next.**

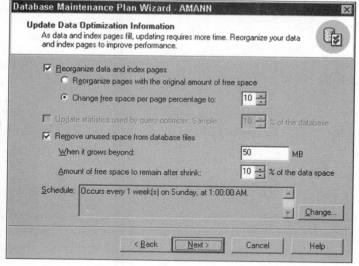

Figure 15-1:
Specifying
data
optimization
information
in the
Maintenance
Plan Wizard.

You can choose from these options:

- **Reorganize Data and Index Pages:** When SQL Server 2000 stores data and indexes, it stores them in 8KB (kilobyte) pages. Just as your disk drive can become fragmented, so can you data and index pages. Therefore, you can check this option to rebuild these pages. This option cannot be specified in the same maintenance plan as the Update Statistics Used by Query Optimizer option.

  When you created the table or index, you had the option of specifying a `FILLFACTOR` keyword. If you would like to reorganize data and index pages, you have the option of checking the Reorganize Pages with the Original Amount of Free Space option (which is selected by default). Otherwise, you can specify a `FILLFACTOR` by choosing the Change Free Space Per Page Percentage To option. Then you can select the desired percentage, with 10 percent being the default value. Both of these options are enabled only if you choose the Reorganize Data and Index Pages option.

- **Update Statistics Used by Query Optimizer:** Check this option if you want statistical information for indexes to be updated. The SQL Server 2000 optimizer knows which index to choose when executing a query because of the statistical information that it builds. Therefore, the more data that is sampled for the statistical information, the more accurate the index chosen will be. If you choose this option, you can also specify the percentage of data that will be sampled for the statistics rebuild. By default, this percentage is 10 percent, but you may want to make that higher. I would recommend at least 25 percent. However, you should know that the larger the percentage, the more time it will take to rebuild the statistical information. This option cannot be specified in the same maintenance plan as the Reorganize Data and Index Pages option.

- **Remove Unused Space from Database Files:** When SQL Server stores data, it allocates space on the hard disk one chunk at a time. A chunk can be a specific number of megabytes, or a percentage of the current size. However, when data is deleted from the database, the space that is freed up in the database is not reclaimed by the operating system. You can reclaim this space by checking this option.

If you check this option, then you have two additional fields to specify. The first is the When It Grows Beyond field. This field is used to specify how large the database must become before space is automatically removed. By default, this option is specified at 50MB. The second is the Amount of Free Space to Remain After Shrink field. You don't want the database to be shrunk so far that there is no space available for new data. Therefore, you specify the percentage of free space to remain. This field is set at 10 percent by default.

If you select any of the preceding three options, a default schedule is generated that runs the desired options at 1 a.m. every Sunday morning. If you want to change this schedule, click the Change button. For more information on job schedules, see Chapter 14.

4. **Select database integrity options (see Figure 15-2) and click Next.**

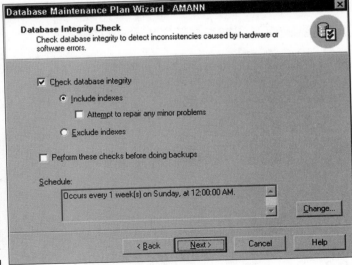

Figure 15-2: Specifying database integrity options in the Maintenance Plan Wizard.

Checking the database integrity fixes internal problems in the database. Using the database integrity options is the same as running the DBCC program. DBCC stands for Database Consistency Checker and is an administrative tool for verifying the integrity of your database. If you wish to check for and fix database integrity issues, check the Check Database Integrity option.

If you select this option, other options become available:

- **Include Indexes:** Select this option if you want indexes to be included in the integrity checks. Also, if you want indexes to automatically be repaired if problems are encountered, click the Attempt to Repair Any Minor Problems check box. The Include Indexes option is selected by default, but the Attempt to Repair Any Minor Problems check box is not.

- **Exclude Indexes:** If, for some reason, you do not want indexes to be checked and/or fixed for problems, select this option. However, it is a good idea to know whether problems exist with your indexes.

- **Perform These Tests Before Doing Backups:** If this option is not checked and problems are found, you can back up the problems. Doing so may be desirable because sometimes you want your backups to be an exact replica of the state of your database at a specific point in time. This option is not checked by default.

Again, if you selected to check the database integrity, a default schedule is populated that runs the integrity checks every Sunday, but at midnight, not at 1 a.m. If you want to change this schedule, click the Change button. For more information on job schedules, see Chapter 14.

5. **Select database backup options (see Figure 15-3) and click Next.**

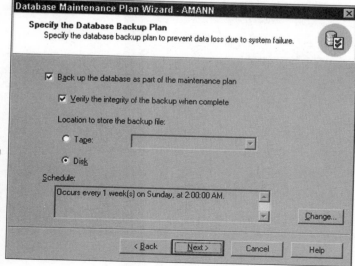

Figure 15-3:
Specifying backup plan options in the Maintenance Plan Wizard.

If you want the database to be backed up as part of the plan, check the Backup the Database As Part of the Maintenance Plan option.

If you select this option, other options become available:

- **Verify the Integrity of the Backup on Completion of the Backup:** Although having this option enabled makes the maintenance plan take more time to perform, you should check this option if you want to know that your backup was successful. This option is checked by default.

- **Tape:** Check this option if you want to back up to a tape drive. This option is disabled if you don't have a tape drive installed. Select from the drop-down list of available tape devices.

- **Disk:** Check this option if you want to backup your database to a disk drive. You will be prompted in the next step as to the disk location.

If you selected to back up the database, a default schedule is generated that runs the backup every Sunday, but at 2 a.m., not midnight or 1 a.m. as with the other options. If you want to change this schedule, click the Change button. For more information on job schedules, see Chapter 14.

6. **Select database backup disk directory information (see Figure 15-4) and click Next.**

   This option appears only if you selected to back up the database to disk, not tape.

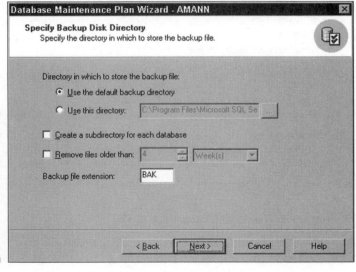

Figure 15-4: Specifying database backup disk directory information in the Maintenance Plan Wizard.

You can choose from these options:

- **Use the Default Backup Directory:** This option, which is chosen by default, will backup to the default folder of \MicrosoftSQLServer\ MSSQL\Backup on the drive where you installed SQL Server 2000.

- **Create a Subdirectory for Each Database:** This option, if chosen, will automatically create a subdirectory, or subfolder, under the selected backup directory for each database. Subdirectories can be easier to manage than all files being placed in a single folder but this option is not chosen by default.

- **Remove Files Older Than:** So that your disk drive doesn't grow uncontrollably and fill up, you can opt to delete backups after a specific amount of elapsed time has passed. If you choose this option, you specify this interval, with a default value of 4 weeks.

- **Backup File Extension:** The default backup file extension is BAK, but you can change it if you wish. I don't recommend changing this because BAK is a standard that most people will recognize.

7. **Select transaction log backup disk directory information and click Next.**

   This option appears only if you selected to backup to disk, not tape.

   You can choose from these options:

   - **Use the Default Backup Directory:** This option, which is chosen by default, will back up to the default folder of \MicrosoftSQLServer\ MSSQL\Backup on the drive where you installed SQL Server 2000.

   - **Create a Subdirectory for Each Database:** This option, if chosen, will automatically create a subdirectory, or subfolder, under the selected backup directory for each database. This option is not chosen by default.

   - **Remove Files Older Than:** So that your disk drive doesn't grow uncontrollably and fill up, you can opt to delete backups after a specific amount of elapsed time has passed. If you choose this option, you specify this interval, with a default value of 4 weeks.

   - **Backup File Extension:** The default backup file extension is TRN, but you can change it if you wish. I don't recommend changing this because TRN is a standard that most people will recognize.

8. **Select transaction log share information (see Figure 15-5) and click Next.**

   This option appears only if you selected to log ship the transaction log.

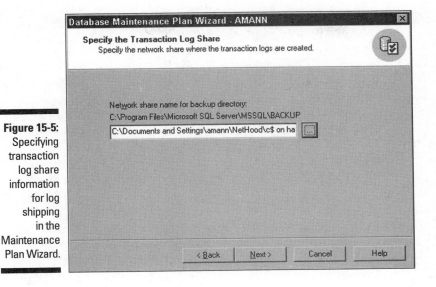

Figure 15-5:
Specifying
transaction
log share
information
for log
shipping
in the
Maintenance
Plan Wizard.

Enter or select a valid network share name for transaction log shipping.

9. **Specify log shipping destination information and click Next.**

This option appears only if you selected to log ship the transaction log.

To specify log shipping destinations (which is where you will ship the logs to), click the Add button. Doing so brings up the Add Destination Database dialog box, as shown in Figure 15-6.

Then, you can fill in or select from the following fields:

- **Server Name:** Select from the available registered SQL Servers. Selecting a server populates most of the rest of the available fields with data from that server. You cannot ship a transaction log to the same database that you are shipping from.

- **Directory:** Enter the directory (or folder) for the log to be shipped to. By default, this is the `\MicrosoftSQLServer\MSSQL\Backup` folder on whatever drive you installed SQL Server on. Note that this is the folder on the selected destination server.

- **Create New Database:** Select this option if you want the log to be shipped to a new database. This option is selected by default. This makes some other fields become enabled.

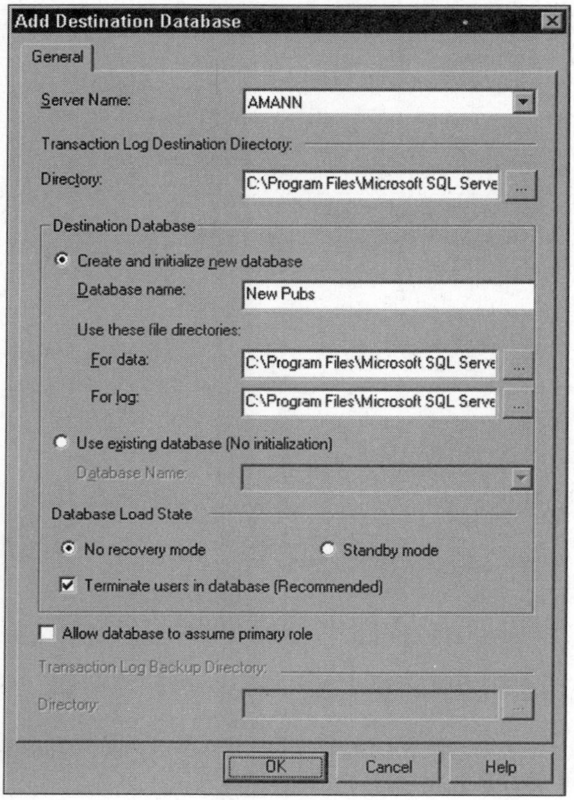

Figure 15-6:
Adding
destination
information
for log
shipping
in the
Maintenance
Plan Wizard.

The first is the Database Name. By default, the database name entered is the same as the one selected for log shipping. Enter the directory information for the data and log to be created in the For Data and For Log fields, respectively. By default, both of these are set to the \Microsoft SQL Server\MSSQL\Data directory of wherever SQL Server 2000 was installed on the destination server.

- **Use Existing Database:** Select this option if you want the log to be shipped to an already created database. If you choose this option, select the desired database from the Database Name drop-down list. If you choose this option, you cannot also choose the Allow Database to Assume Primary Role option.

- **No Recovery Mode:** Select this option to ship the transaction log but keep the database from being available for use. This option is selected by default.

- **Standby Mode:** Select this option to ship the transaction log and make the database available for use (but read-only).

- **Terminate Users in Database:** Because log shipping can happen only if there are no users currently using the database, you must check this option to ensure that the log shipping does not fail. If you don't check this option, you are assuming that there will be no users on the system at the time the log shipping takes place.

- **Allow Database to Assume Primary Role:** Check this option if you want the destination database to have the capability of assuming the primary role or becoming the active database. If you choose this option, you must also specify the directory to back up the transaction log. This option can be used only if you select the Create New Database option.

10. **Specify database initialization options and click Next.**

    This option appears only if you selected to log ship the transaction log and to create a new database.

    SQL Server 2000 initializes the new database from a backup. Therefore, you can specify these options:

    - **Take Full Database Backup Now:** Click this option if you want to use the current schema configuration of the source database. This option is selected by default.

    - **Use Most Recent Backup File:** Click this option if you don't want to use the current schema configuration of the source database but rather the schema that existed in a backup. If you choose this option, you must specify the location and filename of the backup to use.

11. **Specify log shipping schedules (see Figure 15-7) and click Next.**

    This option appears only if you selected to log ship the transaction log.

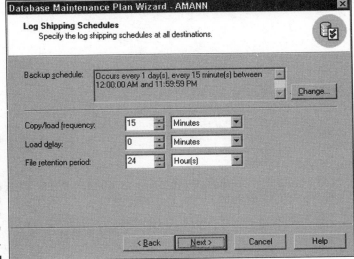

Figure 15-7:
Specifying
log shipping
schedules
in the
Maintenance
Plan Wizard.

SQL Server 2000 initializes the new database from a backup. Therefore, you can specify these options:

- **Backup Schedule:** By default, shipped logs will be backed up every 15 minutes. If you want to change this schedule, click the Change button. For more information on job schedules, see Chapter 14.

- **Copy/Load Frequency:** Specify how often the logs will be shipped and loaded into the destination database. The default is every 15 minutes.

- **Load Delay:** Specify how old the transaction log must be before it can be loaded. By default, loading is immediate, but you may want to indicate that the log must be five minutes old (or some other number). Setting a delay helps to ensure that there are transactions in the log. The time for loading should be determined based on the activity on your server.

- **File Retention Period:** Specify how long the shipped log must be kept before it is deleted. By default, this is 24 hours.

12. **Specify log shipping thresholds (see Figure 15-8) and click Next.**

This option appears only if you selected to log ship the transaction log.

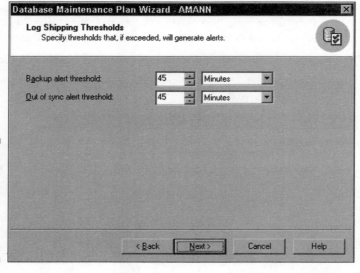

Figure 15-8:
Specifying
log shipping
thresholds
in the
Maintenance
Plan Wizard.

A log shipping threshold is used to determine the point at which an administrative alert should be sent. You can specify these options:

- **Backup Alert Threshold:** Specify the number of minutes that are allowed to elapse since the last transaction log backup was made before an alert is generated. By default, this value is 45 minutes.

- **Out of Sync Alert:** Specify the number of minutes that are allowed to elapse since the last transaction log backup was made and subsequently loaded before an alert is generated. By default, this value is also 45 minutes.

13. **Select the log shipping monitor server (see Figure 15-9) and click Next.**

    This option appears only if you selected to log ship the transaction log.

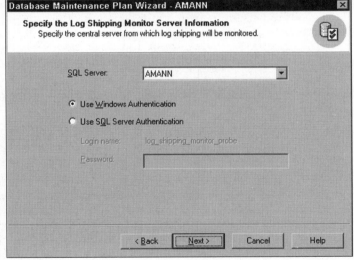

Figure 15-9:
Specifying log shipping monitor server in the Maintenance Plan Wizard.

The status of log shipping process is monitored by a server. This server is specified using the screen shown in Figure 15-9. You can specify these options:

- **Use Windows Authentication:** Select this option if you want the monitor server to be authenticated by using the Windows NT or Windows 2000 authentication. This option is selected by default.

- **Use SQL Server Authentication:** Select this option if you want the monitor server to be authenticated by using a SQL Server login. If you choose this option, you must specify the password. The login name has already been configured for you as log_shipping_monitor_probe.

14. **Select the desired options for reports and click Next.**

    You can choose from these options:

    - **Write Report to a Text File in Directory:** Check this option if you want to generate reports about the maintenance plan. If you check this option, you must also specify, in the provided text box, the folder location to place the text files. By default, this folder is `\Program Files\Microsoft SQL Server\MSSQL\LOG` on the drive where you installed SQL Server 2000. To search for a folder, click the ellipsis (. . .) button. Additionally, you can opt to delete old report files by checking the Delete Text Report Files Older Than option. Specify the amount of elapsed time that must occur before files are deleted. By default, this is `4 weeks`.

    - **Send E-Mail Report to Operator:** Check this option if you want e-mails to be sent to an operator containing the same information in the report that can also be sent to a text file. To add a new operator, click the New Operator button. To select an existing operator, click the ellipsis (. . .) button. If you want to learn more about operators, check out Chapter 14.

15. **Okay, you're almost home! Select the desired maintenance history options and click Next.**

    Maintenance history is a database that stores the activities and status of each of the maintenance plan jobs. You can write the maintenance plan history to a local and/or remote server. You can choose from these options:

    - **Write History to the msdb.dbo.sysdbmaint_history Table on this Server:** Check this option if you want to store the maintenance history on the local server. Checking this option enables the Limit Rows in the Table To check box, which allows you to limit the number of rows that are stored for a maintenance plan's history. The reason for this is to keep the database from growing out of control. By default, this is `1000` rows.

    - **Write History to the Server:** Check this option if you want to store the maintenance history on a remote server that you specify. To select the server, click the ellipsis (. . .) button. Checking this option enables the Limit Rows in the Table To check box, which allows you to limit the number of rows that are stored for a maintenance plan's history. The reason for this is to keep the database from growing out of control. By default, this is `10000` rows.

16. **Review your choices in the Database Maintenance Plan Wizard Summary dialog box and click Next.**

    Enter the name of the new maintenance plan in the Plan Name text box or accept the default value. Then, review the summarized text box of your choices.

17. **Whew! You made it! Click Finish to create your maintenance plan.**

    To complete the wizard, review the parameters that you have chosen for the new login. If you want to change any information, click the Back button.

Editing a Maintenance Plan

Editing a maintenance plan is as simple as changing the parameters that I detail in the "Using the wizard" section, earlier in this chapter. To change any of these parameters, follow these simple steps:

1. **Start the SQL Server Enterprise Manager by choosing Start⇨Programs⇨ Microsoft SQL Server⇨Enterprise Manager.**

2. **Expand the tree so that you see the Management folder; then select the Database Maintenance Plans folder by clicking it.**

    For more information about expanding the tree, see the Introduction of this book.

3. **Select the desired maintenance plan.**

4. **Choose <u>A</u>ction⇨Properties.**

    Alternatively, you can right-click the desired maintenance plan in the Database Maintenance Plans folder or the desired maintenance plan shown in the right pane; then click Properties.

    All these methods bring up the Database Maintenance Plan dialog box, as shown in Figure 15-10, which presents fields in a series of tabs. The number of tabs that are presented depends on the options chosen in the Maintenance Plan Wizard. To use the wizard, refer to the descriptions of the fields and options in the "Using the wizard" section, earlier in this chapter.

Figure 15-10:
Editing your
maintenance
plan.

Deleting a Maintenance Plan

Deleting a maintenance plan not only deletes the plan itself but also the history and jobs associated with it. To delete a maintenance plan, follow these steps:

1. **Start the SQL Server Enterprise Manager by choosing Start⇨Programs⇨ Microsoft SQL Server⇨Enterprise Manager.**

2. **Expand the tree so that you see the Management folder; then select the Database Maintenance Plans folder by clicking it.**

   For more information about expanding the tree, see the Introduction of this book.

3. **Select the desired maintenance plan.**

4. **Choose Action⇨Delete.**

   Alternatively, you can right-click the desired maintenance plan in the Database Maintenance Plans folder or the desired maintenance plan shown in the right pane; then click Delete.

All these methods present a confirmation dialog box allowing you to back out if you are not sure that you want to delete the maintenance plan.

If your maintenance plan includes log shipping, you must remove the log shipping first before deleting the plan. To remove log shipping, you can edit the maintenance plan and click the Log Shipping tab. Then click the Remove Log Shipping button.

Viewing Maintenance Plan History

As mentioned earlier, when you create a maintenance plan, you can opt to write history information to a history database. Obviously, if you write this information, you may have the need to read it.

The screen that allows you to read your maintenance plan history logs is more of a search tool than anything else. To bring up the Maintenance Plan History dialog box, follow these steps:

1. **Start the SQL Server Enterprise Manager by choosing Start⇨Programs⇨ Microsoft SQL Server⇨Enterprise Manager.**

2. **Expand the tree so that you see the Management folder; then select the Database Maintenance Plans folder by clicking it.**

   For more information about expanding the tree, see the Introduction of this book.

3. **Select the desired maintenance plan.**

4. **Choose <u>A</u>ction⇨Maintenance Plan History.**

   Alternatively, you can right-click the Database Maintenance Plans folder or anywhere in the right pane; then click Maintenance Plan History.

You can click anywhere in the right pane because you are not bringing up a history for a specific maintenance plan. You are bringing up the history of all plans for a server. You can then filter by a specific maintenance plan, if you want.

All these methods bring up the Database Maintenance Plan History dialog box shown in Figure 15-11.

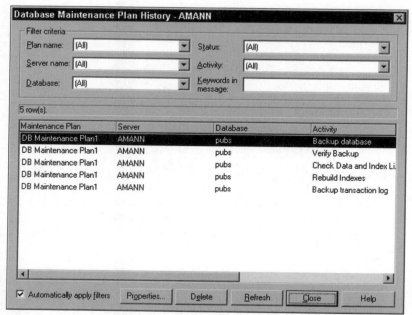

Figure 15-11:
Viewing the
maintenance
plan history.

5. Select the desired search criteria.

By default, all maintenance plan histories will be shown. If you want to search, or filter, on specific attributes, you can filter on these fields:

- **Plan Name:** This drop-down list shows the names of all maintenance plans in the history database.

- **Server Name:** This drop-down list shows the names of all servers that have maintenance plans in the history database.

- **Database:** This drop-down list shows the names of all databases that have maintenance plans in the history database.

- **Status:** This drop-down list allows you to select from succeeded, failed, or all.

- **Activity:** This drop-down list shows the possible activities that have been performed in any maintenance plan whose history is stored on the server. One such activity is Backup Transaction Log.

- **Keywords in Message:** Allows you to manually enter keywords that must appear in the message of the maintenance plan history.

- **Automatically Apply Filters:** This option performs an immediate search whenever you change any of the filter criteria except

Keywords in Message. This check box is checked by default. You may want to uncheck this if your history database is quite large and you have many filters to apply. In such a case, you would uncheck this box and click the Refresh button when you are ready to search.

6. **Choose the desired action button.**

There are five possible action buttons that you can click to aid in managing your history logs. They are as follows:

- **Properties:** Allows you to view the status and all related data for the selected historical item (see Figure 15-12), known as an *entry*. This option performs the same function as double-clicking the desired historical item.

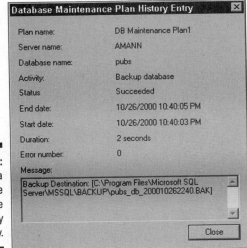

Figure 15-12:
Viewing a Database Maintenance Plan History Entry.

- **Delete:** Allows you to delete the selected historical item from the database. You are prompted to confirm this action.
- **Refresh:** Re-queries the database, applying the criteria that you have selected.
- **Close:** Simply closes the dialog box.
- **Help:** Brings up SQL Server help for the dialog box.

Part VI
The Part of Tens

The 5th Wave   By Rich Tennant

RICHTENNANT

Fixed Up
DATING SERVICE

"OK, make sure this is right. 'Looking for caring companion who likes old movies, nature walks and quiet evenings at home. Knowledge of configuring a 32-bit Microsoft Client for NetWare Networks in Windows 98, a plus.'"

In this part . . .

Okay, say that you've read all my babble on Microsoft SQL Server 2000 and (believe it or not) you're still having problems. This part shows you not only resources available to you to extend SQL Server 2000 but also some of the best tools to help you get your job done. In this part, I even show you where you can get additional consulting help if you need it.

Chapter 16

Ten Microsoft SQL Server Resources

In This Chapter

▶ Consulting additional help

▶ Checking out cool web pages

▶ Solving problems in discussion groups

*I*f you would you like additional information about SQL Server, check out this short chapter to find some further resources.

Consulting

The company that I work for, Internosis, where I am a Principal Architect, specializes in custom e-commerce solutions using Microsoft technologies. Internosis is a world-class consulting organization that I am very proud to be a part of. Internosis leverages a proven process in delivering client value and is both the 1999 and 2000 Microsoft Certified Solution Provider (MCSP) Partner of the Year in the Mid-Atlantic and the 2000 MCSP Partner of the Year in New England. Check out our SQL services at `http://www.internosis.com/solutions/ecommerce/SQL2000`.

If you want to strengthen client relationships, optimize efficiency, solve a business problem, or find out more about some of the innovative solutions that we have delivered for our prestigious clients, just drop me a line. I'd be more than happy to put you in touch with the right person who can help you; contact me using the information that I provide in the "About the Author" section at the beginning of this book.

Web Page Research

Every Microsoft SQL Server 2000 user needs access to online Web pages to keep current in the latest technology, as well as with new products and resources. This section shows some useful Web pages.

I have found that the most useful resources on the subject of Microsoft SQL Server (and other Microsoft products) are produced by Microsoft itself. Therefore, I list more Microsoft Web pages than any other resource in this chapter.

The mother of all SQL sites: Microsoft SQL Server

```
www.microsoft.com/sql
```

This page is, of course, the SQL Server home page from Microsoft, and it provides much in the way of resources for Microsoft SQL Server. Check this page often for news and information about SQL Server 2000 and future releases.

Microsoft's .NET strategy and products (including SQL Server)

```
www.microsoft.com/net/default.asp
```

As an IT professional, you need to keep up with the latest and greatest on Microsoft's .NET framework and strategy. You can get information about any of the .NET products from links on this page.

Microsoft files for downloading

```
ftp://ftp.microsoft.com/Softlib/mslfiles
```

This Web page is a Microsoft FTP (File Transfer Protocol) page that allows you to browse and download free files from Microsoft, including SQL Server files. For an index of the files available in this directory, view the index.txt file, which is located in the parent directory, ftp://ftp.microsoft.com/Softlib/index.txt.

Microsoft's TechNet site

www.microsoft.com/technet/

The Microsoft TechNet Web page is a great resource to learn how to evaluate, support, or implement Microsoft technology solutions. This page includes Microsoft SQL Server and .NET products. Some features of this Web page may not be free.

Microsoft Developer Network (MSDN) Online

http://msdn.microsoft.com/default.asp

The Microsoft Developer Network (MSDN) Web page is a great resource for finding out information about specific developer-related issues about SQL Server and other Microsoft technologies. Some features of this Web page are not free.

The Development Exchange

www.sql-zone.com/

The Development Exchange (DevX) Web site provides much useful information, not only on SQL Server but on development tools as well. Some features of this Web page may not be free.

Discussion Groups

Discussion groups, also known as *newsgroups,* have become quite a good resource for Microsoft SQL Server, all versions. A discussion group is useful mainly because you can get lots of people's opinions — and you don't even have to pay for them. You post a message regarding a problem you may be having. With luck, someone will respond who has experienced the very same problem.

What goes on in a newsgroup?

In newsgroups, anybody can post anything. Groups can take on a particular character or a distinguishing characteristic. Newsgroups can even have several personalities within them. You learn who knows something and who doesn't. Some people are helpful whereas others seem to want only to show off. Often, you notice an atmosphere of kidding around and name calling, which can sometimes indicate rifts in the newsgroup. At other times, the kidding around just signifies a sense of camaraderie among people who are used to one another. Newsgroups are great places to trade information and find useful techniques. The mood changes as different people participate at different times.

The way that you access a news group is to use a news reader, such as Microsoft News, which is installed automatically with many programs, such as Internet Explorer 5.0. You need to configure your news reader to access a news server. Usually, your Internet service provider has a news server in the format of `news.domain.com|net`, which is a common format but by no means a mandatory one. After you point your news reader to a news server, you can use it to download a list of newsgroups. The following section lists popular newsgroups.

microsoft.public.sqlserver.programming

This Microsoft newsgroup specializes in programming issues with all versions of Microsoft SQL Server.

microsoft.public.sqlserver.misc

This Microsoft newsgroup specializes in miscellaneous or general issues with all versions of Microsoft SQL Server.

comp.databases.ms-sqlserver

This newsgroup specializes in general issues with all versions of Microsoft SQL Server.

Chapter 17

Ten Popular Ways to Give SQL Server More Pizzazz

In This Chapter
▶ Tools that add on to the SQL Server product itself
▶ Tools that work in conjunction with SQL Server

Microsoft thought of many things with SQL Server 2000. However, some vendors provide add-on tools that extend the SQL Server 2000 capabilities even further (hard to believe, isn't it?). This chapter lists ten of the add-on tools and products that work in conjunction with SQL Server that I consider the most popular tools. I present these tools in no particular order and I'm not specifically endorsing any product. Also, I don't list any specific version numbers for the products, because they can certainly change often. I suggest you go to the Web sites. Many of these vendors have free trial versions that you can download. Each of the products is a trademark or service mark of its manufacturer.

Microsoft — Visio

`www.microsoft.com/office/visio`

Visio Professional and Enterprise Editions are excellent graphics tools that allow you to create drawings by using stencils and shapes. In addition, Visio allows you to create SQL Server databases as well as reverse-engineer diagrams from existing databases. Visio provides these major benefits:

- ✔ Many shapes and symbols
- ✔ Multiple wizards and add-ons
- ✔ The capability to read your network and generate network diagrams

- Database diagramming and design
- Much, much, much more — check it out!

Seagate Software — Crystal Reports

www.seagatesoftware.com/products/crystalreports

Crystal Reports is an industry-standard, award-winning tool from Seagate Software that allows you to report on data from Microsoft SQL Server by enabling you to manipulate data in many different ways. You can drill down on data and provide multiple views. Crystal Reports even integrates with Microsoft Visual Studio. Crystal Reports supports:

- Visual Studio development environment
- Events and callbacks
- Most Microsoft technologies and products
- Microsoft Visual Studio .NET
- Report Creation APIs

Sylvain Faust — SQL Programmer

www.sfi-software.com

SQL Programmer is an award winning productivity tool from Sylvain Faust that is designed to make manipulating SQL Server objects easier, including stored procedures, triggers, functions, views, and indexes. SQL Programmer was awarded the *Visual Basic Programmer's Journal* 1998 and 1999 *Reader's Choice Merit Award*. Some of the exciting features include:

- Documentation generation
- Script generation
- Multiple database server connections
- Team programming
- Full version control
- Much more!

Quest Software — SQL Navigator for SQL Server

www.quest.com/sql_navigator_ss

SQL Navigator for SQL Server from Quest Software allows you to easily create and manage your SQL Server databases. If you have used the Oracle version of this tool, you'll like the SQL Server version also. Main features include:

- Browses database objects
- Allows you to bookmark your code
- Uses an integrated debugger
- Is "workspace-oriented" for opening multiple connections and objects

BEI Corporation — Ultrabac

www.ultrabac.com/product/default.htm

Also known as ultrabac.com, Ultrabac is a product that backs up your SQL Server databases and provides these key benefits:

- Integrates with regular scheduled network backups
- Is compatible with Microsoft clusters
- Supports RAID 0, 1, 0+1, 3 and 5
- Can use shared tape devices

Embarcadero Technologies — DBArtisan

www.embarcadero.com/products/Administer/dbdatasheet.htm

DBArtisan, from Embarcadero Technologies, allows you to easily administer SQL Server databases. DBArtisan won the *PCWeek* Analyst's Choice Award in 1999 and the *DBMS Magazine* Reader's Choice Award for several years.

Among its features are the following:

- Allows concurrent management of databases
- Is great for all experience levels
- Contains great reporting features
- Manages security

Embarcadero Technologies — ER/Studio

www.embarcadero.com/products/Design/erdatasheet.htm

ER/Studio, also from Embarcadero Technologies, allows you to model and design your databases. This product features:

- Construction of logical and physical data models
- Cross-project domain and model reuse
- Manage data model scope changes
- Multilevel design capabilities

Great Plains Software — Dynamics

www.greatplains.com/dynamics/productinfo.asp

Dynamics, from Great Plains Software, is a tool that provides Financial Management and runs on Microsoft SQL Server. The main features provided by Great Plains Dynamics are as follows:

- Bank reconciliation
- eBanking
- Invoicing
- Inventory
- Payroll
- Much more!

Legato Systems — Networker

www.legato.com/products/protection/networker/networker6/
nwmodules/sql.cfm

Networker for SQL Server protects your SQL Server database applications at the database, transaction log, and file group level. Networker for SQL Server provides these benefits:

- Centrally managed indexes
- High performance backups
- 24/7 database availability during backups
- The use of Microsoft clusters

TNT Software — Event Log Monitor

www.tntsoftware.com/products/emon22/Default.asp

Although this product does not directly integrate with SQL Server, many times you need to view the event log when troubleshooting SQL Server and Windows 2000 issues. Therefore, this product seems appropriate to be listed here. The Event Log Monitor from TNT Software allows you to generate alerts for conditions that are generated in your event logs. Event Log Monitor provides these features:

- Real-time monitoring
- Central console processing
- Reporting

Part VII
Appendixes

In this part . . .

Here I provide you with some additional resources. Sometimes it's great to have everything you need in one place. You'd probably write me lots of hate e-mail if I put this stuff in the chapters themselves. In these appendixes, I include wizard flowcharts and an explanation of what you can expect to find on this book's CD.

So, here ya go!

Appendix A

Wizard Flowcharts

● ●

*T*his appendix contains flowcharts of many of the wizards (in alphabetical order) that make Microsoft SQL Server 2000 easier to use than ever before. Sometimes a flowchart is very valuable when understanding the ramifications of making certain choices.

Configure Publishing and Distribution

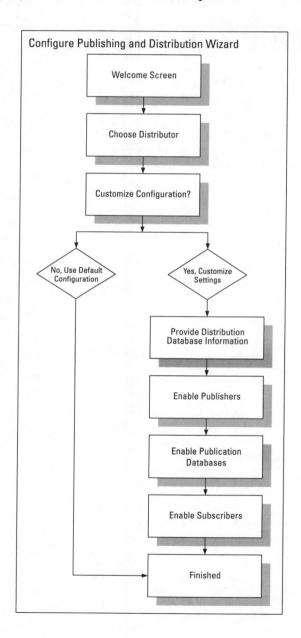

Copy Database

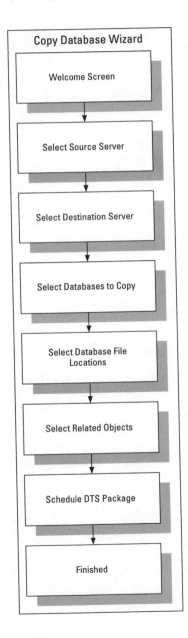

Create Alert

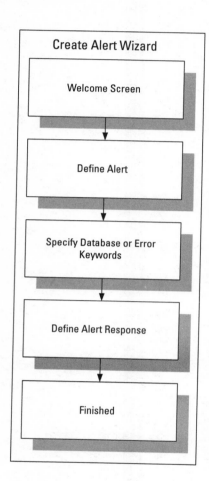

Create Database

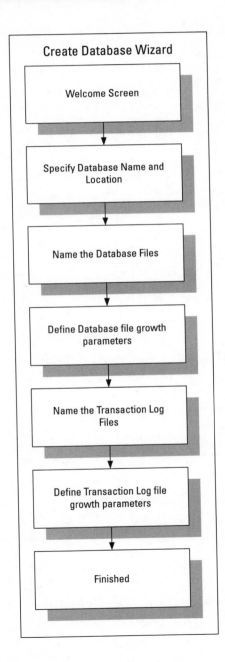

Create Database Backup

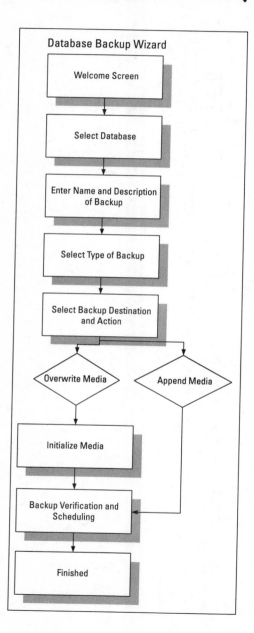

Create Index

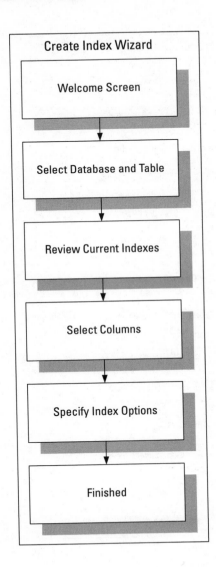

Create Job

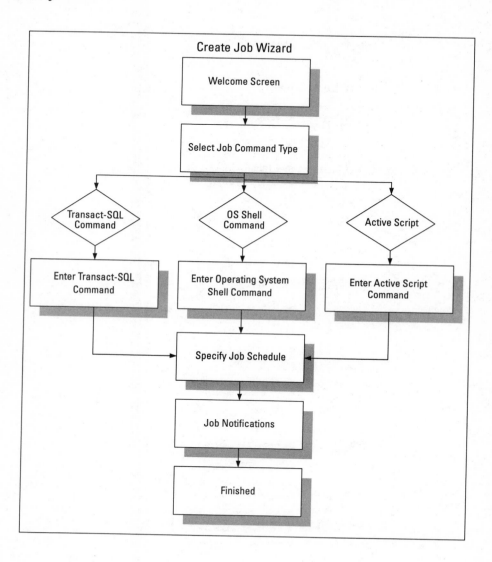

Create Login

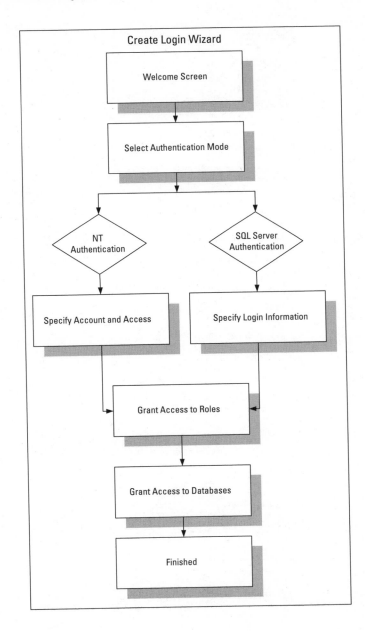

Create Publication

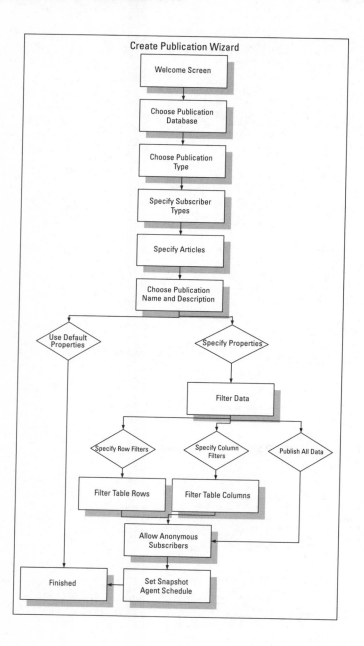

Create Stored Procedure

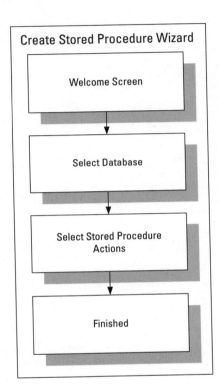

Create View

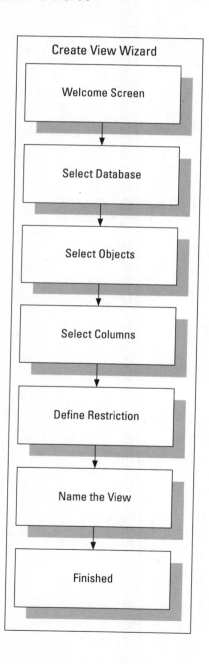

Database Maintenance Plan

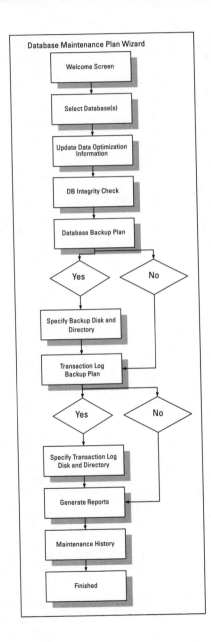

Disable Publishing and Distribution

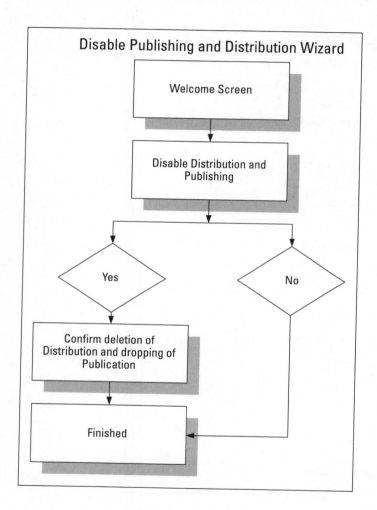

DTS Import/Export

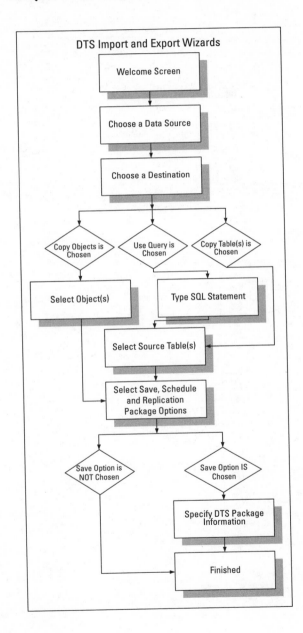

DTS Import and Export Wizards

- Welcome Screen
- Choose a Data Source
- Choose a Destination
  - Copy Objects is Chosen
  - Use Query is Chosen
  - Copy Table(s) is Chosen
- Select Object(s)
- Type SQL Statement
- Select Source Table(s)
- Select Save, Schedule and Replication Package Options
  - Save Option is NOT Chosen
  - Save Option IS Chosen
- Specify DTS Package Information
- Finished

Full-Text Indexing

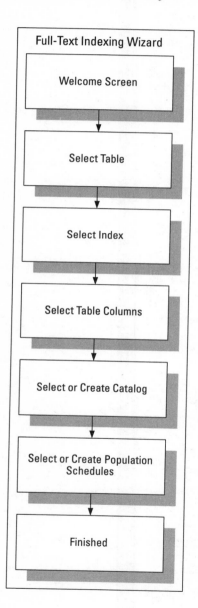

Full-Text Indexing Wizard

- Welcome Screen
- Select Table
- Select Index
- Select Table Columns
- Select or Create Catalog
- Select or Create Population Schedules
- Finished

Pull Subscription

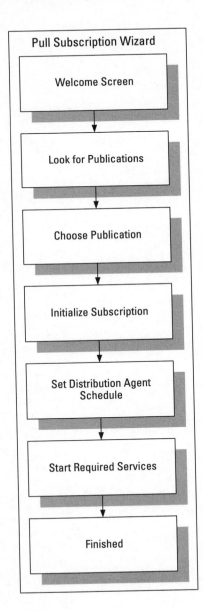

Push Subscription

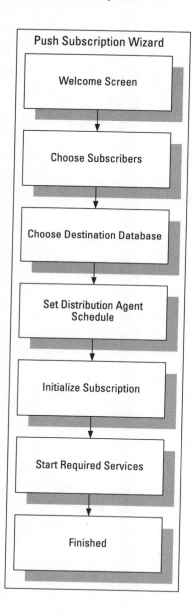

Web Assistant

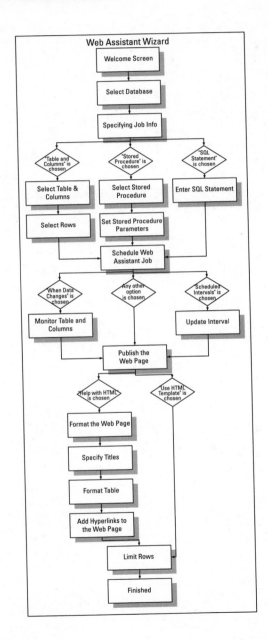

Appendix B

About the CD

*O*n the CD-ROM:

✔ I have included Microsoft SQL Server 2000 120-Day Evaluation. For more information about Microsoft SQL Server and its features, check out the Web site at `www.microsoft.com/sql`.

System Requirements

Make sure that your computer meets the minimum system requirements listed below. If your computer doesn't match up to most of these requirements, you may have problems using the contents of the CD.

✔ A PC with a Pentium 166 MHz or faster processor.

✔ Microsoft Windows NT Server 4.0, or Microsoft Windows 2000 Server.

✔ At least 64MB of total RAM installed on your computer. For best performance, we recommend at least 128 MB of RAM installed.

✔ 95-270MB (Depending on components installed.) of hard drive space available to install all the software from this CD. Typical installation requires 250MB.

✔ Microsoft Internet Explorer 5.0.

✔ Internet Information Services.

✔ A monitor with VGA or higher resolution.

800 x 600 or higher resolution (required for SQL Server graphical tools).

✔ A modem with a speed of at least 14,400 bps.

If you need more information on the basics, check out *PCs For Dummies,* 7th Edition, by Dan Gookin; *Windows NT Server 4 For Dummies*, by Ed Tittel; *Windows 2000 Server For Dummies*, by Ed Tittel, Mary T. Madden, and James Michael Stewart (all published by IDG Books Worldwide, Inc.).

Using the CD with Microsoft Windows

To install the items from the CD to your hard drive, follow these steps.

1. **Insert the CD into your computer's CD-ROM drive.**

2. **If the compact disc does not autorun, double-click autorun.exe in the root directory of the compact disc.**

3. **Choose Browse Setup/Upgrade Help to view addition installation instructions or click on SQL Server 2000 Components to begin installation.**

What You'll Find

Shareware programs are fully functional, free trial versions of copyrighted programs. If you like particular programs, register with their authors for a nominal fee and receive licenses, enhanced versions, and technical support. Freeware programs are free, copyrighted games, applications, and utilities. You can copy them to as many PCs as you like — free — but they have no technical support. GNU software is governed by its own license, which is included inside the folder of the GNU software. There are no restrictions on distribution of this software. See the GNU license for more details. Trial, demo, or evaluation versions are usually limited either by time or functionality (such as being unable to save projects).

Here's a summary of the software on this CD arranged by category. If you use Windows, the CD interface helps you install software easily. (If you have no idea what I'm talking about when I say "CD interface," see "Using the CD with Microsoft Windows.")

If you use a Mac OS computer, you can take advantage of the easy Mac interface to quickly install the programs.

Microsoft SQL Server 2000 120-Day Evaluation

Microsoft Corporation

For Windows NT Server or Windows 2000 Server. 120-Day Evaluation version. Use Microsoft SQL Server 2000 120-Day evaluation to assist you while you read. You have the opportunity to work along with the examples in the book to . . .

- Build a database
- Set up rules
- Work with stored procedures
- Use the Query Analyzer
- And much more!

For additional information on Microsoft SQL Server 2000, view the Web site at `http://www.microsoft.com/sql`

If You've Got Problems (Of the CD Kind)

I tried my best to compile programs that work on most computers with the minimum system requirements. Alas, your computer may differ, and some programs may not work properly for some reason.

The two likeliest problems are that you don't have enough memory (RAM) for the programs you want to use, or you have other programs running that are affecting installation or running of a program. If you get error messages like `Not enough memory` or `Setup cannot continue`, try one or more of these methods and then try using the software again:

- **Turn off any antivirus software that you have on your computer.** Installers sometimes mimic virus activity and may make your computer incorrectly believe that it is being infected by a virus.

- **Close all running programs.** The more programs you're running, the less memory is available to other programs. Installers also typically update files and programs; if you keep other programs running, installation may not work properly.

- **In Windows, close the CD interface and run demos or installations directly from Windows Explorer.** The interface itself can tie up system memory, or even conflict with certain kinds of interactive demos. Use Windows Explorer to browse the files on the CD and launch installers or demos.

- **Have your local computer store add more RAM to your computer.** This is, admittedly, a drastic and somewhat expensive step. However, if you have a Windows 95 PC or a Mac OS computer with a PowerPC chip, adding more memory can really help the speed of your computer and enable more programs to run at the same time.

If you still have trouble installing the items from the CD, please call the Customer Care phone number: 800-762-2974 (outside the U.S.: 317-572-3993).

Index

• A •

ABSOLUTE keyword, 214
access, remote data, 284–289
Action Wizard, 17
ad-hoc server connection, 286–287, 289
ADO (ActiveX Data Objects), 209
AFTER keyword, 113
Agent, 20
alerts, 293, 305–306
  conditions, 307–308
  errors, 307
  Event Alert, 307
  Performance Condition Alert, 307
  raising, 306
  responses, 308, 310
  severity, 307
aliases, 188
  Client Network Utility, 37
ALTER statement, 160
ambiguous joins, 187
Analysis Services, 20
analysis services enhancements, 9
architecture, new features, 10–11
articles, 268
  selecting for publication, 272
  subscribing to, 273–276
ASC keyword, 167
ASP (Active Server Pages), 218–221
atomicity, transactions, 71
authentication, 202

• B •

Backup Device Properties dialog box, 243–244
Backup Wizard, 246
backups, 14
  complete, 246
  configuring, 246–248
  databases, 17
  destination, 247
  device setup, 242–244
  differential, 246
  expiration, 249
  failover clustering, 242
  incremental, 18
  log shipping, 255
  maintenance, 317–318
  media set labels, 249–250
  optional data, 248–250
  passwords, 14
  performing, 245–250
  reasons for, 241
  restoring, 14
  restoring data, 250–252, 254–255
  scheduling, 247–248
  tape drives, 244
  transaction log, 247
  verifying, 248
base-level objects, 75
batches, 204
BEGIN TRANSACTION statement, 191
BEGIN...END statement, 129
BEI Corporation, Ultrabac, 339
BINARY BASE64 keyword, 185
binding, 47
  rules, 171

Books Online, 13, 40
BREAK statement, 132–133
browsers, metadata and, 15
building databases, 76, 78–86

• *C* •

Cartesian products, 67
cascading constraints, 15
CASE...WHEN statement, 129
CASE...WHEN...ELSE...END statement, 130
categories, SQL, 160
change tracking, full-text catalogs and, 119
char datatype, 165
CHECK constraints, 100, 104
  configuration, 106
  Enterprise Manager, 104–106
  SQL, 106–107
clauses, 159, 175
  constraint clauses, 166
  FOR XML, 185
  FROM, 187
  GROUP BY, 168
  ORDER BY, 187
  WHERE, 175
Client Network Utility, 36–39
  aliases, 37
  protocols, 36–37
CLOSE statement, 216
closing, cursors and, 216
clustered indexes, 49, 108, 167–168
CLUSTERED keyword, 167
code execution, Transaction-SQL, 136
collation, 11, 82, 164
columns, 43
  constraints, 164
  identity columns, 89
  indexed, 11
  indexes, 166
  keys and, 50
  primary keys and, 45
  properties, 163

rules, 103–104
sort order, 167
table design, 87
traces, 28–29
views, 169
Web Assistant, 259
COM (Common Object Model), 208
comments, 135
commit phase, DTC service, 279
Commit phase (transaction two-phase commit), 72
COMMIT TRANSACTION statement, 191
complete backup, 246
compound selects (queries), 186–187
conditions
  alerts, 307–308
  rules, 171
configuration, check constraints, 106
Configure Publishing and Distribution Wizard, 269–270
Connect to SQL Server dialog box, 202
connectivity, 208–210
consistency in transactions, 71
constraint clauses, 166
constraints
  cascading, 15
  CHECK, 100
  check constraints, 104–107
  columns, 164
  tables, 164
consulting resources, 333
CONTAINS keyword, 196
CONTAINSTABLE keyword, 197
CONTINUE statement, 134
control-of-flow statements, 127–134
Copy Database Wizard, 17
copying databases, 17
Create Database Backup Wizard, 17
CREATE DATABASE statement, 161–162
Create Database Wizard, 76, 78–81
CREATE DEFAULT statement, 172
CREATE INDEX statement, 167

Create Login Wizard, 17
Create Publication Wizard, 270–273
CREATE RULE statement, 103, 170–171
CREATE statement, 160
CREATE TABLE statement, 163–165
CREATE TRIGGER statement, 173–175
CREATE VIEW statement, 169
Crystal Reports (Seagate Software), 338
Cube Wizard, 17
cursors
  closing, 216
  deallocating, 216–217
  declaring, 126, 212–213
  navigating with, 210–212
  opening, 213
  removing, 216–217
  Transact-SQL statements and, 212
  types, 211–212

• *D* •

DAO (Data Access Objects), 208
Data Control Language (DCL), 160
data mining, 10, 18
data models, 51–57. *See also* schema
  logical model, 51–52
  physical model, 52
data pages, maintenance, 314
data transformation, 224
Data Transformation Services Wizard, 17
Database Maintenance Plan Wizard, 17,
    312–325
Database Properties dialog box, 82
databases
  building, 76, 78–86
  copying, 17
  DDL and, 161–162
  exporting to, 232–238
  importing to, 225–232
  integrity, maintenance and, 316
  unused space, maintenance and, 315
  views, 169–170

datatypes, 57–60, 165
  char, 165
  length, 90
  new, 11
  nulls, 90
  precision, 90
  table design, 88
  user-defined, 60–62
  varchar, 165
DBArtisan, Embarcadero Technologies, 339
DB-Library, 210
DCL (Data Control Language), 192–195
DCOM (Distributed Common Object
    Model), 208
DDL (Data Definition Language), 160–175
DEALLOCATE statement, 216–217
deallocating cursors, 216–217
declaration
  cursors, 126, 212–213
  local variables, 126
  table definition variables, 127
declarative referential integrity, 46
DECLARE CURSOR statement, 212–213
DECLARE keyword, 126
Default Properties dialog box, 93
default values, 93
  Enterprise Manager, 94–95
  Query Analyzer, 95
defaults, 47
Define Transformation of Published Data
    Wizard, 18
DELETE object permission, 194
DELETE statement, 182–184
  triggers and, 48
deleting, objects, 96–97
denormalized data, 49–51
DENY statement, 192
derived fields, 55
DESC keyword, 167
Design Table menu, 105
Design Table screen, 88

designing tables, 87–88, 90–92
  columns, 88
  datatypes, 88
  Query Analyzer, 91
destination, backups, 247
destination table, 230
DevX (Development Exchange) Web
  page, 335
differential backup, 246
Dimension Wizard, 18
dimensions, 10
Disable Publishing and Distribution
  Wizard, 18
discussion groups, 336
displaying information, 135
distributed nontransactional queries,
  277, 285
  ad-hoc server connection, 286–287
  linked servers, 285–286
distributed queries, 14, 277
  DTC service and, 278
Distributed Transaction Coordinator, 20
distributed transactional queries,
  278–279, 287
  ad-hoc server connection, 289
  linked servers, 287–288
distributed transactions, 72
distributor, 268
DML (Data Manipulation Language), 160,
  175–191
documentation, 12
DROP keyword, 96–97
DROP statement, 160
DROP_EXISTING keyword, 168
DTC service, distributed queries and, 278
DTS (Data Transformation Services),
  224–225
  enhancements, 12
  package, 230
durability, transactions, 71
duty schedule, operators, 304

dynamic cursor, 211
Dynamics (Great Plains Software), 340

ELEMENTS keyword, 185
Embarcadero Technologies
  (DBArtisan), 339
 ER/Studio, 340
English Query, 13, 32
Enterprise enhancements, 13
Enterprise Manager, 21–22
  building databases, 81–86
  check constraints, 104–106
  default values, 93
  foreign key creation, 107–108
  full-text catalogs, 120, 122–123
  rules, 100–103
  table design, 87, 90–91
  triggers, 114–116
ER/Studio (Embarcadero
  Technologies), 340
error handling, 137–138
errors, alerts, 307
Event Alert, 307
Event Log Monitor (TNT Software), 341
events, 22
  traces (Profiler), 27–28
EXECUTE object permission, 194
EXECUTE statement, 178
executing
  extended procedures, 149
  system procedures, 146
executing code, Transact-SQL, 136
expiration, backups, 249
exporting, 223
  to databases, 232–238
extended procedures, 146–147
  creating, 150–152
  executing, 149
  properties, 148–149

• F •

failover clustering, 242
failures, job steps, 298
FETCH keyword, 214
fields, 43, 163
  derived, 55
  read-only, 54
  read-write, 55
filegroups, 75–76
files, growing, 79–81
FILLFACTOR keyword, 168
filters, traces, 30
firing triggers, 48, 113–119
1NF (First Normal Form), 50
FIRST keyword, 214
flow charts. *See* Appendix A
FOR XMLl clause, 185
foreign keys, 46–47
  Enterprise Manager, 107–108
  relationship, 107–108
FREETEXT keyword, 196
frequency of jobs, 299–301
FROM clause, 187
full outer joins, 190
full-text catalogs, 119–120, 122–123
  change tracking, 119
  Enterprise Manager, 120, 122–123
Full-Text Indexing Wizard, 18, 120
full-text queries, 195–199
functions
  OPENQUERY, 178
  OPENROWSET, 178
  rowset, 183
  system functions, 138–139
  Transact-SQL, 138–142
  user-defined, 10, 139–142

• G •

GLOBAL keyword, 213–214
glossary (Books Online), 13

GOTO statement, 131–132
GRANT statement, 192
Great Plains Software, Dynamics, 340
GROUP BY clause, 168
groups, repeating, 50
growing files, 79–81

• H •

handling errors, 137–138
hard-coded data, 178–179
Help, 40
history, maintenance, 324
  viewing, 327–329
HTML (Hypertext Markup Language), 219
  Web Assistant, 263
HTML page, Web Assistant, 267
HTTP (Hypertext Transfer Protocol), 10

• I •

identity column, 90
IF...ELSE statements, 128–129
IGNORE_DUP_KEY keyword, 168
Import/Export Wizard, 225–238
importing, 223
  to databases, 225–232
inactive entries in transaction log,
    backups, 249
incremental backups, 18
Incremental Update Wizard, 18
incrementing, 164
index pages, maintenance, 314
Index Tuning Wizard, 18
indexed views, 10
indexes, 48–49, 108–109, 166
  clustered, 49, 108, 167–168
  computed columns, 11
  nonclustered, 49, 108, 167–168
  Query Analyzer, 112–113
  table scans and, 48
  tuning, 18

information display, 135
inner joins, 188–190
INSENSITIVE keyword, 212
INSERT object permission, 194
INSERT statement, 167, 177–179
  triggers and, 48
instances, multiple, 11
INSTEAD OF keyword, 113
INSTEAD OF statement, 174
integrity, referential integrity, 46
isolation levels, transactions, 279
  READ COMMITED, 279
  READ UNCOMMITED, 279
  REPEATABLE READ, 279
  SERIALIZABLE, 279
isolation, transactions, 71–73

• J •

jobs, 293
  completion, 301–303
  failures, 298
  frequency, 299–301
  new, 294–303
  output files, 298
  retries, 298
  steps, 295–299
JOIN keyword, 187
joins
  ambiguous, 187
  inner joins, 188–190
  outer joins, 190–191

• K •

keys, 43–44
  columns and, 50
  foreign keys, 46–47
  primary keys, 45–46
keyset-driven cursor, 212
keywords
  ABSOLUTE, 214
  AFTER, 113

ASC, 167
BINARY BASE64, 185
CLUSTERED, 167
CONTAINS, 196
CONTAINSTABLE, 197
DECLARE, 126
DESC, 167
DROP, 96–97
DROP_EXISTING, 168
ELEMENTS, 185
ENCRYPTION, 170
FETCH, 214
FILLFACTOR, 168
FIRST, 214
FREETEXT, 196
GLOBAL, 213–214
IGNORE_DUP_KEY, 168
INSENSITIVE, 212
INSTEAD OF, 113
JOIN, 187
LAST, 214
NEXT, 214
NONCLUSTERED, 167
NOT NULL, 166
ON, 187
PAD_INDEX, 168
PRIOR, 214
RELATIVE, 214
SORT_IN_TEMPDB, 168
STATISTICS_NORECOMPUTE, 168
UNIQUE, 167
WITH CHECK OPTION, 170
XML, 185

• L •

language enhancements, 14
LAST keyword, 214
left outer joins, 190
legacy data, 225
Legato Systems, Networker, 341
libraries, networks, 35

links, servers, 279–288
local variables, declaring, 126
lock modes, 68–69
locking, 68–70
locking hints, 178
log shipping, 14
  backup, 255
  maintenance and, 321–323
logical data model, 51–52
logical names, 87
look-up tables, 54

• *M* •

maintenance, 311
  backups, 317–318
  data pages, 314
  database integrity, 316
  Database Maintenance Plan Wizard,
    312–325
  deleting plan, 326–327
  editing plan, 325
  history, viewing, 327–329
  history options, 324
  index pages, 314
  log shipping and, 321–323
  Query Optimizer statistics, 314
  reports, 324
  transaction log, 318–319
  unused space, databases, 315
Maintenance Plan History dialog box,
    327–329
many-to-many relationships, 67–68
media set labels, backups, 249–250
memory, 11
merge publications, 268, 271
metadata browsers, 15
metadata services, 15
Microsoft cluster services, 242
Microsoft Search, 20
Microsoft SQL Server 2000 120-Day
    Evaluation version, 366–367

Microsoft Visio, 337
Microsoft Windows, CD bundle and, 366
Migrate Repository Wizard, 18
migration, 18
Mining Model Wizard, 18
modeling, 15
MSCS (Microsoft cluster services), 242
MSDN (Microsoft Developer Network)
    Online Web page, 335

• *N* •

naming
  conventions, 64–65
  logical names, 87
  physical names, 87
  triggers, 173
NET strategy Web page, 334
Net-Library, 11
Networker (Legato Systems), 341
networks
  Client Network Utility, 36–39
  libraries, 35
  Server Network Utility, 33–35
New Alert Properties dialog box, 306
New Job Properties dialog box, 294
New Job Step dialog box, 295
New Operator Properties dialog box, 304
newsgroups, 336
NEXT keyword, 214
nonclustered indexes, 49, 108, 167–168
NONCLUSTERED keyword, 167
non-noise words. *See* full-text catalogs
normalization
  1NF (First Normal Form), 50
  2NF (Second Normal Form), 50
  3NF (Third Normal Form), 50
  denormalized data, 49, 50, 51
NOT NULL keyword, 166
notifications, operators, 305
null values, 166
nulls, datatypes and, 90

• O •

object browsers, Query Analyzer, 206
object permissions, 194–195
objects
  base-level, 75
  deleting, 96–97
  schema, 43–49
  security, 97
ODBC (Open Database Connectivity), 208
OLAP Project Wizard, 18
OLE DB (Object Linking and Embedding for
    Databases), 209
OLE DB providers, 11
ON keyword, 187
one-to-one relationships, 66–67
Open dialog box, 23
opening
  cursors, 213
  traces (Profiler), 23–24
OPENQUERY function, 178
OPENQUERY statement, 285
OPENROWSET function, 178
operators, 175–177, 293, 303–304
  duty schedule, 304
  notifications, 305
  properties, 304
ORDER BY clause, 187
outer joins, 190–191
  full outer joins, 190
  left outer joins, 190
output file, jobs, 298
overhead, 211
owner, views, 169

• P •

PAD_INDEX keyword, 168
Partition Wizard, 18

partitioning, 18
passthrough queries, 285
passwords, backups, 14
Performance Condition Alert, 307
performance hits, 51
Performance Monitor, 32–33
permissions, 97
  objects, 194–195
  statements, 193
physical data model, 52
physical names, 87
pivot tables, 10
precision, datatypes, 90
prepare phase, DTC service, 279
Prepare phase (transaction two-phase
    commit), 72
primary keys, 45–46
  columns and, 45
  identity column, 90
PRINT statement, 135
PRIOR keyword, 214
procedures. *See also* stored procedures
  extended, 146–147
  system procedures, 144–146
Profiler, 22–30
  traces, 23–30
programming, metadata enhancements, 15
Project Wizard, 18
projects, 18
properties
  backup devices, 243–244
  column constraints, 164
  columns, 163
  extended procedures, 148–149
  jobs, new, 294–295
  linked servers, 280
  operators, 304

Rule Properties dialog box, 101
  stored procedures, 153
  table constraints, 164
  Trigger Properties dialog box, 115
protocols
  Client Network Utility, 36–37
  Server Network Utility, 34
publications
  merge, 268, 271
  snapshop, 269, 271
  transactional, 268, 271
publisher, 268
publishing Web data, 257–267
  to another computer, 268–276
Pull Subscription Wizard, 274–276
pull subscriptions, 268
push subscriptions, 268

• *Q* •

queries, 184–191. *See also* distributed
    queries; English Query
  compound selects, 186–187
  distributed, 14
  executing, 202–204
  full-text, 195–199
  passthrough, 285
  results, 204
  simple selects, 186
  speed, 166–169
  transactions and, 191–192
Query Analyzer, 31, 201
  authentication, 202
  building databases, 85–86
  default values, 95–96
  executing queries, 202–204
  indexes, 112–113
  new features, 16
  results, 204
  table design, 91–93
  templates, 206–207
  Windows NT authentication, 202
Query Optimizer, maintenance and, 314
query plans, 201
querying data, 184–191
Quest Software, SQL Navigator for SQL
    Server, 339

• *R* •

RAISERROR statement, 137–138
raising alerts, 306
RDBMS (Relational Database Management
    System), 9
RDO (Remote Data Objects), 209
RDS (Remote Data Service), 209
READ COMMITED isolation level, 279
read-only fields, 54
read-write fields, 55
records, 45, 163. *See also* rows
  inserting, 178
redundant data, 50
referential integrity, 46, 173–175
  declarative, 46
relational databases, 43
relational model, 49–51
relationships, 66–68
  Cartesian products, 67
  foreign keys, 107–108
  many-to-many, 67–68
  one-to-many, 67
  one-to-one, 66–67
RELATIVE keywords, 214
remote data access, 284–289
REPEATABLE READ isolation level, 279
repeating groups, eliminating, 50
replay options, traces, 24
replication
  enhancements, 16
  triggers and, 174
reports, maintenance, 324

resolution tables, 68
resources
  consulting, 333
  discussion groups, 336
  newsgroups, 336
  Web pages, 334–335
responses, alerts, 308, 310
restoring backups, 14
restoring from backup, 250–252, 254–255
  as database, 251
result sets, 210
  Web data, 259
results (queries), 204
retries, job steps, 298
RETURN statements, 130
REVOKE statement, 192
right outer joins, 190
ROLLBACK TRANSACTION statement, 192
rows, 45. *See also* records
  text, 11
  Web Assistant, 260
rowset functions, 183
Rule Properties dialog box, 101
rules, 47, 99–100
  binding, 171
  columns, 103–104
  conditions, 171
  Enterprise Manager, 100–103
  SQL, 103–104
  user-defined datatypes, 103
running traces, Profiler, 23–24

• S •

scalability, utilities, 14
scheduling backups, 247–248
schema
  data models, 51–57
  objects, 43–49
SCROLL keyword, 212
SCSI hard drives, MSCS and, 242
Seagate Software, Crystal Reports, 338

searches, 20
  full-text searching, 11
  Transact-SQL commands, 195–196
2NF (Second Normal Form), 50
security, 10
  linked servers, 281–282
  objects, 97
  stored procedures, 155
Security Delegation, 14
SELECT object permission, 194
SELECT statement, 184–191
Select Wizard dialog box, 39–40, 76
SERIALIZABLE isolation level, 279
Server Network Utility, 33–35
  libraries, 35
servers
  ad-hoc connections, 286–287, 289
  linking, 279–288
  options, 282–283
Service Manager, 19–21
SET TRANSACTION ISOLATION LEVEL
    statement, 279
severity, alerts, 307
shareware, 366
simple select, queries, 186
snapshot publications, 269, 271
sort order, columns, 167
SORT_IN_TEMPDB keyword, 168
source table, 230
SQL (Structured Query Language), 159.
    See also Transact-SQL
  categories, 160
  check constraints, 106–107
  rules, 103–104
  system procedures and, 145
  triggers, 116–119
SQL For Dummies, 159
SQL Navigator for SQL Server (Quest
    Software), 339
SQL Profiler, 17
SQL Programmer (Sylvain Faust), 338
SQL Project Wizard, 18

SQL Server Backup dialog box, 245
SQL Server Web site, 334
SQL-DMO (Structured Query Language-
      Distributed Management Objects), 209
square brackets ([ ]), 92
statements, 160
   ALTER, 160
   BEGIN TRANSACTION, 191
   BEGIN...END, 129
   BREAK, 132–133
   CASE...WHEN, 129
   CASE...WHEN...ELSE...END, 130
   CLOSE, 216
   COMMIT TRANSACTION, 191
   CONTINUE, 134
   control-of-flow, 127–134
   CREATE, 160
   CREATE DATABASE, 161–162
   CREATE DEFAULT, 172
   CREATE INDEX, 167
   CREATE RULE, 103, 170–171
   CREATE TABLE, 163–165
   CREATE TRIGGER, 173–175
   CREATE VIEW, 169
   DEALLOCATE, 216–217
   DECLARE CURSOR, 212–213
   DELETE, 182–184
   DENY, 192
   DROP, 160
   EXECUTE, 178
   GOTO, 131–132
   GRANT, 192
   IF...ELSE, 128–129
   INSERT, 167, 177–179
   INSTEAD OF, 174
   OPENQUERY, 285
   permissions, 193
   PRINT, 135
   RAISERROR, 137–138
   RETURN, 130
   REVOKE, 192

ROLLBACK TRANSACTION, 192
   SELECT, 184–191
   SET TRANSACTION ISOLATION
      LEVEL, 279
   UPDATE, 167, 179–182
   USE, 163
   WAITFOR, 133
   WHILE, 131
STATISTICS_NORECOMPUTE keyword, 168
steps, jobs, 295–299
Storage Design Wizard, 18
stored procedures, 143
   extended procedures, 148–149
   security, 155
   system procedures, 144–146
   Web data, 259
Stored Procedures Properties dialog
      box, 153
subscriber, 268
subscribers, types, 271
subscriptions, articles, 273–276
Sylvain Faust, SQL Programmer, 338
system functions, 138–139
system procedures, 144–146
   availability, 144
   executing, 146
   SQL and, 145
system requirements, 365

• *T* •

table definition variables, 127
table design, 87–88, 90–93
   columns, 88
   datatypes, 88
   Query Analyzer, 91–93
table hints, 178
table scans, 48
tables, 163–166. *See also* fields; records
   constraints, 164
   destination table, 230

tables *(continued)*
  fields, 163
  look-up, 54
  new, 163
  pivot tables, 10
  records, 163
  resolution tables, 68
  source table, 230
  updating, 179–182
  Web Assistant, 259
tape drives, backups, 244
TechNet Web site, 335
templates, 206–207
  traces, 25–26
text, rows, 11
3NF (Third Normal Form), 50
tiers, 63
TNT Software, Event Log Monitor, 341
Trace Properties dialog box, 25, 27
traces (Profiler), 23
  columns, 28–29
  description information, 26–27
  events, selecting, 27–28
  filter data, 30
  new, 24–30
  opening, 23–24
  replay options, 24
  running, 23–24
  saving results, 26–27
  stop time, 27
  template names, 26
  templates and, 25
Transact-SQL, 125, 159
  batches and, 204
  cursors, 212
  DCL and, 192
  DDL and, 160
  executing code, 136
  functions, 138–142
  statement permissions, 193
  templates and, 206–207
  text searches, 195–196

  variables, 125–127
  Web data, 259
transaction log
  backups, 247
  inactive entries, deleting, 249
  maintenance, 318–319
transactional publications, 268, 271
transactions, 71–73
  atomicity, 71
  consistency, 71
  durability, 71
  isolation, 71–73
  isolation levels, 279
  queries and, 191–192
  two-phase commit, 72
transformation. *See* data transformation
Trigger Properties dialog box, 115
triggers, 11, 48, 113–119, 173–175
  AFTER keyword, 113
  Enterprise Manager, 114–116
  firing, 48
  INSTEAD OF keyword, 113
  names, 173
  replication and, 174
  SQL, 116–119
troubleshooting CD, 367
two-phase commit, transactions, 72

• U •

UDL (Universal Data Link), 210
Ultrabac (BEO Corporation), 339
UNIQUE keyword, 167
update intervals, Web Assistant, 262
UPDATE object permission, 194
UPDATE statement, 167, 179–182
  triggers and, 48
Usage Analysis Wizard, 18
Usage-Based Optimization Wizard, 18
USE statement, 163
User-Defined Data Type Properties dialog
  box, 62

user-defined datatypes, 60–62
  rules, 103
user-defined functions, 10, 139–142
utilities
  Client Network Utility, 36–39
  scalability, 14
  Server Network Utility, 33–35

• V •

varchar datatype, 165
variables
  local, 126
  table definition, 127
  Transact-SQL, 125–127
verification, backups, 248
views, 169–170
  columns, 169
  indexed, 10
  owners, 169
Virtual Cube Wizard, 18
Visio, Microsoft, 337
Visual Basic 6 For Dummies, 218

• W •

WAITFOR statement, 133
Web Assistant, 257–266
  columns, 259
  HTML, 263
  HTML page access, 267
  job access, 266
  rows, 260
  tables, 259
  update intervals, 262
Web data, publishing, 257–267
  to another computer, 268–276
  result sets, 259
  stored procedures and, 259
  Transact-SQL statements, 259
Web pages
  ASP, 218–221
  DevX (Development Exchange), 335

files for downloading, 334
Microsoft Developer Network (MSDN)
    Online, 335
NET strategy, 334
resources, 334–335
SQL Server, 334
TechNet, 335
WHERE clause, 175
  rules text, 102
WHILE statement, 131
Windows CE, 16
Windows NT authentication, 202
Winsock Proxy, Server Network Utility, 35
WITH CHECK OPTION keyword, 170
WITH ENCRYPTION keyword, 170
wizards
  Action, 17
  Backup, 246
  Configure Publishing and Distribution,
      269–270
  Copy Database, 17
  Create Database, 76, 78–81
  Create Database Backup, 17
  Create Login, 17
  Create Publication, 270–273
  Cube, 17
  Data Transformation Services, 17
  Database Maintenance Plan, 17, 312–325
  Define Transformation of Published
      Data, 18
  Dimension, 18
  Disable Publishing and Distribution, 18
  flow charts. *See* Appendix A
  Full-Text Indexing, 18, 120
  Import/Export, 225–238
  Incremental Update, 18
  Index Tuning, 18
  Migrate Repository, 18
  Mining Model, 18
  new, 17, 18
  OLAP Project, 18
  Partition, 18
  Project, 18

wizards *(continued)*
  Pull Subscription, 274–276
  Select Wizard dialog box, 39–40
  SQL Project, 18
  Storage Design, 18
  Usage Analysis, 18
  Usage-Based Optimization, 18
  Virtual Cube, 18
  Web Assistant, 257–266

XML (Extensible Markup Language)
  support, 15
XML encoding, 15
XMLDATA keyword, 185

120-Day Evaluation License for Microsoft SQL Server 2000

IMPORTANT-READ CAREFULLY: This Microsoft Evaluation License Agreement ("Evaluation License") is a legal agreement between you (either an individual or a single entity) and Microsoft Corporation for the Microsoft software product identified above, which includes computer software and may include associated media, printed materials, and "online" or electronic documentation ("Software Product"). BY INSTALLING, COPYING, OR OTHERWISE USING THE SOFTWARE PRODUCT, YOU AGREE TO BE BOUND BY THE TERMS OF THIS EVALUATION LICENSE. IF YOU DO NOT AGREE TO THE TERMS OF THIS EVALUATION LICENSE, DO NOT INSTALL, COPY, OR USE THE SOFTWARE PRODUCT.

The Software Product is owned by Microsoft or its suppliers and is protected by copyright laws and international copyright treaties, as well as other intellectual property laws and treaties. THE SOFTWARE PRODUCT IS LICENSED, NOT SOLD.

1. GRANT OF LICENSE. The Software Product includes software that is installed and provides services on a computer acting as a server ("Server Software", and the computer running the Server Software shall be referred to as the "Server"); software that allows an electronic device ("Device") to access or utilize the services or functionality provided by the Server Software ("Client Software"); and "Tools." The "Tools" consist of the following components of the Software Product: Management Tools, Books-Online and Development Tools.

    Provided that you comply with all terms and conditions of this Evaluation License, Microsoft grants to you the following rights under this Evaluation License solely for purposes of demonstration, testing, examination and evaluation of the Software Product for the limited period specified below:

    (a) You may install only once and use the Server Software on each computer used by you or (for entities) each computer within your organization. The Software Product may contain several copies of the Server Software, each of which is compatible with a different microprocessor architecture. You are only authorized to use the copy of the Server Software that is appropriate for your Server.

    (b) You may install only once and use each of the Client Software and the Tools on each Device used by you or (for entities) each Device within your organization.

    (c) You may not install the Software Product (or any component thereof) more than one time on the same computer or same Device.

    (d) Solely for purposes of your use of the Software Product as authorized under this Evaluation License, you may permit an unlimited number of authorized Devices to access or otherwise utilize the services or functionality of the Server Software.

    (e) YOUR RIGHT TO USE THE SOFTWARE PRODUCT SHALL BE EFFECTIVE FROM THE DATE YOU FIRST INSTALL ANY PORTION OF THE SOFTWARE PRODUCT ON ANY DEVICE FOR A PERIOD OF ONE HUNDRED TWENTY (120) DAYS. THE SERVER SOFTWARE IS TIME SENSITIVE AND WILL NOT FUNCTION UPON EXPIRATION OF THE 120-DAY PERIOD. NOTICE OF EXPIRATION WILL NOT ACTIVELY BE GIVEN, SO YOU NEED TO PLAN FOR THE EXPIRATION DATE AND MAKE A COPY OF AND REMOVE YOUR IMPORTANT DATA BEFORE EXPIRATION. If you desire to use the Software Product after your evaluation is completed, you will need to acquire a validly licensed copy of the non-evaluation version of the Software Product (and Client Access Licenses for Microsoft SQL Server 2000, if appropriate).

    (f) The SOFTWARE PRODUCT is "NOT FOR PRODUCTION USE". You may not demonstrate, test, examine, evaluate or otherwise use the Software Product in a live operating environment or with data that has not been sufficiently backed up.

    (g) All rights not expressly granted are reserved by Microsoft.

2. DEMAND FOR EXAMINATION. Microsoft hereby requests that you fully examine the Software Product during the term of this Evaluation License so that you will be fully familiar with it before obtaining a copy of the non-evaluation version of the Software Product. Only your full examination now will determine whether or not the non-evaluation version will be merchantable or fit for your particular purposes.

3. ADDITIONAL LIMITATIONS. You may not reverse engineer, decompile, or disassemble the Software Product, except to the extent such foregoing restriction is expressly prohibited by applicable law notwithstanding this limitation. You may not rent, lease, lend, or transfer the Software Product. You may not disclose the results of any benchmark test of either the Server Software or Client Software to any third party without Microsoft's prior written approval.

4. INTELLECTUAL PROPERTY RIGHTS. All ownership, title and intellectual property rights in and to the SOFTWARE PRODUCT (including but not limited to any images, photographs, animations, video, audio, music, text and "applets" incorporated into the SOFTWARE PRODUCT), and any copies you are permitted to make herein are owned by Microsoft or its suppliers. All ownership, title and intellectual property rights in and to the content which may be accessed through use of the SOFTWARE PRODUCT is the property of the respective content owner and may be protected by applicable copyright or other intellectual property laws and treaties. This Evaluation License grants you no rights to use such content. For each copy of the Software Product you are authorized to use above, you may also reproduce one additional copy of the Software Product solely for archival or restoration purposes.

5. U.S. GOVERNMENT RESTRICTED RIGHTS. All SOFTWARE PRODUCT provided to the U.S. Government pursuant to solicitations issued on or after December 1, 1995 is provided with the commercial rights and restrictions described elsewhere herein. All SOFTWARE PRODUCT provided to the U.S. Government pursuant to solicitations issued prior to December 1, 1995 is provided with RESTRICTED RIGHTS as provided for in FAR, 48 CFR 52.227-14 (JUNE 1987) or FAR, 48 CFR 252.227-7013 (OCT 1988), as applicable.

6. EXPORT RESTRICTIONS. You acknowledge that Product is of U.S. origin. You agree to comply with all applicable international and national laws that apply to the Product, including the U.S. Export Administration Regulations, as well as end-user, end-use and destination restrictions issued by U.S. and other governments. For additional information, see <http://www.microsoft.com/exporting/>.

7. APPLICABLE LAW. If you acquired this Software Product in the United States, this Evaluation License is governed by the laws of the State of Washington. If you acquired this Software Product in Canada, unless expressly prohibited by local law, this Evaluation License is governed by the laws in force in the Province of Ontario, Canada; and, in respect of any dispute which may arise hereunder, you consent to the jurisdiction of the federal and provincial courts sitting in Toronto, Ontario. If this Software Product was acquired outside the United States, then local law may apply.

8. QUESTIONS. Should you have any questions concerning this Evaluation License, or if you desire to contact Microsoft for any reason, please contact the Microsoft subsidiary serving your country, or write: Microsoft Sales Information Center/One Microsoft Way/Redmond, WA 98052-6399.

9. DISCLAIMER OF WARRANTIES. To the maximum extent permitted by applicable law, Microsoft and its suppliers provide the Software Product and any (if any) support services related to the Software Product ("Support Services") AS IS AND WITH ALL FAULTS, and hereby disclaim all warranties and conditions, either express, implied or statutory, including, but not limited to, any (if any) implied warranties or conditions of merchantability, of fitness for a particular purpose, of lack of viruses, of accuracy or completeness of responses, of results, and of lack of negligence or lack of workmanlike effort, all with regard to the Software Product, and the provision of or failure to provide Support Services. ALSO, THERE IS NO WARRANTY OR CONDITION OF TITLE, QUIET ENJOYMENT, QUIET POSSESSION, CORRESPONDENCE TO DESCRIPTION OR NON-INFRINGEMENT, WITH REGARD TO THE SOFTWARE PRODUCT. THE ENTIRE RISK AS TO THE QUALITY OF OR ARISING OUT OF USE OR PERFORMANCE OF THE SOFTWARE PRODUCT AND SUPPORT SERVICES, IF ANY, REMAINS WITH YOU.

10. EXCLUSION OF INCIDENTAL, CONSEQUENTIAL AND CERTAIN OTHER DAMAGES. TO THE MAXIMUM EXTENT PERMITTED BY APPLICABLE LAW, IN NO EVENT SHALL MICROSOFT OR ITS SUPPLIERS BE LIABLE FOR ANY SPECIAL, INCIDENTAL, INDIRECT, OR CONSEQUENTIAL DAMAGES WHATSOEVER (INCLUDING, BUT NOT LIMITED TO, DAMAGES FOR LOSS OF PROFITS OR CONFIDENTIAL OR OTHER INFORMATION, FOR BUSINESS INTERRUPTION, FOR PERSONAL INJURY, FOR LOSS OF PRIVACY, FOR FAILURE TO MEET ANY DUTY INCLUDING OF GOOD FAITH OR OF REASONABLE CARE, FOR NEGLIGENCE, AND FOR ANY OTHER PECUNIARY OR OTHER LOSS WHATSOEVER) ARISING OUT OF OR IN ANY WAY RELATED TO THE USE OF OR INABILITY TO USE THE SOFTWARE PRODUCT, THE PROVISION OF OR FAILURE TO PROVIDE SUPPORT SERVICES, OR OTHERWISE UNDER OR IN CONNECTION WITH ANY PROVISION OF THIS EVALUATION LICENSE, EVEN IN THE EVENT OF THE FAULT, TORT (INCLUDING NEGLIGENCE), STRICT LIABILITY, BREACH OF CONTRACT OR BREACH OF WARRANTY OF MICROSOFT OR ANY SUPPLIER, AND EVEN IF MICROSOFT OR ANY SUPPLIER HAS BEEN ADVISED OF THE POSSIBILITY OF SUCH DAMAGES.

11. LIMITATION OF LIABILITY AND REMEDIES. Notwithstanding any damages that you might incur for any reason whatsoever (including, without limitation, all damages referenced above and all direct or general damages), the entire liability of Microsoft and any of its suppliers under any provision of this Evaluation License and your exclusive remedy for all of the foregoing shall be limited to the greater of the amount actually paid by you for the Software Product or U.S.$5.00. The foregoing limitations, exclusions and disclaimers shall apply to the maximum extent permitted by applicable law, even if any remedy fails its essential purpose.

12. NOTE ON JAVA SUPPORT. THE SOFTWARE PRODUCT MAY CONTAIN SUPPORT FOR PROGRAMS WRITTEN IN JAVA. JAVA TECHNOLOGY IS NOT FAULT TOLERANT AND IS NOT DESIGNED, MANUFACTURED, OR INTENDED FOR USE OR RESALE AS ONLINE CONTROL EQUIPMENT IN HAZARDOUS ENVIRONMENTS REQUIRING FAIL-SAFE PERFORMANCE, SUCH AS IN THE OPERATION OF NUCLEAR FACILITIES, AIRCRAFT NAVIGATION OR COMMUNICATION SYSTEMS, AIR TRAFFIC CONTROL, DIRECT LIFE SUPPORT MACHINES, OR WEAPONS SYSTEMS, IN WHICH THE FAILURE OF JAVA TECHNOLOGY COULD LEAD DIRECTLY TO DEATH, PERSONAL INJURY, OR SEVERE PHYSICAL OR ENVIRONMENTAL DAMAGE. Sun Microsystems, Inc. has contractually obligated Microsoft to make this disclaimer.

Si vous avez acquis votre produit Microsoft au CANADA, la garantie limitée suivante vous concerne :

RENONCIATION AUX GARANTIES. Dans toute la mesure permise par la législation en vigueur, Microsoft et ses fournisseurs fournissent le Produit Logiciel et tous (selon le cas) les services d'assistance liés au Produit Logiciel ("Services d'assistance") TELS QUELS ET AVEC TOUS LEURS DÉFAUTS, et par les présentes excluent toute garantie ou condition, expresse ou implicite, légale ou conventionnelle, écrite ou verbale, y compris, mais sans limitation, toute (selon le cas) garantie ou condition implicite ou légale de qualité marchande, de conformité à un usage particulier, d'absence de virus, d'exactitude et d'intégralité des réponses, de résultats, d'efforts techniques et professionnels et d'absence de négligence, le tout relativement au Produit Logiciel et à la prestation ou à la non-prestation des Services d'assistance. DE PLUS, IL N'Y A AUCUNE GARANTIE ET CONDITION DE TITRE, DE JOUISSANCE PAISIBLE, DE POSSESSION PAISIBLE, DE SIMILARITÉ À LA DESCRIPTION ET D'ABSENCE DE CONTREFAÇON RELATIVEMENT AU PRODUIT LOGICIEL. Vous supportez tous les risques découlant de l'utilisation et de la performance du Produit Logiciel et ceux découlant des Services d'assistance (s'il y a lieu).

EXCLUSION DES DOMMAGES INDIRECTS, ACCESSOIRES ET AUTRES. Dans toute la mesure permise par la législation en vigueur, Microsoft et ses fournisseurs ne sont en aucun cas responsables de tout dommage spécial, indirect, accessoire, moral ou exemplaire quel qu'il soit (y compris, mais sans limitation, les dommages entraînés par la perte de bénéfices ou la perte d'information confidentielle ou autre, l'interruption des affaires, les préjudices corporels, la perte de confidentialité, le défaut de remplir toute obligation y compris les obligations de bonne foi et de diligence raisonnable, la négligence et toute autre perte pécuniaire ou autre perte de quelque nature que ce soit) découlant de, ou de toute autre manière lié à, l'utilisation ou l'impossibilité d'utiliser le Produit Logiciel, la prestation ou la non-prestation des Services d'assistance ou autrement en vertu de ou relativement à toute disposition de cette convention, que ce soit en cas de faute, de délit (y compris la négligence), de responsabilité stricte, de manquement à un contrat ou de manquement à une garantie de Microsoft ou de l'un de ses fournisseurs, et ce, même si Microsoft ou l'un de ses fournisseurs a été avisé de la possibilité de tels dommages.

LIMITATION DE RESPONSABILITÉ ET RECOURS. Malgré tout dommage que vous pourriez encourir pour quelque raison que ce soit (y compris, mais sans limitation, tous les dommages mentionnés ci-dessus et tous les dommages directs et généraux), la seule responsabilité de Microsoft et de ses fournisseurs en vertu de toute disposition de cette convention et votre unique recours en regard de tout ce qui précède sont limités au plus élevé des montants suivants: soit (a) le montant que vous avez payé pour le Produit Logiciel, soit (b) un montant équivalant à cinq dollars U.S. (5,00 $ U.S.). Les limitations, exclusions et renonciations ci-dessus s'appliquent dans toute la mesure permise par la législation en vigueur, et ce même si leur application a pour effet de priver un recours de son essence.

DROITS LIMITÉS DU GOUVERNEMENT AMÉRICAIN

Tout Produit Logiciel fourni au gouvernement américain conformément à des demandes émises le ou après le 1er décembre 1995 est offert avec les restrictions et droits commerciaux décrits ailleurs dans la présente convention. Tout Produit Logiciel fourni au gouvernement américain conformément à des demandes émises avant le 1er décembre 1995 est offert avec des DROITS LIMITÉS tels que prévus dans le FAR, 48CFR 52.227-14 (juin 1987) ou dans le FAR, 48CFR 252.227-7013 (octobre 1988), tels qu'applicables.

Sauf lorsqu'expressément prohibé par la législation locale, la présente convention est régie par les lois en vigueur dans la province d'Ontario, Canada. Pour tout différend qui pourrait découler des présentes, vous acceptez la compétence des tribunaux fédéraux et provinciaux siégeant à Toronto, Ontario.

Si vous avez des questions concernant cette convention ou si vous désirez communiquer avec Microsoft pour quelque raison que ce soit, veuillez contacter la succursale Microsoft desservant votre pays, ou écrire à: Microsoft Sales Information Center, One Microsoft Way, Redmond, Washington 98052-6399.

Installation Instructions

To install the items from the CD to your hard drive, follow these steps.

1. Insert the CD into your computer's CD-ROM drive.

2. If the compact disc does not autorun, double-click autorun.exe in the root directory of the compact disc.

3. Choose Browse Setup/Upgrade Help to view addition installation instructions or click on SQL Server 2000 Components to begin installation.

For more information, see the "About the CD" appendix.